HOWARD BARKER

COLLECTED PLAYS

VOLUME ONE

CLAW
NO END OF BLAME
VICTORY
THE CASTLE
SCENES FROM AN EXECUTION

CALDER · LONDON
RIVERRUN PRESS · NEW YORK

First published in Great Britain in 1990 by
John Calder (Publishers) Limited

and in the U.S.A. in 1990, by
Riverrun Press Inc.
c/o Whitehurst & Clark, 100 Newfield Avenue, Edison, N.J. 08837

This second impression published in 1994 by
Calder Publications Limited
Reprinted in 2002 by Calder Publications Limited, 51 The Cut, London SE1 8LF
Copyright © Howard Barker 1977-1990

Performing rights are strictly reserved

Applications for USA and Canadian amateur and stock rights
in *Scenes from an Execution* only should be made to:

Samuel French Inc, 45 West 25th Street, New York, NY 10010-2751

Applications for a licence to perform the other plays in this volume should
be made to:

Judy Daish Associates Ltd, 83 Eastbourne Mews, London W2 6LQ

ALL RIGHTS RESERVED

British Library Cataloguing in Publication Data

Barker, Howard 1946–
  Collected plays.
  Vol. 1
  I. Title
  822.914

ISBN 0-7145-4161-3

Library of Congress Cataloguing in Publication Data

Barker, Howard.
  (Plays)
  Collected plays/Howard Barker,
  p. 18.6cm
  Contents: v.1 Claw; No end of blame; Victory; The castle; Scenes from
  an execution.
  ISBN 0-7145-4161-3 (v.1)
  I.Title. PR6052.A6485A19 1990
  822 '.914 — dc19   88-36769
                              CIP

Typeset 9/10pt Times by Pure Tech Corporation, Pondicherry, India.
Printed in Great Britain by Bookcraft, Midsomer Norton, Nr Bath.

CONTENTS

CLAW
An Odyssey

CHARACTERS

MRS. BILEDEW	A Woman of London
BILEDEW	Her Husband
NOEL BILEDEW	Her Son
NORA	An Ally
POLICEMAN	
CHRISTINE	A Waitress
FIRST ASSASSIN	
SECOND ASSASSIN	
CLAPCOTT	A Minister of State
ANGIE	His Wife
POLICE MOTORCYCLIST	
SPECIAL BRANCH OFFICER	
LILY	A Male nurse
LUBSY	A Male nurse

ACT ONE

Scene One

Widely scattered across the stage, bricks and rubble.

Enter, scruffily dressed and holding a baby and a suitcase, MRS. BILEDEW. The baby is crying. She picks her way over the bricks, looks around, bends down and extracts from the rubbish a framed wedding photograph. She blows the dust off it, stands it up against some masonry.

MRS. BILEDEW: Shut up, miserable little bleeder! (*She looks at the child.*) Horrible yellow muck caked round your eyes . . . (*Pause*) Makes you feel sick. (*She puts the baby down on the ground.*) Well, here we are. Unpack. Spread out your little treasures. Vera Biledew has come home. (*The baby cries.*) With a little nuisance picked up on the way. (*Pause*) Well, was I supposed to go without for five whole years? Was he going without? Like hell he was. Got bastards all the way across the continent. (*Pause*) Well, would have had, if he hadn't got captured at Dunkirk. (*She kneels down and begins unpacking the suitcase, spreading out little items along the ground, a hand mirror, lighter, clock, hairbrush.*) To start off with he'll want to bash my face in. I expect I'll lose a few teeth, maybe get my arm broken. Then he'll just get used to it. Or piss off altogether, I don't know. If he stays I'll have to have half a dozen kids of his, just to make up for it. And when he's lying on top of me I'll have to say, 'Oh, no, you're killing me!' For a few months, anyway. He always wanted to think I was dying. Pleased him. (*The child cries again.*) All right, we're home!

She carries on unpacking. Enter left, in battered army uniform, VICTOR BILEDEW. He keeps his hands in his pockets, kicks the floor resentfully. Then he watches her coldly for a few seconds.

BILEDEW: I should kick your head in.

MRS. BILEDEW (*looks up*): You look well, Vic. (*Pause*)

BILEDEW: You never wrote.

MRS. BILEDEW: Nothing to say . . .

BILEDEW: Five years behind barbed wire! (*Pause*)

MRS. BILEDEW: You know what I'm like with letters . . . I started one . . . then I left it . . . I meant to pick it up again . . . it's here somewhere . . . (*She starts to look.*)

BILEDEW: Don't bother.

MRS. BILEDEW: No . . . (*She smiles.*) Well, I'm here now . . . (*Pause. BILEDEW looks at the baby.*)

BILEDEW: Whose is that? (*Pause*)

MRS. BILEDEW: Ours. (*Pause*)

BILEDEW: Ours?

MRS. BILEDEW (*aside*): I could lie to him. I could say I found it in the ruins of a house, after a raid, clinging to its dead mother's tits . . . (*Pause. She turns back to him.*) Whose do you think?

BILEDEW: Jesus . . . (*Pause*)

MRS. BILEDEW: We'll get a prefab, I expect. On the edge of the common. The house was damp, if you remember. I'm not sorry it got blitzed. Apart from your mum, that was sad . . . (*Pause*)

BILEDEW: Oh, Christ . . .

MRS. BILEDEW (*looks up at him*): Victor . . . (*Pause*) Come on, Victor . . . swallow your pride . . . (*He sways slightly, eyes closed. She watches him, then goes back to her work, emptying the suitcase.*) Munitions work was horrible. But I saved a few quid. Put it in the post office. (*BILEDEW walks over to where the child is lying, gazes down at it. Slowly, deliberately, he bends down and picks up a brick.*) My skin went funny, and I was nearly in an accident. They reckoned twenty girls died in that blast. And hundreds without arms and legs. (*BILEDEW is motionless, holding the brick, gazing at the child.*) The boss went to the funeral. He was crying, I was surprised to see. But we got the day off. That was nice.(*Suddenly BILEDEW throws the brick aside. She turns to him. He is weeping bitterly, silently. Pause.*) You better go down for the ration books.

Pause. and spotlight on NOEL BILEDEW, *in a silver suit and thick-lensed spectacles.*

NOEL: So I was saved, not for the first time, from a violent death, and the old man spared the guilt of child murder, which knowing him and his appetite for misery, would undoubtedly have led him to hang himself, or swallow glass, or something very loud and obvious. (*He goes out. Pause.*)

MRS. BILEDEW: Victor never did hit me. But he never spoke to Noel.

BILEDEW: Why Noel?

MRS. BILEDEW: *In Which We Serve.*

BILEDEW: What?

MRS. BILEDEW: *In Which We Serve.*

BILEDEW: I've been behind barbed wire for five years.

MRS. BILEDEW: Noel Coward. A week before he popped out I was taken to the flicks. And there was Noel. It just seemed obvious. (*Pause.* BILEDEW *nods. She looks at him.*) Some feller took me to the flicks.

BILEDEW: You said. (*Pause*)

MRS. BILEDEW: A bloke, Victor. (*Long pause*, BILEDEW *doesn't react.*) Be jealous, Victor! Knock me round the head. (*Pause*) For your own good . . . (*Pause*)

BILEDEW: On Tuesdays we played football in the yard. I was goalie. English and Poles versus Americans. The ball was made of rags tied up with string. Somebody kicked it very wide. It rolled, and stopped half across the white line where the guard patrolled. No prisoner was allowed across the line. It was a rule. But they all shouted at me, go on Victor, don't hang about. So I went up to the line and stood there and waited, just in case. But they all kept on at me, just pick it up! So I leant over and picked it up. (*Pause*) And the guard came. And he kicked me in the privates. (*Pause. He starts to roll a cigarette.* MRS. BILEDEW *shrugs, looks at the baby*). We can't have kids. (*Pause. She looks at him.*) I can't. (*Long pause.*)

MRS. BILEDEW: All right, Victor. We won't have kids. Now go and get the ration books. (*Pause, then he slowly walks out right.*)

An armchair, a paraffin heater, a fireplace, are brought on and assembled like a room. MRS. BILEDEW *attends to the paraffin heater.*

Enter NOEL, *in shorts, school blazer, and thick-rimmed glasses. He stands with his hand in his pockets.*

NOEL: Coronation just went by.

MRS. BILEDEW: Did it?

NOEL: Loads of horses. Coppers with funny outfits on.

MRS. BILEDEW: Pass us the paraffin.

NOEL (*handing her a can*): When they'd gone there was horse-muck everywhere. People went and picked it up. Put it in their handkerchiefs . . .

MRS. BILEDEW: Worth money that is. Find some matches.

NOEL: At school they gave us a pencil and a mug. They said always to treasure 'em, even when the lead ran out. They said I was to put the mug on the mantlepiece.

MRS. BILEDEW: I'm not stopping you. (*Pause*)

NOEL: I've got thirty of 'em.

MRS. BILEDEW: Thirty mugs!

NOEL: I did a swap.

MRS. BILEDEW: What for?

NOEL: A look.

MRS. BILEDEW: At what?

NOEL: Joan Preston. Behind the lavatories.

MRS. BILEDEW: You dirty little sod!

NOEL: I gave her half!

MRS. BILEDEW: You give 'em back!

NOEL: I got you thirty mugs!

MRS. BILEDEW (*grabbing him*): You take 'em back!

NOEL: You always say we haven't got no china.

MRS. BILEDEW: You heard me. Take 'em back.

NOEL (*pulling free*): No. (*Long pause. They glare at one another.*)

MRS. BILEDEW: No point in giving 'em back now, I s'pose . . .?

NOEL: Course not. I'll get 'em in. (*He goes out, returns with a cardboard box full of Coronation mugs, and begins lining them up on the mantlepiece.*) All right, aren't they?

As NOEL stands admiring them, enter BILEDEW, with a news-paper. He sits in the armchair, reads. Gradually his eyes travel to the mantlepiece. Pause.

BILEDEW: What's that?

MRS. BILEDEW: What?

BILEDEW: Them.

MRS. BILEDEW: Mugs. (*She turns to NOEL.*) Did you get them matches? Like an iceberg in this house.

BILEDEW: What mugs?

MRS. BILEDEW: Never mind about the mugs. Have you got a job or not?

BILEDEW: I had offers.

MRS. BILEDEW: And you accepted them? (*Pause.* BILEDEW *is still staring at the mugs.*)

BILEDEW: Considering.

MRS. BILEDEW: Blimey! Six months on the dole and you're —

BILEDEW (*angrily*):   Considering! (*Pause*) No rush . . .

MRS. BILEDEW: Give us three quid. No, make it four.

BILEDEW: What for?

MRS. BILEDEW: Coal. Food. Electricity.

BILEDEW: I can't.

MRS. BILEDEW: And you're considering! He goes out, he comes home with a tea service. You go out, you come home with nothing. He's nine. How old are you?

BILEDEW: Nicked!

MRS. BILEDEW: Not nicked, so there! Fair deal! (*Pause.* BILEDEW *looks back at his paper.*)

BILEDEW: I'm not a workhorse. I've got a life. (*Pause*)

MRS. BILEDEW (*aside*):   I should have stayed in Birmingham. I had offers. We might have had a car by now, me and whoever I was with. A Vauxhall with a sunroof, and them white wall tyres . . . matches! (NOEL *runs out.*)

Scene Two

Lights up on BILEDEW, *standing alone before the fireplace.*

BILEDEW: I met this fellar. And he said had I read *Das Kapital.* Das what? I said. About the opression of the working man, he said. No, I hadn't read it. Read it, he says. All right, I start. I get the first line, and then the second line. The third line I'm not so sure of, but I carry on. The fourth line I skip. I know odd words, the sense I haven't got. I skip the next two lines. I give up that paragraph. I carry on. I can't get it — the second paragraph, that is. I turn over. Now I'm angry. I skip that page, and start another, but I don't know what it's all about, I'm lost now, I am fucking angry, I am so fucking angry I throw it on the bloody floor! (*Pause*) It stays there. She doesn't move it. I don't move it. Gets tea stains on the cover. Papers put on top of it. But it's still there . . . niggling me. I'm sitting there, I look at it, from a distance, then I get up, I pick it up, I open it, and start again. I get the first line, and then the second line. The third line I'm not sure of, and the fourth line — I'm so bloody ignorant! (*Pause*) So I go back to this feller. I cannot read *Das Kapital*, I say. I'm ignorant. And he holds out the Manifesto of the Communist Party. No thanks. It's short, he says. I'll go through it with you. And for half and hour after dinner he goes through it with me. Daily. In the canteen. In all that racket. Karl Marx's words . . .

Enter MRS. BILEDEW.

MRS. BILEDEW: Noel's been expelled.

BILEDEW (*indifferently*):   Go on . . .

MRS. BILEDEW: Chucked out of school!

BILEDEW: I saw it coming. It had to happen.

MRS. BILEDEW: Get him a job.

BILEDEW: What as?

MRS. BILEDEW: Apprentice him.

BILEDEW: I'm not the Personnel Manager.

MRS. BILEDEW: You're in with the shop steward.

BILEDEW: We're friends.

MRS. BILEDEW: Help him! (*Enter* NOEL, *in a leather jacket, some sizes too large. He stands, hands in pockets. She turns to him.*) You silly sod. (*Pause*) A week before your 'O' levels!

NOEL: No future in it. The accumulation of qualifications is a blind alley, as far as I can see.

MRS. BILEDEW: On his expulsion form they called him deceitful. Said he hid behind his spectacles! Said he used his handicap as a means of challenging authority!

NOEL: Gym teacher confiscated my camera . . .

MRS. BILEDEW: Apparently he took pictures of girls in the showers.

NOEL: They were flattered. They were queuing up to volunteer.

MRS. BILEDEW: He was selling 'em to newsagents.

BILEDEW: Why tell me! I saw it coming. (*They glare at one another.*)

MRS. BILEDEW: Well, what are you going to do?

NOEL: I want some tea. And then I'll think about my future.

Whether I shall make the effort to be a good citizen. Or drop coppers down manholes, rev my motorbike round village squares and prey on old men coming home from betting shops. (*Pause.* BILEDEW *is looking at him as he relishes the image.* MRS. BILEDEW *goes out to make tea.*)

BILEDEW: To what end? (*An astonished silence. Slowly* NOEL *turns to look at* BILEDEW, *mouth agape. Pause.*)

NOEL: Blimey! (*Pause*) He spoke! (*Pause*) To me! (*Pause*) He spoke! (*He rushes to the door.*) Phone a doctor! Get an ambulance! He's speaking to me! (*Enter* MRS. BILEDEW.)

NOEL: Listen! (*He holds a finger to his lips, goes up to* BILEDEW *and cupping his ear, puts it up to* BILEDEW's *face. Pause, expectantly.*)

BILEDEW: Waste.

NOEL: Hear that!

MRS. BILEDEW (*delighted*): Victor, I'm so glad! (*She goes towards him, arms outstretched.*)

BILEDEW: Clear off!

MRS. BILEDEW (*repulsed*): Oh dear . . .

BILEDEW: Leave us alone. (*Pause. Then she goes out, looking at* NOEL. *For some time* NOEL *and* BILEDEW *just look at one another.*) You're not my son.

NOEL: That had dawned on me.

BILEDEW: Even your mother doesn't know who your father was.

NOEL: I'm not bothered. Maybe I never had one. Maybe I'm immaculate.

BILEDEW: From the moment I set eyes on you I hated you. I wished you dead. When you had scarlet fever I went to the church and prayed. Not for you.

NOEL: No . . .

BILEDEW: Against you.

NOEL: Right.

BILEDEW: I hoped the devil would hear me and carry you off.

NOEL: I think he's rather fond of me.

BILEDEW: You ruined my happiness. For sixteen years I've looked at you and felt murder in my heart.

NOEL: Nice character . . .

BILEDEW: You felt it, did you? Scorching you across the breakfast table? Coming through the wall at nights from the bedroom where I was sweating in the dark?

NOEL: I'm used to being hated. From the first day I went to the Infants school they had it in for me. Because of these. (*He touches his glasses.*) They never gave me a chance. They never said, Noel, what are you good at? What stamps do you collect? Will you be in our team, Noel? They hated me. Straight off. Like a disease.

BILEDEW: I pitied you.

NOEL: Don't strain yourself.

BILEDEW: Even while I hated you.

NOEL: Yeah, well — no surprises so far, then.

BILEDEW: I haven't come to my point yet.

NOEL: Oh . . . (*Pause*)

BILEDEW: I am right, am I not, in believing you to be resentful? (NOEL *shrugs.*) You are angry, Noel. Correct me if I'm wrong. (*He shrugs again.*) Well, what I'm saying is, I don't think you should waste your anger. Don't pour away your precious anger, Noel. Use it. (*Pause*) For the workers.

NOEL (*looks at him, curiously*):   Workers?

BILEDEW: Your people. Your own class.

NOEL: Come on —

BILEDEW: They need your anger —

NOEL: They can have it!

BILEDEW: Serve them!

NOEL: Serve who? The sods who hid my glasses so I wandered round the playground with my hands outstretched, calling out 'Boss eyes' and 'Blind git' and making me fall on my face? Help them! I was never Noel to them, just four eyes, who always managed to step in their puke! (*Pause*)

BILEDEW: All the more reason to assist in their improvement, Noel. In an unjust society, the weak will always be the persecuted. Just as they brutalized you, so they are brutalized by the system. But when the system falls, so will all forms of cruelty, and boys with bad eyesight will be loved, even by their cuckolded stepfathers . . . (*Puase*

NOEL: Too late for me . . .

BILEDEW: Avenge yourself . . . (*Pause*)

NOEL (*turning to the audience*):   So there I was, at sixteen, thinking about the uprising of the proleteriat, and wondering, if the old man had a point, how I was to lead them to the light, cast off their chains and so on, and channel my hatred into the appropriate political response. (*He has now taken off his jacket and extends his arms.*)

Enter MRS. BILEDEW, *holding another jacket, which she slips on him. As she does so, she notices a badge on the lapel.*

MRS. BILEDEW: What's this!

NOEL: A badge.

MRS. BILEDEW: Don't come it! What's it mean?

NOEL: Young Communists. (*Pause. Then she rips it off.*) My badge!

MRS. BILEDEW (*tossing it across the stage*):   Don't let me catch you going near that lot again!

NOEL: Why not?

MRS. BILEDEW: Join a youth club if you must go out.

NOEL: I like it there.

MRS. BILEDEW: You like them? You like low characters who want to make the world as miserable as them?

NOEL: They like me there. They call me Trotsky. Because of these. (*He touches his glasses.*)

MRS. BILEDEW: Noel . . . you could do well . . . get away from this . . . you've got brains, not like the old man . . . he's got nothing . . . he's dried up . . . in bed, lying beside him, it's like lying with a corpse . . . (*Pause*) No need for you to be like that. You can get out of it. Don't waste yourself. Be free . . .

Enter NORA, *a girl of seventeen.*

NORA: 'ello.

NOEL: Nora . . .

NORA: Coming down the Y.C.L?

NOEL: Dunno.

NORA: Haven't seen you.

NOEL: Haven't been.

NORA: Why not? (*He shrugs. She looks at him, grinning.*) Trotsky! (*She laughs. He laughs, feebly. Pause.*)

MRS. BILEDEW: Did you want something!

NORA: Not specially. (*Pause*) Oh, well . . . (*She is about to go.*)

NORA: I s'pose — (*He looks at his mother.*) Going out for a bit. Fresh air. (*Without waiting for her response he goes out behind* NORA. *She watches ruefully. Pause.*)

BILEDEW: Crushing him. (*Pause*) What he has. (*Pause*) Crushing him.

MRS. BILEDEW: Saving him. For better things.

BILEDEW: You hope.

MRS. BILEDEW: You can't have him. You've had me. You've parked your corpse on me for sixteen years, squeezing the joy out of me. But you're not having him. Oh, no. (*Pause. He looks at the oil heater.*)

BILEDEW: Needs some more paraffin. It's flickering. (MRS. BILEDEW *goes out.*)

Scene Three

A bombsite. Enter NOEL *and* NORA. *They stand around.*

NOEL: Dismal. Our surroundings. Highly dismal.

NORA: Rather live here than in the flats.

NOEL: I like the flats. From the flats you see over the top of the power station. And beyond that, the little lights of Chelsea restaurants . . .

NORA: We'll burn down Chelsea.

NOEL: You will.

NORA: And you.

NOEL: The time's not ripe.

NORA: Maybe . . .

NOEL: So in the meantime, you exploit your opportunities.

NORA: But when the time's ripe —

NOEL: It's not ripe —

NORA: **When** it is —

NOEL: We'll see. (*He walks up and down. She sits on a wall.*) What's your considered opinion on free love?

NORA: Favourable.

NOEL: I mean, the sanctity of marriage, for example? What's your view?

NORA: A capitalist convention, based on property.

NOEL: That's what I think. (*Pause*) Fancy coming into business with me?

NORA: Business?

NOEL: Trade.

NORA: Dirty word.

NOEL: All right — exchange of goods or services. No exploitation of the masses.

NORA: How do you mean?

NOEL: Modelling. (*Pause*)

NORA: How do you mean?

NOEL: Going with men.

NORA (*getting up*): You filthy bastard.

NOEL: Well, you have.

NORA: Have I?

NOEL: The Y.C.L.

NORA: Have I?

NOEL: Come on, been through the Y.C.L. — apart from
        me —

NORA: Have I?

NOEL: Money for jam! (*Pause. NORA looks at him coldly.*)

NORA: You disgusting little parasite.

NOEL: Look, I don't want to die in this bloody hole, I don't
        want to be like my old man or like the silly bleeders in the
        Y.C.L., all waiting, waiting, waiting till the time is ripe. I don't
        want to see the bright lights through the power station smoke if
        the wind should happen to be favourable, I want to be there,
        Nora, I want to be there squatting on their faces, spitting my
        acid in their eyes!

NORA (*just looks at him*):   Don't come to the Y.C.L. We won't
        acknowledge you. (*She turns, starts to go out.*)

NOEL: This is a political action! (*She stops, her back to him.*)
        This isn't theory. This isn't arguing the toss for the millioneth
        time in the Battersea cell of the world revolutionary party. This
        is action, this is carrying anthrax into their woolly nests! (*Pause.
        NORA turns, looks at him for some seconds.*)

NORA: And what's my share?

NOEL: Halves.

NORA: No. (*Pause*)

NOEL: All right. 60/40.

NORA (*grinning*):   Rip their soiled knickers down!

NOEL: Hero of Labour!

NOEL: How do we start?

NOEL: Right here. Tonight. Start small and local, then spread
        our wings.

NORA: There aren't any bourgeois in this street.

NOEL: Of course not. This is just for the experience.

NORA (*taking a deep breath*):   All right.

NOEL: First geezer comes along, I proposition him.

NORA: Suppose he's horrible?

NOEL: Got to start somewhere, haven't we? No point in alien-
        ating ourselves because of some aesthetic prejudice. This is an
        apprenticeship. (NORA *shrugs, unwilling.*) First geezer. And
        no chickening out. Now get behind that wall, all right?

NORA (*looking astonished*):   Can't do it in the street, can we?

It's illegal. (*Pause. Then she holds out her hand. He helps her over the wall.*)

NOEL: Comfortable?

NORA: It's filthy in here!

NOEL: Oh. Christ . . .

NORA: Suppose there's rats?

NOEL (*impatiently*):   No rats! (*Pause*) Now just hold on.

NORA: It's dark.

NOEL: Shut up. (*He walks up and down, hands in pockets, whistling.*)

NORA: Maybe we should have gone up to town . . .

NOEL: There's someone coming. Get ready! (*There are measured footsteps offstage, then they stop and a torch flashes, finds NOEL.*) Hello?

NORA: Who, me?

Enter a POLICEMAN. *He goes to within a couple of feet of NOEL, the torch still on him.*

PC: What's your game?

NOEL: Nothing.

PC: Oh. Like bombsites, do you?

NOEL: They're all right. (*Pause. Then they both start speaking at once and stop. Pause.*)

PC: I'm not keeping you.

NOEL: No . . . (*He doesn't move.*)

PC (*looking closer*):   What's the matter with your eyes?

NOEL: Nothing.

PC (*looking closer*):   Can you see?

NOEL: Yeah.

PC (*taking a step backward, then another*):   Tell me when I go out of focus.

NOEL: What's this —

PC: Just interested. (*He takes more steps.*) Now? (*Another step.*) Now? Don't tell me you can see me now!

NOEL: Look here —

PC: Don't get shirty. Just never seen lenses like them before. Terrible drawback. Eyes like fish in goldfish bowls . . .

NOEL (*under pressure*):   Do you like girls? (*Pause. The POLICEMAN walks back, stands close to NOEL.*)

PC: What did you say?

NOEL: Do you like girls?

PC (*coldly*):   Don't be impertinent, four eyes.

NOEL: If you want one . . . she's yours for a quid . . . (*Long pause.*)

PC: Who is?

NOEL: Over there. (*Pause*)

PC: Not your game, this, is it, son?

NOEL: Not really . . .

PC: New to it. Importuning me. Must be new to it.

NOEL: A quid. (*Pause*)

PC: Your girl friend, is it? (*He nods in the direction of the wall.*) Over the wall? (NOEL *nods.*) New to it, is she? (NOEL *nods.*) **Brand** new? (NOEL *nods again. Pause. The* POLICEMAN *reaches into his inside pockets, takes out his wallet and hands over a pound note. Then he surreptitiously goes to the wall, and looking either way quickly, hops over it.* NOEL *wipes his mouth nervously.*)

NOEL: So I did it. I had proved to myself I could do it. There was nothing could stop me going on. To bigger things. I was down for Chelsea. With my first pound note! (*He holds it up to the light, smiles, then takes out his own wallet and slips it in.*) Tell her it was ten bob. After all that risk. (*He puts the wallet away. The* POLICEMAN *reappears, slowly climbing over the wall.* NOEL *looks up.*) All right? (*The* POLICEMAN *approaches him, then suddenly punches him savagely in the stomach.* NOEL *collapses at once, with a small groan and lies still on the ground. The* POLICEMAN *removes* NOEL's *wallet and taking the pound note, tosses the wallet on the ground.*)

PC: Importuning me. Four eyes.

NORA: How could you! Of all the people in the world, you had to pick that — lumpenproletariat! I froze. My flesh was creeping. I felt so degraded. How could you degrade me with a class enemy like that!

NOEL (*weakly*): My glasses . . .

NORA: I'm contaminated . . .

NOEL: I'm hurt.

NORA: Good. And give me my cut.

NOEL: I can't.

NORA: All right, I'll take your jacket until you give me what you owe me. (*She strips off his jacket and starts walking away.*)

NOEL: I'll freeze!

NORA: Hooray! (*She goes out.* NOEL *gradually sits up, feels around for his glasses, finds, them, puts them on. He climbs to his feet, stands swaying a few moments.*)

NOEL: He hit me! I was struck! I won't be struck! Never again will I be struck, I vow that! (*He sobs with anger, clenching his fists, then raises an arm to the sky.*) I'll tear their skin off first, I'll rip their faces off their skulls, I'll be a great claw ripping them, slitting their bellies like ripe fruits! Hear me, formerly Trotsky of the Y.C.L., declare it on this night, note it in your calendars, I'll claw them first!

Scene Four

The tea room of a department store. A table with silverware and stiff white tablecloth. Two cane chairs.

As lights come on, MRS. BILEDEW, *dressed in an ill-fitting item of haute-couture, is waltzing around with an imaginary partner. She revolves for some moments, then as the tune comes to an end, she stops, claps, and returns to her seat, where she sits with a distinctly lonely and bored expression. She pours herself a cup of tea.*

Enter WAITRESS *with a tray laden with pastries.* MRS. BILEDEW *points to several, which are transferred to her plate. The* WAITRESS *goes out.*

MRS. BILEDEW: Every afternoon. At Fortnum's. Waited on. Then at five, collected by taxi, and driven home, bursting with pastries. Belching angelica and glacé cherries. Burping double Devon cream. (*She bites into a cream puff. The voice of* BILEDEW *is heard.*)

BILEDEW: Where's the money coming from, that's what I'd like to know.

MRS. BILEDEW: Here they treat you like you're someone. Pick up your cream horn if you drop it. And give you another one.

BILEDEW: Crime! Profits of crime!

MRS. BILEDEW: Shut up, Biledew!

BILEDEW: Sordid gains of criminal activities!

MRS. BILEDEW: I'll sort you out when I get home! (*Pause*) Can't say I've made that many friends, though I'm on nodding terms with the other regulars. It's the surroundings, the chandeliers, this lovely linen, and the music . . . it's like a dream . . .

Enter NOEL, *in a leather jacket emblazoned with a huge red claw.*
He grabs a chair and sits back to front on it.

NOEL: Claw's here.

MRS. BILEDEW (*shocked*):   Don't sit like that!

NOEL: Why not?

MRS. BILEDEW: In here!

NOEL: S'all right.

MRS. BILEDEW: I have to sit here every day.

NOEL: Go to Harrods. Go to Freebody's.

MRS. BILEDEW: Please, Noel . . . (*Reluctantly he gets up,*
turns the chair round, and sits facing the table, but begins tipping
it back on its back legs. She watches him.) I don't think you
should visit me.

NOEL: Why not?

MRS. BILEDEW: Uncouth. (*Pause*) You'll break that chair
. . . Your father thinks you're in crime . . . (*Pause*) Are you in
crime? (NOEL *looks at her. The* WAITRESS *enters.*)

CHRISTINE: Yes, please?

NOEL (*looks her up and down. Pause*):   What's your name?

CHRISTINE: Christine.

NOEL: You could do better, Christine.

MRS. BILEDEW: Take no notice of him.

CHRISTINE: Do you want tea?

NOEL: Show me your thighs. (CHRISTINE *walks smartly*
away. He looks after her.)

MRS. BILEDEW: You disgusting beast! What are people going
to think of me! I'm happy here, don't ruin it for me. (*Pause.*
NOEL *shrugs. Pause. He tips his chair back, taps a spoon on a*
plate.)

NOEL: Don't expect I'll see much of you in the future.

MRS. BILEDEW (*surprised*):   Why?

NOEL: Social mobility.

MRS. BILEDEW: I'm your mother.

NOEL: I'm moving on.

MRS. BILEDEW: You have moved on.

NOEL: Further.

MRS. BILEDEW (*suddenly distraught*):   You're my boy . . .

NOEL: I'll send you hampers.

MRS. BILEDEW: How could you —

NOEL: This table's yours — in perpetuity.

MRS. BILEDEW: Noel, please — (*Suddenly, angrily,* NOEL

*thumps the table with his fist, making the crockery jump. There is
a silence. The* WAITRESS *appears.*

CHRISTINE: Yes, please?

NOEL (*looking at her*):   Christine, do you want to earn fabulous
wages? Do you want to own more things? Eat out with celeb-
rities? (*She walks away again. Pause*)

MRS. BILEDEW: Don't leave me with the old man . . .
please . . . I couldn't bear it . . . stuck with him . . . his dead
face — the television droning on . . . I'm not young any more,
Noel . . . (*Pause*) I carried you down the A1 on my back.

NOEL: As an investment? As a maturing policy?

MRS. BILEDEW: I'm human, Noel!

NOEL: Don't boast about it! (*Pause*)

MRS. BILEDEW: You don't . . . love me . . . at all, then . . .
(*Pause*) You don't feel anything . . . (*Suddenly, angrily,* NOEL
thumps the table with his fist again, shaking the crockery. The
WAITRESS *enters.*)

CHRISTINE: Yes! (*Pause.* NOEL *looks at her.*)

NOEL: Can you simulate an orgasm?

MRS. BILEDEW: Here, what is this?

CHRISTINE (*looks at him, weighing him up*):   What's it worth?

NOEL: Prosperity. Draw up a chair.

MRS. BILEDEW: What about me?

NOEL: In a minute. (*The* WAITRESS *drags a chair to the table.*
MRS. BILEDEW *experiences a moment of clarity.*)

MRS. BILEDEW: You are mixed up with criminals!

BILEDEW: I told you so!

NOEL: This is purely a formality, Christine. I'm afraid I need to
see your thighs.

MRS. BILEDEW: You dirty minded little sod!

BILEDEW: This is where your cream horns come from!

CHRISTINE (*as she pulls up her skirt*):   I take it this is high class
modelling. I don't want any of your common clientele.

NOEL: Nothing beneath a barrister.

CHRISTINE: How's that?

NOEL: All right.

CHRISTINE: Only all right?

NOEL: I don't expect you'll make Miss World.

CHRISTINE: I do not wish to be Miss World. I'm after a decent
income like anybody else.

MRS. BILEDEW: Noel are you living off . . . of girls?

MRS. BILEDEW (*distraught, rises to her feet, speaks out to the
audience*):   I could have ripped the clothes off me, I could have

chucked my handbag, crocodile skin shoes and silk gloves in the gutter, I could have washed my mouth out with carbolic soap, I felt so sick and weary, so let down and dirty . . . (*Pause*)

BILEDEW: I told you so . . .

MRS. BILEDEW: And then I thought . . . what's done is done. There is no justice or I would have got my rewards long before now. What am I getting so high and mighty for, I had my little bit of happiness from his bad ways, this table in Fortnum and Mason's all due to him, not from the government or the charity of the rich, but by courtesy of Noel Biledew. You have to take what you can get, I'll pay for it at Judgement Day if I have to. I'm not young. I'll go along with it and what I don't like shut my eyes to. Lifting my little finger doesn't shake the stars, does it? (*She sits down again.*) Noel —

NOEL: Claw. (*Pause*)

MRS. BILEDEW: What? . . .

NOEL: My name. Is Claw. (*Pause*)

MRS. BILEDEW: I'm sorry I got difficult.

NOEL: This is Christine. She's signed with me.

MRS. BILEDEW: That's nice.

NOEL: Christine. My mum.

CHRISTINE: Pleased to meet you.

NOEL: I have found a niche for mum. She is going to take charge of wardrobes.

MRS. BILEDEW: Oh, Noel — I'm so happy, Claw . . .

NOEL: Christine, order some cakes. (CHRISTINE *clicks her fingers. Enter* BILEDEW, *holding a large, framed portrait of Karl Marx. They all gaze at him. He is heaving with emotion. Pause.*) Who let you in?

MRS. BILEDEW: This isn't any old tea bar, Biledew.

NOEL: Have you been walking down the streets with that? You must have looked a silly sod.

MRS. BILEDEW: Wait for me outside. By the No.68 bus stop. Quickly! Go on! (BILEDEW *sways on his feet, as if intoxicated with grief.*)

BILEDEW: He weeps!

NOEL (*to* CHRISTINE):   Cream slice?

BILEDEW: You betray him! You worms, crawling on the sweet carcass, you maggots in the watery filth!

CHRISTINE: Horrible old thing!

MRS. BILEDEW: Biledew, you are embarassing us in front of other people.

CHRISTINE: That's the idea. We get a lot of it in here. Show-offs, hippies, them bald-headed monks and that . . .

NOEL: Pull up a chair.

CHRISTINE (*shrinking*):   No thanks!

MRS. BILEDEW: Biledew, go home!

BILEDEW: I have come here on a mission. To destroy degeneracy.

NOEL: Haven't you misread the texts?

BILEDEW: How would you know?

NOEL: I have had acquaintance with the works. It seems to me the point of old weirdbeard's diagnosis was to hasten the corruption, not run after it with a dustpan and broom. Which confers on me the status of a hero, so sit down and shut your gob.

MRS. BILEDEW: ⎫
CHRISTINE: ⎭ Hear, hear.

BILEDEW: Oh, rancid worm, bred under my own roof —

NOEL (*rising to his feet*):   Not worm! Jaguar! Swift disemboweller of lazy herds! Red claw in the intestines of the overfed! (BILEDEW *glares at him, trembling, then with a cry of* 'Bastard!', *he brings down the heavy portrait on* NOEL's *head. There are screams from* MRS. BILEDEW *and* CHRISTINE, *the lights go out and the* 'Internationale' *erupts, then ceases.*)

Scene Five

BILEDEW *is alone on stage, hands hanging at his sides, under a spotlight.*

BILEDEW: Watching him at breakfast, I couldn't force the food down me for thinking how he was conceived in some bedroom, some room in some street somewhere in Birmingham, some room which is still there with the same wallpaper for all I know, and how she lay there under him moaning all night or afternoon for all I know with her clothes across a chair, or chucked on the floor because of their hurry and how he had all he wanted from her, pushing her like some warm thing against the wall, that same wallpaper still there in that room in the middle of that city somewhere where it happened on that night . . . (*He dries. The voice of the* MAGISTRATE *is heard.*)

MAGISTRATE: Had the attack occurred in some back street, in some low dive or public house, I would feel less disposed to allow my indignation to affect my judgement, but you calculatedly and deliberately chose to carry out this deed before the eyes of gentle and inoffensive persons taking tea, and I can only assume you did so in the furtherance of some misguided notion of class conflict, as the blunt instrument employed suggests. I am therefore withdrawing any influence of clemency that might have mollified my judgement. I sentence you to seven years. (*Pause*)

BILEDEW: I . . . I . . . my wife . . . during the war . . . in some bedroom with . . . the wallpaper . . . it's floral, I see it now . . . big roses with —

MAGISTRATE: Take him down.

BILEDEW: In Birmingham . . . I craved to know . . . what room it was . . . what window . . . was there running water in the room . . .

MAGISTRATE: Go down! (BILEDEW *is silent for a moment, gathers himself together. Suddenly he bursts out singing the* 'Red Flag', *noisily and out of tune.*

MAGISTRATE: Go down! Take him down!

Scene Six

The BILEDEW *home. Lying on a couch,* NOEL, *his head bandaged. A door slams off.*

MRS. BILEDEW (*off*): Claw! Claw!

NOEL: I'm kipping.

MRS. BILEDEW (*entering, in coat*): Biledew got seven years!

NOEL: Not bad.

MRS. BILEDEW: Seven years!

NOEL: Not bad. For attempted filicide.

MRS. BILEDEW: The poor old sod . . . my heart went out to him, he looked so frail beside the policeman, so hunched and undernourished. I expect people thought I never fed him properly. (*She takes her coat off.*) Seven years in some damp cell, with God knows who for company. He never had much

comfort, never knew real luxury, always said no to an electric
blanket or a bottle in the bed.

NOEL: He'll be in good condition for his deprivations, then.

MRS. BILEDEW: I wept . . . I called out to him but he looked
right through me . . . he looked so small . . . (*She sits in the
chair, clasping her knees.*)

NOEL: He might like prison. Reading is encouraged, I believe.

MRS. BILEDEW: I'll visit him. And meet him at the little door
when he comes out. Can't do more than that, can I? (*She jumps
up gaily.*)

NOEL: Scarcely. With your responsibilities.

MRS. BILEDEW: I was wondering, what with the vast increase
in our turnover, if maybe we weren't — over-extending?

NOEL: Big words for you.

MRS. BILEDEW: I mean . . . .you're doing very nicely.

NOEL: Quite adequate.

MRS. BILEDEW: You're rich . . .

NOEL: Relatively.

MRS. BILEDEW: You have a car.

NOEL: I have a car.

MRS. BILEDEW: That's good going.

NOEL: Good going — That's good going, is it?

MRS. BILEDEW: I'm happy, Claw . . .

NOEL: That's wonderful.

MRS. BILEDEW: Be happy too.

NOEL: I will be. Happiness is before me, glowing like the
sunset on a choppy sea, drawing me on . . .

MRS. BILEDEW: What to?

NOEL: Chelsea. The love nests of H.M. Government.

MRS. BILEDEW: Oh, Claw, what for?

NOEL: You wouldn't understand. Satisfaction is within arm's
reach for you.

MRS. BILEDEW: I'm glad.

NOEL: Of course.

MRS. BILEDEW: I only thought . . . for a young man . . . you
have so little fun . . . that's all . . .

NOEL: I'm anticipating it.

MRS. BILEDEW: But here . . .

NOEL: No, not here . . . just prowling here . . . (MRS. BILEDEW
looks at him, pityingly, then turns to go.) I have a dream. (*She stops,
in the doorway.*) To be a sort of Cecil Beaton . . . in big hats
. . . and white suits . . . with chiffon neckscarves blowing in the
wind . . . on beaches in Jamaica . . . with women and celeb-

rities . . . and flash bulbs popping at me . . . and my memoirs
in the 'Sunday Times' . . .

MRS. BILEDEW: That's nice . . .

NOEL: And then, in front of everybody . . . I would disem-
bowel myself . . . and chuck my innards in Mick Jagger's
gob . . . (*Pause.* MRS. BILEDEW *looks at him, lying there,
lost in thought.*)

MRS. BILEDEW: I'll put the kettle on. (*She goes out, returns at
once with a tray and puts it down.*) If anybody had told me that
Noel, or Claw, as he prefers to be called, wasn't absolutely
normal I'd have scratched their eyes out. But there is this matter
of that nasty blow, and who knows what effect that might have
had on the brain. Still, I'm his mother, and I'll stick by him.
(*She goes out. Suddenly there is a sound of splintering glass.
Enter right, two* ASSASSINS. *One holds a megaphone the other
a pistol. While one goes methodically through the room smashing
everything in sight and grinding it under his feet, the other, taking
up a convenient position, addresses the audience through the
megaphone.* NOEL *instantly covers his face.*)

FIRST ASSASSIN: Into the peacefulness of a suburban street,
the rude interruption of a Mafia punishment squad, hand picked
for its ruthlessness and total lack of human sympathy. No moral
code restrains them, no pity glimmers in their eyes, they are a
punishment squad issuing in this vivid way an unambiguous
message — GET OFF OUR PATCH! (*The* FIRST ASSASSIN
lowers his megaphone. NOEL *remains perfectly still, hands over
eyes. Then the* SECOND ASSASSIN *goes into the kitchen, and
drags in a terrified* MRS. BILEDEW.)

MRS. BILEDEW: You've got the wrong house! What have we
done!

FIRST ASSASSIN (*raising his megaphone*):   Typically the trans-
gressor adopts a policy of injured innocence.

MRS. BILEDEW (*forced to her knees*):   Don't hurt me! Don't
kill me! Don't hurt me, please!

FIRST ASSASSIN: There follows a succession of appeals to the
humanity of the assassins, the rejection of which inevitably
evokes despair, or sometimes even loss of consciousness.

MRS. BILEDEW (*as the* SECOND ASSASSIN *levels his
pistol*):   Oh, God...

FIRST ASSASSIN: A shot is fired, a signal for the car doors to
be opened and the squad to make an orderly retirement to their
vehicles.

The SECOND ASSASSIN *fires one shot, into* MRS. BILEDEW's
*hand. She screams. They withdraw. Sound of car doors slamming
and a vehicle roaring away.* MRS. BILEDEW *gets up, clutching
her hand.* NOEL *hasn't moved.*

MRS. BILEDEW: Bastards! (*She walks about, picking up odd
items, dropping them again.*) My home! My things! My little bits
I scraped together, not worth nothing, no use to nobody, things
I had to struggle for, not much, but my little things! (*She sobs
for a few moments.*) Noel . . .

NOEL: Claw . . .

MRS. BILEDEW: Noel to me! (*He removes his hands from his
eyes.*) I'm not cleaning this lot up. You can do it. (*She picks up a
chair, sits in it.*)

NOEL: I was afraid they'd smash my glasses. People always
want to smash my glasses.

MRS. BILEDEW: I've been shot!

NOEL: I know . . .

MRS. BILEDEW: Well, do something!

NOEL (*getting up*):   I'll get one of the girls.

MRS. BILEDEW: I want an ambulance!

NOEL: That's out of the question, you know that.

MRS. BILEDEW: I'll bleed to death.

NOEL: Run it under the tap. I won't be long. (*He grabs his
overcoat. She goes into the kitchen. He is about to go out when he
stops.*) When I heard that shot, I thought — Claw, you are a
dead man. Though of course rationally I knew all the time that a
bullet travels faster than sound, and were the shot aimed at me I
should have heard it only after the impact. But all the same I
experienced a great peace, like all the seas had drained
away . . . (*He ponders.*)

MRS. BILEDEW (*off*):   It hurts!

NOEL: (*snapping out of his mood, and buttoning his coat*): This is a
sign, of course. This is a clear warning. (*Enter* MRS. BILEDEW,
*her hand wrapped in a tea towel. She sits on the sofa, rocks to
and fro.*) **Not** to give in. **Not** to scuttle away, but to go higher,
use my long strides to bound into the exclusive areas where I
belong . . .

Suddenly MRS. BILEDEW *collapses.* NOEL *looks at her,
shocked. He lifts up her legs, laying her along the sofa, puts a
cushion under her head and hurries out.* MRS. BILEDEW, *deliri-
ous, talks to herself out loud.*

MRS. BILEDEW: Biledew . . . what have we reared? To think
   I carried him, down the A1 in that awful winter, hitching lifts
   from blokes who stuck their hands up me . . . just to be shot in
   the hand . . .

Enter NOEL, *followed by* NORA, *altogether more professional in
style and manner from her previous appearance. Seeing the room
she stops and gasps.*

NORA: Blimey!
NOEL: She isn't dead.
NORA: What a shambles . . .
NOEL: See to her!
NORA (*gazes round*):   What a going over . . .
NOEL: Send 'em a postcard with your congratulations on, why
   don't you?
NORA: Sorry.
NOEL: My old mother has been shot and all you do is stand and
   gawp!
NORA (*quickly sitting beside her on the sofa*):   Sorry. (*She is
   quite helpless and squeamish.*) How are you? How do you feel?
NOEL: Jesus Christ! Bind up her hand! (*She flusters, looking
   round.*) Oh, the leadweight of their intellects . . . and me like
   lightning on the icecap . . .
NORA: Is there a bandage in the . . .?
NOEL: Tear up a sheet. Like they do it on the pictures. And tip
   some Dettol over it. (NORA *rushes out.* NOEL *collapses in the
   chair.* NORA *enters, dragging a sheet.*)
NORA: Can't tear it. (NOEL *is motionless.*) Claw . . . (*Pause.
   He looks at her.*) Can't tear it. (*He looks blankly at her for a
   moment, then gets up, takes the sheet and rips it.*) Couldn't find
   the Dettol. Is bleach all right?
NOEL: Kills germs, don't it? That's all we want.

They go to MRS. BILEDEW *and sit beside her.* NOEL *douses her
hand with the bleach, then* NORA *begins tying the bandage.*
NOEL *watches her for some seconds. She ends with a knot.*

NORA: There. Done it.
NOEL: That was nice.
NORA: What?
NOEL: Watching you do that. Gave me funny feelings in my
   head. (*Pause*)

NORA: Oh . . .

NOEL: I never felt that . . . warm tingling in my head. (*Pause*)

NORA: Got a client at half past three . . . (*Long Pause. NOEL looks at her.*)

NOEL: Undress.

NORA (*incredulous*):   What?

NOEL: Please. Take your clothes off.

NORA (*more so*):   What?

NOEL: I'm asking you.

NORA: That's very nice, but I've got a client coming here at —

NOEL: Take 'em off! (*Pause*)

NORA: No. (*Pause*)

NOEL: Why not?

NORA: I don't want to.

NOEL: Blimey, you're doing it all bloody day!

NORA: That's for money!

NOEL: All right, I'll pay.

NORA: I couldn't take it.

NOEL: Look, I'm your employer!

NORA: I think that's how it should be left — (*She gets up.*)

NOEL (*on his feet too*):   Nora! (*She stops still. Pause.*)

NORA: I just . . . I really do not fancy you. (*Pause. He looks incredulous now.*)

NOEL: But you're a prostitute . . .

NORA: That's different. That's not personal. If you were a stranger, I might even do it as a favour, but I am acquainted with you, and that puts a different light on it. (*Pause*)

NOEL: Look . . . I'm not ashamed to admit that I . . . for various reasons I'm not all that . . . I'm a virgin . . . (*Pause*)

NORA: Christ . . .

NOEL: Funny, ain't it?

NORA: Jesus . . .

NOEL: So you see, I . . . if you would be so kind as to allow —

NORA: Oh, no, I couldn't possibly. Not now. It wouldn't be right. With me.

NOEL: It would.

NORA: No, not with me. With a nice girl —

NOEL: I don't know one.

NORA: I'm sure you will.

NOEL: Just then — watching you tie that bandage — I felt, I told you I felt warm, I never felt like that before, I felt so close to you.

NORA: Please, Claw . . .

NOEL: Call me Noel . . .
NORA: Out of the question.
NOEL: Look, don't turn me down, please —
NORA: I've got a client. I'm sorry —
NOEL: Please, Nora —
NORA: I'm sorry, no! (*She goes out, slams the door.*)
NOEL: (NOEL *staggers to the middle of the stage, his hands slowly extend in front of him, then in a paroxysm of despair.*) Oh give me wings, give me throttle, melting the tarmac to a sea of fire, the sleeve valves pissing carbon in the frosty air!

There is a roar of a full-throttled motorbike. His teeth clenched, his eyes half closed, NOEL *mimes riding a powerful machine along a bumpy road. The roar accelerates into a climax, there is a sickening skid but instead of a crash, the thud of a heavy steel door.* NOEL *retains a pre-death posture, handlebars askew, jaw twisted. Enter shuffling in prison clothes,* BILEDEW. *He looks at* NOEL.

BILEDEW: Thinks he's T.E. Lawrence. Wants to rub out with the seedy panache of a hero of imperialism. No such luck. For you, the bitter, hard path of the class struggle, which you are twisting your intestines into knots to miss. You cannot miss! It is written, your individualist daydreams lead only to the pit of self-disgust.
NOEL: Shut up.
BILEDEW: Wake up — 'Claw'.
NOEL (*still retaining posture*):   Shut up. I did not ask you to write to me on your snotty prison notepaper.
BILEDEW: Then read my thoughts.
NOEL: What for!
BILEDEW: Contentment.
NOEL: What's that?
BILEDEW: Contentment is to align yourself with the prevailing flow of history.
NOEL: Done you a lot of good, ain't it?
BILEDEW: I am happy.
NOEL: With your low expectations, happiness was a walkover.
BILEDEW: Must stop now, though I have much more to say.
NOEL: I wasn't going to read it anyway.
BILEDEW: Revolutionaries are the tallow in the candle of our dreams.
NOEL: What?
BILEDEW: I made that up.

NOEL: Who said you were a daft old git?

BILEDEW (*going out again, slowly*):   Have love, Noel, have love . . .

The steel door slams.

ACT TWO

Scene One

The drawing room of an expensive Chelsea residence. CLAPCOTT, *a Home Secretary, is seated in an armchair. He is working through a paper, ticking off items. His patience is eroded. Suddenly, he throws back his head.*

CLAPCOTT: Paroles, paroles, bloody paroles! Everybody's on parole! (*He looks back at the list, draws a thick line cruelly across a name.*) Well, no! Not you! You stay and rot! (*Pause. He reads on.*) Let you out, you go and murder somebody, makes me look a bloody fool. (*Pause*) Social workers are in league with 'em. (*He works on.*) More convicts out than in, as far as I can see. (*He ticks, stops, draws a cruel line.*) Not you! Remember you. Swore to castrate the judge if I remember rightly. 'No gaol will hold me!' Loud mouthed yob. Now crawling on your knees after parole. Loathsome specimen. (*He carries on, stops. He takes some whisky, looks at his watch, yawns, carries on.*) Yes . . . yes . . . (*He ticks names.*) Oh, yes . . . yes . . . yes . . . timid little embezzlers . . . yes . . . yes . . . yes . . . (*He stops.*) Child murderers! What's got into them! I distinctly said no one's crucifying me for some itchy fingered child killer. (*He draws a line through it.*) Impertinence. (*He looks up.*) Wandering round commons with their doodles out, get carried away, impale some infant, costs a fortune finding them. (*Pause*) My eyes are tired . . . (*He ticks away, squinting.*) Must get some drops . . . (*He ticks some more, then impatiently.*) The rest are noes. (*He draws a long, diagonal line through, then drops the file on the floor.*) No gratitude in any case. Don't even have the decency to send a note. Don't expect literacy, just a little gratitude. (*The front door slams.*)

ANGIE (*off*):   Oo — oo!

CLAPCOTT *groans, takes a swig of whisky. Enter in long fur-trimmed coat,* ANGIE. *She is forty-five, bright-eyed, energetic.*

CLAPCOTT: You weren't coming back tonight.

ANGIE (*slipping off her coat*):   His wife's in town. He said did I want a hotel, I said no, let's do without the physicals, he looked put out, like some school boy done out of his afters. Anyway, I wasn't interested. He looked podgy, I felt sick after the cassata, he got me a taxi, and here I am. (*She goes out with the coat, returns, sits down.*)

CLAPCOTT: I was rather planning on being alone tonight.

ANGIE: I'll go to bed.

CLAPCOTT: If you would.

ANGIE: Or do you want it?

CLAPCOTT: The bed? No, I don't want the bed.

ANGIE: Didn't think you would. Never shit on your own door-step. That's what you learn at public school.

CLAPCOTT (*coldly*):   How would **you** know?

ANGIE: Well, isn't it?

CLAPCOTT: Did you go to public school?

ANGIE: You know bloody well I didn't.

CLAPCOTT: Shut up, then.

ANGIE: Oh, dear. A rotten evening with the prison files. Two hours with the parole list and you're behaving like an East-bourne magistrate.

CLAPCOTT (*measured*):   I've been sitting here, quietly engaged in work involving the hopes and happiness of several hundred people, my eyes are tired, my mind is full of doubts of the most serious nature, and you come in, quite unexpectedly, jibbering like an inebriated whore and expect me to be entertaining —

ANGIE: Never!

CLAPCOTT: You have been whoring, haven't you? As good as?

ANGIE (*icily*):   Never entertaining. Not from the first day that we met. **Never entertaining**. (*Pause*)

CLAPCOTT: You didn't have to marry me.

ANGIE: You pestered me.

CLAPCOTT: You didn't **have** to marry me.

ANGIE: No . . .

CLAPCOTT: Well, then.

ANGIE: I was led on. By the insinuations of the press. The burst of flashbulbs blinded my discrimination. It was all too glamorous. And I was all too young, and innocent . . .

CLAPCOTT: Innocent! At twenty-six? A dancer in a chorus line, too innocent? You went into it wide-eyed with avarice . . . (*Pause*)

ANGIE: You wouldn't leave me alone. You never have.

CLAPCOTT: That's my misfortune. It was one of those things.

ANGIE: A ghastly, everlasting, chemical attraction.

CLAPCOTT: I've paid the price.

ANGIE (*recollecting*):   The earnest, puppy politician, and the long-legged chorus-girl . . . (*Suddenly she sits forward.*) Shall we get the cuttings out?

CLAPCOTT: No.

ANGIE: Oh, go on!

CLAPCOTT (*glaring at her*):   No.

ANGIE: No . . . (*Pause*)

CLAPCOTT: Look, why don't you go to bed?

ANGIE: Who's coming? (*He doesn't answer.*) An expert in ballistics? An authority on urban terrorism? A high-level conference, lasting late into the morning . . . Oh, the bloody glamour of it all . . . (*With inspiration.*) Can I stay?

CLAPCOTT: No. You cannot.

ANGIE: I'm not tired . . .

CLAPCOTT: We did agree, I think —

ANGIE: Oh, yes. I don't embarass you, and you give me a free hand in exchange . . .

CLAPCOTT: That's fair.

ANGIE: Oh, yes, appallingly. A real political deal.

CLAPCOTT: You've got the country cottage, jammed with second-hand car dealers, Hells Angels, Hippies, Christ knows what, go where you like with who you like, rubber-stamped moral disaster, but at least we keep it civil. All I ask is kindly do not fart around in my sphere. I don't think that's unreasonable.

ANGIE: Oh, no . . .

CLAPCOTT: You signed a bit of paper.

ANGIE: I know I did. We went together with it to the bank.

CLAPCOTT: Exactly. (*He looks at his watch.*) Now, if you don't mind — I have a visitor.

ANGIE (*getting up*):   I know all that, Gee-Gee, but I do sometimes get a little curious . . . the murmur of political voices in the drawing room . . . the hum of the conspiracy which keeps the lousy rotten show on the road . . . (*Pause*) Can't I sit in?

CLAPCOTT: No.

ANGIE: I wouldn't speak.

CLAPCOTT: This is a top-level —

ANGIE: Well, of course it is!

CLAPCOTT: I don't ask to sit in on your seedy weekends.

ANGIE: No . . . I will say that for you. you're not a masochist.

CLAPCOTT: Go to bed . . .

ANGIE: Are you? (*Pause*)

CLAPCOTT: My work. Above all things. The rest — is rubbish. (*Pause*) Goodnight. (ANGIE *starts to go out, stops, turns.*)

ANGIE: You know, you should have divorced me. When the PM told you to. When you were nobody. (*She goes out. He reminisces.*)

CLAPCOTT: Third from the end . . . in the chorus line of 'Carousel' . . . with legs that never ended . . . I couldn't tear my eyes off her . . . and hair like copper . . . when the spotlights caught it . . . took my breath away . . . every movement seemed like an appeal to me . . . We married in St. Martins . . . in February . . . it was snowing in the wind . . . newspaper photographers, wetting themselves with anticipation . . . and she came up the aisle and stood beside me . . . the organ was still playing and I whispered . . . what colour are your panties? No colour, she said . . . what . . . transparent, I gasped . . . No . . . none, she said . . . I was fainting at the thought of it . . . (*Pause*) Prime Minister called me in his office. Old beaver glared at me . . . half spectacles catching the sunlight filtering through the Horseguards . . . Georgie, he said, keep a tight rein. I must have looked confused. Your actress, he said. Got itchy hips . . . (*Pause*) She was in the bath . . . shaving her legs, to be precise . . . and I went in and said . . . evidence has reached me, you are carrying on with somebody. Simply. Briefly. Like that. And then she abused me. Consistently abused me, for about half an hour . . . screaming . . . breaking things . . . and at the end of it I locked her in her room . . . and my nerves were like hot needles . . . and I went and drank myself silly in the summerhouse . . . (*Pause*) And then it became regular. We went to a psychiatrist. She said I was inadequate, which isn't true. At least in my opinion . . . though I appreciate these things are relative. And then one day, the PM called me in . . . half spectacles catching the sunlight filtering through the Horseguards . . . and he said . . . Georgie, you've got a right one there . . . unstable marriages . . . terrible handicaps to promotion in the government. I'm afraid I can't give you the Treasury. I felt a prickling sensation in my eyes . . . the room was blurred . . . I was crying . . . I blinked, desperately blinked. He fobbed me off with Under-Secretary to the Colonial Office, as it was then. I wished to Christ I'd never set eyes on 'Carousel'. I wished the whole damned chorus line to buggery. All I wanted was to get home and do the bitch an injury. (*Pause*) There she was, shaving her legs. Your whoring, I said, has cost me the Treasury, I remember she just looked at me and one word escaped from her lips. 'Yippee . . .'

He recollects it bitterly for some moments, but his thoughts are interrupted by the door bell. He gets up, goes out. Suddenly, conspiratorially, ANGIE enters in a dressing gown, and with a glance over her shoulder, secretes herself behind the thick velvet curtains.

Enter CLAPCOTT, *followed by* NOEL, *wearing a well cut dark suit, and expensive, tinted lenses with gold frames. He is carrying a briefcase. He looks around him, taking everything in.* CLAPCOTT *turns the key in the lock.* NOEL *seems surprised.*

CLAPCOTT: Security. Somebody's always after maiming you, kidnapping you, torturing you. Can't mow the lawn without some maniac wanting to blow your head off. These are rotten times. Whisky?

NOEL: Thank you.

CLAPCOTT (*goes to the bottles*):   Periodical. This loss of faith. Sort of moral vacuum. Just our bad luck to be stuck in the middle of an all-time low. Ice?

NOEL: Thank you.

CLAPCOTT: Took a ten day course in unarmed combat. Bloody farce. Rolling about on coconut matting in the basement of the Home Office. (*He hands him a drink.*) Everywhere I went I had this police van trailing me, loaded with matting. They unrolled it and I snatched a lesson whereever I happened to be. Got bruises all along my spine. Try me.

NOEL *looks surprised.* CLAPCOTT, *without waiting for his acquiescence, flings open the small drawer and removes a small pistol.*

CLAPCOTT: Don't worry. Take the bullets out. (*He removes the magazine, throws it on the table. Then he hands the pistol to* NOEL.) Now. Threaten me! (NOEL *holds it, unconvincingly.*) Wave it about. Try to hate me. Be an Arab. Look violent. (NOEL *adopts a stance.*) Good. Now to start with I just play it cool. I lull you into a sense of false security. (*Pause*) How does it go? Er . . . hang on . . . Yes, right. (*He quotes from memory.*) I want you to know, from the bottom of my heart, that the problems of your people — (*He stops.*) You are an Arab? If you're Irish I have a different text, you see . . . okay . . . that the problems of your people are forever uppermost in my thoughts, and I am at this moment — that's the bit, you see, imply some new development — in secret negotiations with the Liberation Front — (*He stops, goes to* NOEL, *pushes his gun hand down a little.*) By now your gunhand is supposed to drop a bit . . . that's it . . . you're lulled, you see . . . (*He goes back to his original position.*) — in secret negotiations with the Liberation Front for the immediate release of all those members who — (*Suddenly he makes a dive for* NOEL's *gun but fails miserably to secure it. Instead he crashes head first into the armchair.*) Don't shoot! (*He covers his head with his hands.* NOEL *just aims the pistol at him.* CLAPCOTT *slowly gets up.*) You were expecting it. The idea is to confuse them by implying that their action is superfluous. One assumes they speak good English, obviously. (*He holds out his hand for the gun.*) If we miss we have to cry 'Don't shoot!' as a sort of last appeal. (*He replaces the magazine, puts the gun away in the drawer.*) They don't hold out much hope for that. (*He rubs his back for a moment.*) Now then . . . in a word . . . (*He sits, expectantly.*) Long legs. (*He indicates the other chair.* NOEL *sits.*) I don't go for the dumpy stuff.

NOEL: You didn't go for Rosie, then?

CLAPCOTT: No legs. And dull as ditchwater.

NOEL: Really? She is a graduate.

CLAPCOTT: Of where?

NOEL: Essex, I think . . .

CLAPCOTT: I don't call those things universities. Anyway, she prattled too much. Thought she could help keep tabs on left-wing clients. Wanted to be a spy or something. Bored me stiff.

NOEL (*opening his briefcase with a snap*):   I'm sorry.

CLAPCOTT: Who was that one at party conference? (NOEL *takes out a thick, glossy file of pictures.*)

NOEL: Stacey?

CLAPCOTT: I wouldn't know, but she had legs.

NOEL: I have a picture here, somewhere . . .

CLAPCOTT: Big   mouth . . . black   hair . . . the   common touch . . .

NOEL (*finding the picture*):   Yes . . . her. (*He holds up the picture.* CLAPCOTT *tips his head to one side.*)

CLAPCOTT: Could be . . .

NOEL: I thought perhaps you'd care for something new.

CLAPCOTT: Well, yes, of course . . .

NOEL: I was thinking, maybe Lindsay . . . or Annabelle . . .

CLAPCOTT (*getting up*): Show me. (*He takes the book.*) Red hair?

NOEL: Natural.

CLAPCOTT: Really?

NOEL: Can I get myself a drink?

CLAPCOTT (*gazing at the picture*): Yes, of course . . . (NOEL *goes to the bottles.*) Any education?

NOEL: Swiss.

CLAPCOTT (*intrigued*): Oh . . . foreign accent?

NOEL: No, just a finishing school. But she can do it if you want.

CLAPCOTT: I'd like that.

NOEL: I'll make a note of it.

CLAPCOTT: Yes, do. (*He flicks through.*)

NOEL (*returning with drink*): That's settled, then.

CLAPCOTT: I think so . . . (*He stops at a picture.*) Who is this?

NOEL (*looking over his shoulder*): Ahh . . . that's Nora.

CLAPCOTT (*disparagingly*): Nora . . .

NOEL: Yes. We began as a team, and I've kept her ever since.

CLAPCOTT: Spoils the catalogue.

NOEL: Yes . . . a sentimental thing, that's all.

CLAPCOTT: Rubbish . . . body like a rabbit's arse . . .

NOEL: Mind you, there have been offers.

CLAPCOTT: Can't think why. Face like cat's spew. (*Suddenly, from behind the curtains, the loud, measured voice of* ANGIE.)

ANGIE: You vile pig . . . (*There is a startled pause.* CLAPCOTT *instantly knows the situation.* NOEL *looks, with dismay, at the source of the voice.* CLAPCOTT *takes* NOEL *gently by the arm.*)

CLAPCOTT: I'm very sorry. I must ask you to go.

ANGIE: Don't go! (NOEL *stares at the curtain.*)

CLAPCOTT: If you would please, Biledew —

ANGIE: Sod it, stick around!

CLAPCOTT (*to* NOEL): This must seem bizarre, but I really must insist — (*He begins pushing* NOEL *to the door.*)

ANGIE: Top level meeting! Gee-Gee, you are a shit!

CLAPCOTT (*turning angrily*): Shut up, damn you! (*At last* ANGIE *sweeps back the curtain and steps out.*)

ANGIE (*to* NOEL): I'm Angie. How d'you do? (*She puts out her hand.* NOEL *takes it, looking into her eyes. They freeze for a few bars of a musical routine. She lets go of his hand.*) Gee-Gee keeps me hidden, don't you, dear? Like some shameful syphlitic relative, secreted in the attic. Actually I am his wife, as of 15th Febraury, 1952.

CLAPCOTT: I'm sorry you had to be subjected to this, Biledew, I'm sure you won't want to —

ANGIE (*pulling a face*):   Bile — dew? What an awful name.

NOEL: I inherited it.

ANGIE: Well, change it then. I was called Myrtle Ackroyd, but I changed it to Angie Diamond. Anyone can do it.

NOEL: I like my name.

CLAPCOTT (*staring at her*):   Lurking behind curtains, like a cheap thief . . .

ANGIE: I had a longing to experience the agony and tension of a major political decision. It's not my fault if I was tricked.

CLAPCOTT: You're drunk.

ANGIE: No. I have just had a blinding flash of insight. Into the tawdry circumstances of your life.

CLAPCOTT: Biledew, if you don't mind —

ANGIE: Oh, no, he can't go now! He might leave with completely the wrong impression. He might let it be known that we're not — compatible!

CLAPCOTT: You treacherous, insensitive bitch.

ANGIE: With his contacts there'd be a scandal strong enough to lift the fart-filled skirts of the Tory party and then where would poor Gee-Gee be?

CLAPCOTT: This disgusting, interminable squabbling . . .

ANGIE: Oh yes, the terrible squalor of domestic truths, compared to your mutual — purity . . . he must be shocked. Can I look through the catalogue? (*Without waiting for permission, she grabs up the catalogue.*) Who was it now, Lindsay, or Annabelle . . . (*She flicks through.*) Long legs are mandatory . . . (*She stops.*) Oh, the monotony of his predilections. Hair — red. Bust--36. (*She looks at* NOEL.) Has he asked for chorus costumes?

CLAPCOTT: Shut up.

ANGIE: He has a very stable chemistry, does Gee-Gee. Always bolts the same old dish. (*She tosses the book down on an armchair, looks at* NOEL.) You must find Gee-Gee and his cronies awfully pitiful. I mean, I knew he got his oats somewhere, but through a — what **do** you call yourself?

NOEL: A pimp. (*Pause*)

ANGIE (*impressed*): Do you . . . (*Pause*)

CLAPCOTT: All right, so you've made a great discovery. Congratulations. Your dirty little trick's paid off.

ANGIE (*sitting with deliberate poise*): Don't worry. It's not possible for you to sink in my estimation.

CLAPCOTT: Don't imagine that bothers me!

ANGIE: Don't be silly. Of course it does. It's completely wrecked your miserable little edifice of moral superiority. I was rather led to believe you went without. Or had something awfully decent going on. But no. You're pure shit. (*She smiles, turns to look at* NOEL.) How old are you?

NOEL: Twenty-seven.

ANGIE: So young and so — (*Pause*) How much do you make a year?

CLAPCOTT: Don't be impertinent!

ANGIE: In response to public pressure Gee-Gee's working on some legislation to eradicate your type. Aren't you, Gee-Gee?

CLAPCOTT: Go to bed . . . (*Pause*)

ANGIE: Yes . . . I will . . . (*She gets up and goes to the door. She turns to* NOEL.) How much is Lindsay? (NOEL *hesitates*.) How much?

NOEL: Two hundred pounds.

ANGIE: Two hundred pounds. For his miserable little efforts . . . (*She unlocks the door, opens it.*) And there are people living on ten pounds a week . . . (*She goes out, unhurriedly, closing the door behind her.* NOEL *watches her, transfixed.*)

NOEL: I watched her . . . I watched her and I wanted — to bite her arse! (*Pause*)

CLAPCOTT: Well, now you know, don't you? (NOEL *looks at him.*) The private burdens public figures have to bear. Imagine trying to smile with **that** behind you. Like swallowing elastic bands . . . (*He sits down, as if very tired.*) I don't deserve it. Christ knows I've done no wrong. Been ambitious, maybe. Couldn't see a ladder without wanting to climb up it. Not my fault, though . . . Don't know why I'm apologizing, nothing wrong with getting on . . . what the Tory party's all about . . . my father was a self-made man. Came from nowhere. Built a factory. Are you interested?

NOEL: Fascinated.

CLAPCOTT: After the war, looked for a place to conquer, some field where the competition wasn't fierce, and there was the Conservative Party, flat on its back. I got myself a reputation for reliability. Not brilliance, but reliability. They go for that. And they bought me. I had smooth cheeks. And this way of looking at people in the eyes. Always. Right in the eyes. I suppose you noticed that? And the handshake. Like a vice. Not too prolonged, but very firm. You can read a handshake. Mine says — reliability. They never liked Rab Butler in this party. His handshake was like a dying fish. Heath's was the same, but he forced himself.

NOEL: I've never been in a politician's house before. Been in managing directors' houses, and lawyers' houses. They have a smell. Of endless squirming. Mind you, my nose is very sensitive, because my eyes are so weak. Nature's generous like that. My mother's house smelt of panic.

CLAPCOTT: And what does this place smell of?

NOEL: Contempt.

CLAPCOTT (*smiling*): My wife's perfume lingering on the air . . .

NOEL: No, it comes from you.

CLAPCOTT: Really? You're dangerously outspoken for a pimp.

NOEL: I'm entitled to be a bit rude when I feel like it. I'm like a jester. I know a little something about everyone.

CLAPCOTT: Regale me.

NOEL: You'd like that, wouldn't you? Is the PM into bondage? Is the Employment Secretary a fetishist? (*He walks a little way, puts the catalogue back in his briefcase.*) People always want to know who else is swimming in the pitch.

CLAPCOTT: You needn't sound so damned censorious!

NOEL: Did I?

CLAPCOTT: You can't go peddling your wares and then get on your moral high horse when somebody purchases.

NOEL: Why not?

CLAPCOTT: Not fair practice, is it?

NOEL: Even the devil knows a sin.

CLAPCOTT: Sin! (*He laughs.*) A sin! Since when was laying whores a sin! (NOEL *just looks at him.*) A puritanical pimp. Good God . . . How you must suffer, as you cash your cheques . . .

NOEL: Pimping has its penalties. Until a very little while ago I felt sure my libido had done a bunk on me. (*He snaps the case shut.*)

CLAPCOTT: My heart bleeds for you. All that minge about. It must be hell. Now, if you don't mind, I have a couple of expulsion orders to confirm. Two Asians washed up on the Isle

of Grain. (*He reaches for his files, drops them on his lap.*)
Would you see yourself out, there's a good chap. (*He puts on his glasses, cranes forward over the files.*)

NOEL (*aside*): So I left the white slug's drawing room, my heart full of malice, but my head buzzing with the sleek tart who was his wife. And in the hallway — very Clapcott, very Sandersons —

ANGIE: Rock me, baby . . . .all night long . . .

NOEL (*transfixed*): Cast a spell on me . . .

ANGIE: Shake, rattle and roll me . . .

NOEL: Why not, Chuck?

ANGIE: Highway child . . .

NOEL: Have hog, will travel . . .

ANGIE: Battersea Bridge. Hot dogs. At three . . .

NOEL: Burn me . . . (*A few bars of Elvis Presley's* All Shook up'. CLAPCOTT *looks up from his file.*)

CLAPCOTT: Didn't like that specimen. Can't see his eyes. Negotiate by phone in future. Never let the underworld into your home. (*He looks back at the file.*) Well no, Mustafa! (*He draws across the name on his file.*) Back to Karachi you must go! Ee — ay, ee — ay, ee — ay — o!

Scene Two

A layby on the Kingston By-Pass. A motorbike stops.

ANGIE: I've done it quicker. On a Norton.

NOEL: Hold up at the Malden roundabout.

ANGIE: I counted that. (*He shrugs. Pause. She takes out a chocolate bar, begins eating it.*) Last time I was here with a member of the Milwaukee Chapter. He was half apache. I was his squaw for nearly a week. Then he was shot in Birmingham. Or was it drowned in Brighton? We didn't have a lot to say. (*She wanders aimlessly.*) Reaching one's destination is such an anti-climax in this game. Want a bite? (*She extends the bar to him. He takes a bite. Sounds of cars passing.*) I hate the country. It bores me stiff. (*Pause. Then NOEL gets off the bike and heaves it onto its stand.*)

NOEL: Did you want to marry him?

ANGIE: Gee-Gee? Yes, desperately.

NOEL: He's vile.

ANGIE: Oh, yes.

NOEL: I don't see it. He's ugly. He has horrible habits.

ANGIE: He didn't always look that hideous. Well . . . perhaps he did . . .

NOEL: Why, then?

ANGIE: I was such a rotten dancer. That was the key to it. My sense of timing was atrocious, and I never have been able to touch my toes. They were about to chuck me out. Not that he noticed. He was obsessed. Another week and I would have got my cards. Then he proposed . . . And I did so want to be a member of the upper class . . .

NOEL (*surprised*):   Weren't you?

ANGIE: Not then. I was born out of wedlock in the vicinity of Aldershot.

NOEL (*with delight*):   Bastard!

ANGIE: They did get married. He was a private in the Engineers.

NOEL (*smiling with joy*):   Bastard! Beautiful bastard! You common slut . . .

ANGIE: Most people are disappointed when they find that out. They like to think I'm from the top drawer. You'd be amazed at the things they say when they're having me. Or perhaps you wouldn't, in your line . . . (*Pause*)

NOEL: Climbing, slithering, clawing our way up the side of the barrel, then — flip! Over the top, into the real pus, into the real poison . . .

ANGIE: Well, now we're in it, we don't want to go back, do we? (*Pause. NOEL sits.*) My husband wouldn't like to think you're having an affair with me. (*He looks up.*) You are going to have an affair with me?

NOEL: It crossed my mind . . .

ANGIE: I signed a piece of paper saying I would desist from his friends or business acquaintances.

NOEL: You'll have to re-negotiate the contract. I'm an unforeseen condition. (*Pause*)

ANGIE: Well . . . (*She looks at him.*) Unzip a banana . . . (*NOEL looks confused for a moment, then shocked.*)

NOEL: What . . . here?

ANGIE: Yes.

NOEL: The cars . . .

ANGIE: The audacity! (*She smiles, starts to unzip her jacket.*)

NOEL: Wait a minute. I don't think this environment appeals to

me. You know what an uncertain business this can be . . .
however much you might want to . . . People are watching!

ANGIE: Only on their way to Guildford. The merest glimpse, at
sixty miles an hour. It's a Clearway, Noel . . . (*Pause. He is
hesitant.*)

NOEL: Angie . . .

Loud music from a musical dance routine. ANGIE *adopts a chorus
line posture, and high kicks her way behind the shrubbery.*
After a few moments NOEL *tears off his jacket and follows after.
Sound of a distant motorbike, approaching. Laughter from behind
the bushes. The motorbike stops, the engine is switched off.*

A POLICE MOTORCYCLIST *enters. He looks at* NOEL's
*bike, with suspicion. A burst of giggling diverts his attention. He
lies on his belly and crawls towards the edge of the shrubbery.*
Suddenly NOEL *bursts out in song, from* 'South Pacific'.

NOEL: I'm in love, I'm in love, I'm in love, I'm in love, I'm in
love with a won — der — ful . . . guy!

ANGIE: Once you have found him, never let him go . . . Once
you have found him . . .

NOEL: ⎫
ANGIE:⎭   Nev — er let him go!

They exclaim ecstatically. The POLICE MOTORCYCLIST *care-
fully removes his notebook.*

NOEL: We'll murder him.

ANGIE: Pump him full of lead.

NOEL: You beautiful angel . . .

ANGIE: Blow his brains out.

NOEL: You beautiful sinner . . .

ANGIE: Rape him with chrome handlebars.

NOEL: Dismember him.

ANGIE: Cut off his little true blue penis.

NOEL: I love you. I am raging with love for you!

ANGIE: No, not again . . .

NOEL: It hurts . . .

The POLICE MOTORCYCLIST *retreats, and leans against the
motorbike.*

ANGIE: Take me to a restaurant. Some lousy, decrepit restaurant with Pepsi-Cola stickers — (*She appears, sees the* POLICE MOTORCYCLIST, *stops a second, then continues with calculated indifference.*) — and a plastic orange drifting round in urine coloured orange juice. (*She takes out a comb, and begins combing her hair.*)

Enter NOEL, *zipping up his jacket.*

PC: Is this your bike?

NOEL: Don't spoil everything.

PC: I asked you a question. Is this your bike?

NOEL: Don't spoil everything! (*Pause*)

PC (*observing his spectacles*): Can you read a number plate at twenty —

NOEL: You've been listening. You've been standing here watching — and listening.

ANGIE: Noel . . .

NOEL: You filth.

ANGIE: Take me home, Noel, I feel — (*She chooses her word.*) — shagged.

PC (*turning to her*): Well, I'm afraid that isn't on. Just careering home with a half-blind driver, following the uttering of threats against an unknown party, following conspiracy to murder. It's not on.

NOEL: Fuck off! (*Violently, the* POLICE MOTORCYCLIST *turns to* NOEL *and takes a step towards him, but impulsively* NOEL *trips him. He stumbles.*)

ANGIE: Oh, God! (*Grabbing a brick from the foot of a litter bin,* NOEL *hits the* POLICE MOTORCYCLIST *on the helmet.*)

NOEL: Start it! (ANGIE *attempts to kick start the bike.*) Start it! Start it!

ANGIE: I can't! (*The* POLICE MOTORCYCLIST, *sinking at* NOEL's *feet, grabs him round the legs and clings on.*) I can't!

NOEL *hits the* POLICE MOTORCYCLIST *several more times before grabbing the waste bin and ramming it over his head. Then he pulls free and goes to the bike.*

ANGIE *sits on the pillion and* NOEL *kickstarts it, revs up and pushes it off the stand. The stunned* POLICE MOTORCYCLIST *grabs the bike by the rear number plate. There is a roar and* NOEL *slips into gear and drives away, leaving the* POLICE MOTOR-CYCLIST *holding the plate, stumbling round in a circle.*

Scene Three

A café. Sitting at the table, holding hands above a crusty sugar bowl, ANGIE *and* NOEL.
　Enter CHRISTINE, *a slovenly and very pregnant waitress.*

CHRISTINE:　What?
NOEL (*not taking his eyes off* ANGIE):　Orange. Twice. (CHRISTINE *goes off.*)
ANGIE:　Gee-Gee will be — apoplectic.
NOEL:　Let him bleed.
ANGIE:　He's very hot on protecting our policemen. He's chairman of the police widows' fund.
NOEL:　He'll fix it.
ANGIE:　Gee-Gee is a savage. He'll wound you, secretly.
NOEL:　I've got all the cards . . .
ANGIE:　Court jesters are dispensable.
NOEL:　You'll save me. Or we'll all sink together. My claws are in him now. I'll drag him down.

CHRISTINE *returns with two orange squashes in paper cups. She slams them down clumsily.*

CHRISTINE:　Twenty P. (NOEL *reaches into his pocket. With a flash of inspiration,* CHRISTINE *throws a cup of orange in* NOEL's *face.*) I know you! You cheating swine!
ANGIE (*jumping to her feet*):　You stupid bitch.
CHRISTINE:　Sit down! (*She shoves* ANGIE *in the chest. She falls back in her seat.*) Claw, is it? Big Claw, is it? You dirty little bleeder!
ANGIE:　What are you on about?
CHRISTINE:　He ruined my life, that's what! I had a decent job when I met him. High class waitressing with great big tips! Fortnum and Mason's — I could have been the manageress! But no, he had to come and spoil it, the dirty ponce!
NOEL (*wiping his eyes*):　I know you . . .
CHRISTINE:　Yeah, you know me, dropped me, didn't you? When I got pregnant by one of his dirty types, kicked me out when I was four months gone and lost my fiancé —
ANGIE:　I don't see why we need to stay —
CHRISTINE:　Because this bastard ruined me, that's why! 'Claw', who was gonna get so big! And look at him, a dirty little rocker! You have got big!

NOEL: Christine, isn't it . . .

CHRISTINE: He knows my name! How marvellous, after so long! What a memory for tarts! My legs aren't quite so lovely now, with three kids and another on the way. Do you wanna offer me a job? Nothing below a barrister!

NOEL (*avoiding her face*):   How are you, Christine?

CHRISTINE: How am I, Christine . . . you hypocrite . . . seven years since I saw you, and I haven't forgotten your mug, Four Eyes, nor your old mother, you pair of swine. (NOEL *gets up, reaches into his pocket and takes a wallet out. He holds out two five pound notes.*) You scum. Never show your face in here again. I'll set the alsatians on yer. (*She takes the money.*)

Scene Four

CLAPCOTT's *Chelsea drawing-room. A door slams off.*

CLAPCOTT *enters in overcoat and hat. He stops, sniffs the air.*

CLAPCOTT: I know that smell. That smell is cannabis. Thinly disguised beneath an aerosol. (*He goes to the ashtray, picks up a butt, sniffs it.*) Not that she likes the stuff. It gives her head-aches. It's to spite me. She has a policy of pinpricks, which she assumes will eventually drain my veins. (*He removes his overcoat, goes out, hangs it up, returns.*) She is a dismal failure in this, as in everything.

Enter ANGIE, *elegant.*

ANGIE: How was the debate?

CLAPCOTT (*sitting down*):   Skilful. Some decent speeches all round. Opposition ragged, though, as usual.

ANGIE: Then you all had a drink in the Members' Bar.

CLAPCOTT: Of course.

ANGIE: The terrible bitterness of it all! (*She goes to the drinks, pours a whisky.*) Gee-Gee, I want you to block a prosecution. (*She takes the drink to him, holds it out. He doesn't take it.*)

CLAPCOTT: Whose? (*Pause*)

ANGIE: Biledew's. (*He looks profoundly shocked.*) Your pimp . . . is in a bit of bother with the fuzz. (*He gawps at her.*)

I'm sorry, but you might as well know now. So you can nip it in the bud. (*Pause. She thrusts the drink at him. He swallows eagerly.*) All you have to do is to pick up the phone and ring the bloody Chief Commissioner and say — whatever you say — take the heat off, man — Official Secrets Act, or D Notice, or something — I could do it for you —

CLAPCOTT: Stop prattling! (*She shrugs, sits in the other armchair, crosses her legs, taps her fingers. He wipes his mouth.*) What do you know? What has he done?

ANGIE: Struck a copper.

CLAPCOTT: Oh, my God. What with?

ANGIE: A brick.

CLAPCOTT: Oh, Christ!

ANGIE (*impatiently*): He had a helmet on!

CLAPCOTT: Why you? Why did he ring you? Why didn't he tell me? I'm the person he wants if he wants a cover up, not you. Why you?

ANGIE: Well . . .

CLAPCOTT: Well?

ANGIE (*gets up, walks a few paces*): I was with him at the time. (*He gawps again.*) We were fifteen miles from Guildford. In a layby, when this — zealous copper came along . . . (*He looks at her, she looks at him. Pause.*)

CLAPCOTT: I wish you dead. (*Pause*) No more than that. (*Pause*) Just dead. And totally forgotten.

ANGIE: Yes, I understand that. We would have got away with it, but . . . you know what they're like . . . throwing themselves on the bonnets of cars and so on . . . he rivetted himself to the back number plate . . . and it came off. So you see, it's only a matter of time before they — swoop.

CLAPCOTT (*aside*): And I went to the PM's office . . . and the old beaver glared at me . . . half spectacles catching the sunlight filtering through the Horseguards . . . and he said, Gee-Gee, that woman is out to ruin. She'll have your balls off, and carry your castration through the streets. Buy her a fast car, he said. All you can hope for is an accident.

ANGIE: He can't go to court. (*Pause*) Can he? (*Pause*) The copper saw me, Gee-Gee!

CLAPCOTT: No . . .

ANGIE: Thank God. I thought for a moment you were envisaging some — glorious kamikaze exit from the government.

CLAPCOTT: Drowning, in all the sewage which came welling up. . . .

ANGIE: After all, it's not just you, is it? (*He shakes his head.*)
Anyway, I'm sorry I broke our agreement. It was just . . .
Anyway, it happened . . .

CLAPCOTT: Yes . . . (ANGIE *looks at him.*)

ANGIE (*aside*): Sitting there, like some boiled lobster, faintly
blue around the ears . . . and in his belly, pasta and liqueurs
. . . churning slowly . . . while he plots some mean revenge . . .

CLAPCOTT (*aside*): One day, come in, burst in, kicking the
door down like some Operation Motorman, catch them, and
throw acid on their writhing backs . . .

ANGIE (*aside*): Static like beef . . . his podgy hands, made for
fondling pens and the stems of glasses . . .

CLAPCOTT (*aside*): Her bony fingers, the skin more mottled as
she gets older, stained with endless fornication . . .

ANGIE (*aside*): Little food stains on his tie . . . on his flies,
grubby marks . . .

CLAPCOTT: Tired sometimes, has to stay in bed with tonics
. . . and her pubic hair is rather grey . . .

ANGIE: Short-breathed on staircases . . . forgets to change his
underwear . . . (*A pause. They remain still. The music of the old
ragtime tune,* 'I'm Happy, If You're Happy'. *It stops.*)

CLAPCOTT: Finish with him. When I've cleared this. We can't
have this. You know that.

ANGIE: Yes . . .

CLAPCOTT: Impossible. (*He gets up, goes to the telephone and
dials a single digit. She watches him.*) Clapcott. This is a blue
call. Yes. Thank you. (*Pause. He looks to* ANGIE.) I hate this!
(*Pause, then into phone*) Clapcott. Yes. I want a case rubbed
out. (*Pause*) Biledew. Yes. Bile. Dew. (*Pause*) Assault against a
policeman. Yes, I'm sorry too. I understand that very well. I
don't like it either. (*Pause*) Near Guildford.

ANGIE: On the By-pass.

CLAPCOTT: On the By-Pass.

ANGIE: Yesterday.

CLAPCOTT: Yesterday.

ANGIE: 'bout three.

CLAPCOTT: Three-ish. (*Pause*) I'm very well, thank you. And
you? Good. Bye Bye. (*He puts the receiver down, then looks at
her.*)

ANGIE: That was lovely. When it comes to protecting itself the
government machine works like greased lightning.

CLAPCOTT: Never again.

ANGIE: Well, it was for you! You didn't want him bawling from the witness box, did you?

CLAPCOTT: Never again. Whatever the consequences, I make that clear.

ANGIE (*uneasily*):   I hope you don't mind, but as we weren't exactly positive how you'd react, I took the liberty of . . . I'm sorry, Gee-Gee, I've asked him here . . . Noel, I mean . . . is on the premises . . . (*Pause, then suddenly* CLAPCOTT *launches himself at the long curtains where* ANGIE *had hidden herself in Scene 1. He tears them back. There is nothing there.*) Don't be silly.

CLAPCOTT: Bring him in.

ANGIE: Promise not to make a fool of yourself.

CLAPCOTT: Bring him in! (*Pause. Then reluctantly, she goes to the door, opens it and calls.*)

ANGIE: Noel! (*She returns, feigning casualness.* CLAPCOTT *fills his tumbler.* NOEL *enters. He looks at her.*)

NOEL: And I looked at her . . . and she was wonderful . . . (*Pause*)

CLAPCOTT: There is a certain thing known as discretion. In the Tory Party, as in life, discretion is the difference between success and abject failure. If you have integrity, but no discretion, then you are nothing. If you have brilliance, but not discretion, then you are nothing. But if you have nothing else, but you have discretion . . . then you are like unto a god. (*He goes close to* NOEL.) You have nothing. And no discretion, either. You are pure shit. (*They glare at one another for some seconds.* ANGIE *gets up nervously.*)

ANGIE: Can I open a window? (*She goes to the windows, opens them slightly.*)

NOEL (*icily*):   I am your pimp.

CLAPCOTT: Not any more you're not.

NOEL: Always. And forever.

CLAPCOTT: Is that supposed to be some kind of threat?

NOEL: I have my teeth in your fat calf, and I won't let go.

CLAPCOTT: The police are dropping proceedings against you. Your nasty little assault is going unpunished. Scamper off with that and be grateful.

NOEL: Scamper off? Where to?

CLAPCOTT: The tenements you came from. The hovels they bred you in, you rodent. (*Pause*)

NOEL: I'm one of you now. I'm your peer.

CLAPCOTT: It's a common fallacy that extravagance somehow

confers a social status. The pennies you delved in the gutters for don't make you anyone.

NOEL: I am your pimp.

ANGIE: Is there any dry ginger?

NOEL: I am your pimp!

ANGIE: All right. Make do with ice. (*She fills her glass.*)

CLAPCOTT: Sink back into the murk, Biledew. You rose, your face saw daylight. You were privileged.

NOEL: To serve you? To dish out skin for your fat paws to fondle? Privileged to lay out women in your bed, you white cod?

CLAPCOTT: You are disgusted. Not by me. By yourself.

NOEL: Yes!

CLAPCOTT: I am not disgusted. I have whores. I accept that. It's a fact of life. I am not disgusted when I shit. That too's a fact of life. The disgust is all on your side. You are full of self-loathing.

NOEL: I won't let you go. My little rat teeth are locked on you.

CLAPCOTT: Don't try to take on the English ruling class.

NOEL: You! Son of a — what? A one-eyed sweatshop owner!

CLAPCOTT: What a peevish concern for origins. What a fastidious pimp.

NOEL: You phrase-maker. You trickling liar, spewing your poison out . . .

ANGIE: Does anybody want the television on?

NOEL: I'm not some shop steward who you can mock because he can't finish his sentences. I'm on the inside. The filth confronting the filth. I can destroy you, Clapcott.

ANGIE (*getting up, moving to go*): I think I will. (*As she passes him,* NOEL *takes her arm. She stops.*)

NOEL: Give us a whisky, darling. (*She doesn't move.* NOEL *is still glaring at* CLAPCOTT.) Me and her. We've got you taped. (*Pause.* CLAPCOTT *looks at* ANGIE.) Angie . . . tell him we're burying him . . . (*Pause. She doesn't move.*) Tell him. (*Pause*)

ANGIE: I'm sorry, Noel . . .

NOEL: What?

ANGIE: Well, it's not on, is it? . . .

NOEL: What's not?

ANGIE: Well . . . the whole damned thing . . .

NOEL: Not on?

ANGIE: Not really, no. In practical terms. Really. Any more than my apache . . .

NOEL: You hate his guts!

ANGIE: Yes.

NOEL: Well, then! (*He is desperate.*) Glorious bastards! (ANGIE *just looks at him, agonizingly*).

CLAPCOTT: How touching . . . cops and robbers on the By-Pass . . . Easy Rider on the A23 . . .

NOEL: Angie . . .

ANGIE: I like it here . . . (*Pause.* NOEL *stares.*) Not like it here exactly . . . just . . . belong . . .

NOEL: You tricked me.

ANGIE: No, not deliberately . . .

NOEL: Liar.

ANGIE: No. I meant it. I need my moments of — delirium. I just — I can't shift now.

NOEL: Get out.

CLAPCOTT: Do no such thing.

NOEL: Get out.

CLAPCOTT: Stay where you are. (*Pause* ANGIE *looks at* NOEL, *then goes out.*)

CLAPCOTT: Don't go! (*She is out of the room.*) Don't go I said. (*Pause.*)

NOEL (*gritting his teeth, eyes shut*):   And I loved her, while she ripped me, my heart bled . . . I'm going straight to the newspapers. I'm laying everything before them. I'm kicking the shit out of you . . . (*Pause.* CLAPCOTT *turns to him.*)

CLAPCOTT: Organized labour sends the Prime Minister lurching with diahhorea. Union militants keep us up at night, sweating in secret conferences. But scandals, they're the bread and butter of the good society.

NOEL: Like hell. (*Pause*)

CLAPCOTT: You strike me as someone who will shortly commit suicide.

NOEL *stares at him. There is a great roll of drums, and when it stops, the voice of* BILEDEW *singing 'The Red Flag', alone and unaccompanied. The moment he stops,* NOEL *makes a dive for the drawer in which* CLAPCOTT *keeps his revolver.* CLAPCOTT *realises his intention too late, makes a move, but stops as* NOEL *aims the gun at him. Pause.*

NOEL: I'm wiping you. For everyone. And then, maybe, I'll kill myself. (*He lifts the gun to aim at* CLAPCOTT's *head.* CLAPCOTT *closes his eyes, then desperately.*)

CLAPCOTT: Before you do . . . (*There is a pause. He struggles to open his eyes.*) I think you should know . . . that Angie . . . with reference to you, said if there was one thing she was quite certain of . . . it was that you had . . . absolutely no right to —

NOEL's *gun hand has dropped an inch or two.* CLAPCOTT *makes a smart dive, seizing the weapon and aiming it at* NOEL.

NOEL: Shoot me, then! Shoot me! (CLAPCOTT *moves away, backing towards the telephone.* ANGIE *enters. She stands silently near the door.* CLAPCOTT *picks up the receiver.*)
CLAPCOTT: Clapcott. This is a red call.

Immediately the windows are flung open and a SPECIAL BRANCH OFFICER *bursts in, clutching a machine gun.* ANGIE *and* CLAPCOTT *watch him with disdain.*

OFFICER: All right, sir? All right, M'am? (ANGIE *walks to the drinks trolley and picks up a bottle.*) Him, is it? (CLAPCOTT *hands his pistol over to the* OFFICER, *who prods* NOEL *severely.*) Get moving. (*He nods in the direction of the windows.* NOEL *looks at* ANGIE.)
NOEL: Claw loved you. And you pissed all over him. (*He looks at* CLAPCOTT.) You should have shot me. You'll be sorry, I'll gnaw through granite blocks to get to you. No gaol will hold me, Clapcott.
CLAPCOTT: No. No gaol . . . (*The* OFFICER *pushes* NOEL *out through the windows. Pause.* ANGIE *is pouring a drink.*) I was very scared . . . at one point I felt my bowels — the muscles in my bowels — sink down, like in the war, when they dive-bombed us out in Crete . . . but this time I stopped myself.
ANGIE: When he got the gun on you?
CLAPCOTT: When he said he'd tell the papers.
ANGIE: There'll be such a wicked lot of shit flying . . .
CLAPCOTT: I don't think so. The moment he grabbed the gun, I knew, assuming I survived, just what would happen to him. No publicity, no courts, no nothing. Not a squeak. (ANGIE *looks at him. Long pause.*)
ANGIE: Gee-Gee, after all the filth I've been with, no one can twist my womb like you. You freeze my blood.
CLAPCOTT (*looking back at her for some seconds, turns.*):   I'll book a table. (*Pause*) Shall I? (*Pause*) Shall I? (*Pause*) Shall we eat?

ACT THREE

Scene One

A room in an institution. A table laid for one, and a chair. A trolley, with covered dishes and crockery.

After a pause of about ten seconds, LILY *and* LUSBY *enter. They wear short white jackets, like waiters, and have napkins on their arms. They take up positions facing the audience. A silence.*

LILY: And he said was it not the Abercorn where I first met you, sitting looking at the women who congregate there of a Saturday between their shopping, and girls drinking and smoking in short skirts, and I said as likely as not, I had a habit of haunting coffee bars, not being a drinking man but liking noisy places. Then that's the place, he said, I had several in mind, but your familiarity has decided me. The bag is in the basement. I said 'Goodbye, Captain' and he saluted smartly, being trained by the English army he gave great attention to these details as indeed we all did, liking to see ourselves as a crack regiment and not some round-shouldered university-trained amateurs. So in the sunshine of the morning I stepped out with my present whistling 'My Guy' by Mary Wells which had somehow got in my head and couldn't be shook off for nothing, and went up through the shopping precinct and I had to hand it to the Lord he had laid it on real proudly for my debut, as he always had done, my brithday having been fine my mother told me and my wedding so gorgeous you might have thought we were a blessed couple instead of as we were, a three weeks' wonder. The Abercorn was crowded, it seemed I could skip the formality of buying myself a coffee and just dump the bag down, who would notice in that hullabaloo, but I thought better of it, always sticking by instructions and remembering how I had to make a good impression and not cut corners, so I joined the queue, joggling my holdall with their stiff new carrier bags and thinking of this queue only the quickest drinkers, the gulpers to be accurate, would leave intact. Two tarts behind me took my eye, with skirts all up and giggling, to my regret bought steak and kidney and two veg so it was obvious they wouldn't leave complete, and it struck me as being wasteful of good cunt if they were hurt, but I was not in a position to be choosy who should die and who should live. I bought a raspberry milkshake because I knew how hot the tea was in this place. Half-finished beverages look suspicious — and picked a table well towards the back, the blast would have been dissipated if I'd set it near the window. I put the bag between my feet. An old bloke looked at me. I stared back. Two ladies joined me. They were going on about loose covers, whatever they may be. I drank my drink, with one eye on my watch and thinking Lily you are within ten minutes of eternity. That thought ran through my head. It moved me, in a funny way. I suddenly had the thought that the bomb's timing might not be that accurate, and having no wish to be disintegrated by my own hand, got up and pushed my chair in, hot and I thought conspicuous. Outside I broke in to a sweat. I felt a prickling in my back. Supposing just as I stepped out, I was blown to buggery! But I walked stiff as a copper to the corner, and then I ran, oh did I run, the beauty of my running no olympic athlete ever knew, my winged feet carried me across the pavements, past the concrete flower-boxes, human faces were like leaves whirling by me and I thought of all the beauty of the world and life and women and fresh air and it was like the whole world stretched her green hills out to me, Lily filling up his lungs with life and gasping with his ecstasy! And then there was this wicked bang not four blocks away which shook the air, and I sat down and while the sirens wailed it came back to me — the tune, I mean, 'My Guy' by Mary Wells, and I thought why not buy the bloody thing, so I got up and went into the record shop.

Pause of ten seconds. The two NURSES *remain perfectly still. Enter from left,* NOEL. *He is wearing a battered grey suit, plimsolls, and a creased white shirt undone at the neck. He goes directly to the table and sits down. After a moment* LILY *goes to the trolley, takes a jug of fruit juice and pours* NOEL *a glass. He returns the jug and stands near the table, ready to serve. Pause.*

LUSBY: And the guvnor said this kraut Podola weighed ten stone eight pounds on arrival, did he not? Correct, I said, therefore the drop will need to be five feet nine inches according to the tables. The factor you have overlooked, he said — he was a kind man, I never saw him angry, he was like a father to me — the factor you have overlooked, is weightloss. The chances of him putting on weight in the death cell were hundreds to one against in his experience. So he suggested an allowance of a stone for this kraut Podola, which made the drop four feet ten inches, the shortest in my brief experience. (NOEL *finishes the fruit juice,* LILY *removes the glass, then takes a plate of bacon and eggs from the trolley and lays it in front of him. He pours a cup of tea, then delivers it and takes up his original position.*) When we fetched him I said I had this idea we were in for bother, remembering how Bentley had struggled and made such an issue of it, being dragged backwards down the corridor and his heels had actually marked the floor and screaming till you thought your eardrums would cave in, and the guvnor in one of his rare angry moments had said he couldn't think straight and nearly put the knot the wrong side, everybody was on edge, but even so I never could agree with sedatives as this would utterly destroy the atmosphere and mystery of the ceremony, which is after all of great importance to the client and worth doing properly. Hello, Gunther, he said, I loved the way he spoke, you'd think it was a doctor at a child's bedside, and being in a black suit, too, that image of the guvnor always stays with me, and shook his hand, which was rather flabby I remember, then he asked for an examination of the neck in which I took part, stepping forward looking at the haircut and the cleanliness. It looked a bit raw where the clippers had gone, but the smell of soap showed me he had made an effort, and then we waited outside while he relieved himself for the last time, the sound of his urine in the bucket I can hear it now . . . The guvnor wasn't keen on Wandsworth, the chamber being of very mean proportions and in the event of trouble very little room for manoeuvre. He liked Leeds best, he was always happy on the train to Leeds, had kippers in the restaurant car. As I suspected from his mien, Podola bucked at the threshold and had to be manhandled for the twenty yards, the prison governor walking stiff like he couldn't hear it going on. He was not a hard man, this kraut Podola, slight of build, and roped up very easily while bawling in his language some filth I expect, or more likely pleading, and my guvnor looked marvellous, un-ruffled as he drew the knot up to his ear, and then as if by the magic of his touch, the kraut was silent, and hung his head like he was ashamed to have made such a din in front of a man like the guvnor, who was very holy in his way, more holy than the priest in my opinion: there was a sort of faith there, in my guvnor's true talent. And then the priest stopped and stood back, and my hand was on the lever, and the guvnor inched him forward, gently, and I waited for the signal, my eyes fixed on the guvnor's eyes, he had exquisite timing and I was full of admiration for his good taste and dignity, and then at last with a slight nod he signalled me, a gentle dip of his head like some great archbishop blessing me, and I threw the lever, and the kraut went down four feet ten inches to his last erection. And afterwards as always, he shook my hand first, and I felt like kissing his fingers because I was in the presence of a master and I knew it wasn't ever in me to be like him . . .

Pause of ten seconds. NOEL *finishes his breakfast and with a napkin wipes his mouth.* LILY *takes a packet of cigarettes from his pocket and extends it to* LUSBY, *who takes one, at arm's length without moving. They light their own with lighters. A pause of ten seconds.*

LILY: And it was closing time and I had drunk enough to ease myself out of my misery and so felt like Popeye after the spinach, sleek as a tomcat in my plimsolls, and no way in the mood for kipping, or for fucking for that matter, though there were women who would have had me in with their husbands next to us if I'd have asked, being a hero and not keeping it too close to my chest what I had done for the brigade when they had cared to use me. It was moonlight and a perfect evening for a bumping off, of which there were no doubt a few in progress at that moment in back streets and lonely farmhouses, the thought of which aroused in me a longing to be standing in some doorway while the shadow of the dead man came towards me in reply to my soft knock. And so in this frame of mind I wandered with my right hand wrapped around my pistol very eager to do something to somebody or I would have an awful night tossing and turning, which I didn't want, preferring almost anything to a bad night. And so it happened I decided the next person — excepting it should be a woman — should be the one to cop it. And when I spied him some hundreds of yards away my heart sang and I skipped to catch him up because he was in a hurry to get home and tucked up in bed. He was by the advertising hoardings in Dooley Street when I did it to him, in the pale light

of the council flats, beneath an advert for Lamb's Navy Rum, if
I remember, and I can say with honesty I never clapped eyes on
his face. And I turned away from him, not waiting for the blood
but light-hearted as a sparrow, a great weight was off my shoulders and skipped up Liffey Street, cutting through the alley
behind Woolworths, which was where they caught me with the
barrel still warm and the cordite sprinkled in my pocket, and
they threw me face down in the pig-van and took turns sitting on
me as we hurtled through the Creggan with my nose bleeding
and my fingers raw with the chaffing of army boots, and rifle
butts . . .

Pause, then LILY *and* LUSBY *clear* NOEL's *table, loading the
crockery onto the trolley which* LILY *then removes.* LUSBY
remains smoking. NOEL *remains seated. After about ten seconds,*
NOEL *rises to his feet, tense and desperate.*

NOEL: Ludovic Kennedy! I call to you across the spaces from
this Christ-knows-where! Can you hear me, Ludovic? (*He waits
for an answer.* LUSBY *doesn't react.*) Thick, oily hair, with
intellectual silver strands in it, sensitive fingers knotted for
Hanratty on 'Panorama'. A good man fighting for the under-
dog . . . Well, help me, Ludovic! Briefly I arrived here in the
dead of night, in a van with sealed windows. The journey could
have been an hour, maybe two — they took my watch —
anyway that places me within a radius of fifty to a hundred miles
from London, it should be relatively easy to find me if you
looked! To be out of here, I would never grumble no matter
what I went through. I'd have an amputation. I've always said
I'd rather die than have a leg missing. Well, I hereby take that
back. To be out of here I would lose a leg and an arm as well.
No, two legs and an arm. I would be legless to be out of here.
Because I have this feeling I never will be out of here. And no
one will hear me. And no one is wondering where I am. And no
questions are being asked. And I'm not missed. And my name is
not on a newspaper that's blowing across the Common as I
dreamed it was last night, and two kids playing football didn't
pick it up and say 'It's him! Four eyes!' because they'd seen me
exercise my dog round there, my dog which has probably died
of hunger in the flat. My home! My ordinary nothingness! I
would fall down on the grass and kiss it no matter how many
dogs had shit on it, I would lie there rolling in it and it could piss
with rain and yobbos could beat me silly under the railway arch,

and spit on me from passing trains I wouldn't care, my common, my scrubby little patch of grass!

Pause of ten seconds. Enter left, LILY *carrying a newspaper and a light, upright chair. He sits down, starts reading. Pause.*

LUSBY: And it was four o'clock precisely, I knew because I heard Big Ben bashing it out above me, and the guvnor, who had been in the public gallery, smart as a solicitor in his pin-stripe suit, crossed the forecourt of the Houses of Parliament, grey-faced and slow of stride so that I knew before I opened the car door for him that things had gone against us. He sat there in silence for some moments, as the tourists wandered past knocking the wing-mirrors with their cameras, and I felt the tears well up, firstly of pity for the guvnor, then of anger against the world doing this to him. The voting had been 200 for abolition, and 48 against. He took a small flask out of his pocket. 'Drive me home,' was all he said. We drove in silence over Vauxhall Bridge and into Lambeth, past the War Museum, into Kennington, and him so shattered, as if the world had flung dirty water in his face when he had carried out his tasks so beautifully, and me at the height of my apprenticeship left high and dry, and both of us somehow made to feel obscene. 'There's always the colonies,' he said at last. He always called the Commonwealth the colonies. I said it wasn't on for me. I loved England even though she spat on us. (*Pause of ten seconds*)

LILY: It's raining.

LUSBY: Want the light on? (*He goes out left, switching the light on as he goes. Pause*)

NOEL: I feel this is Berkshire. Don't ask me why. It feels like the country, because although the windows are too high — (*Pause*) I was angry, but now I'm scared! Because it seems to me on balance there is no hullabaloo about me going on. That is a dreadful thought, but I must face it they have probably fixed it like they fixed it when I hit the copper, and there was no hullabaloo about that. There's no reason I can think of why I should ever leave here. Not that I would not willingly co-operate in every way including drugs or brain surgery to wipe out my memory, but this has not been offered. I would accept any conditions without hesitation. But they haven't offered anything! (*Pause. Enter* LUSBY *with a newspaper and a light, upright chair. He sits and reads. Pause of ten seconds.*)

LILY: And then they took me to a small room which was hot

and stuffy and above all silent and without saying anything to
me they shut the door. And I thought this was all right and I sat
down and only slowly did I realise it was not silent but there was
a booming going on, I couldn't say from where but it got louder
and it seemed inside me, in my ears and in my body and the
more it frightened me the louder and quicker it boomed until I
thought I'd lose my hearing and then I knew — it was my heart
that I could hear, and the trickling of blood through the
chambers of my heart was like a loud stream and my eyelids
closing like a door slam and I shouted take me out I'll tell you
every fucking thing you bastards and they opened the steel door
and the world rushed in, and they dragged me to a table and I
chattered like a monkey, telling them all the shootings I had
done and all the things I could remember about the Brigade.
And then, expecting to be taken to a long-term prison, I was
asked into a special room and two Englishmen in ordinary suits
said was I interested in a certain privilege. Go on, I said. I have
an appetite for privilege. We're looking for men of your type,
he said, who will be pardoned in exchange for certain services.
My type, I said, and pray what is my type exactly? And they
mentioned this post, in Hampshire, and I said yes, I would be
pardoned by Her Majesty. (*Pause*)

LUSBY: And we were packing our things together, taking the
postcards off the wall, emptying the drawers, removing every
trace of our existence from that little room in Wandsworth
where we made the tea and looked out over the exercise yard,
while the guvnor regaled me with stories about his family
holidays, and we had taken looks at the condemned men
walking down below. And our little room looked miserable,
especially when I thought of all the laughter we'd had there.
The guvnor was flying to South Africa, taking his wife and kids
with him, off to a new life in a new country, but I had nowhere,
no future and no prospects, and was feeling right run down,
when the old black phone rang and a voice said would I care to
step along to room 711A, because some gentlemen would like
to see me there. And I knew at once, in my heart of hearts, that
HM Government wouldn't let a decent worker down, not kick
him in the street like some old lag because his craft had suddenly become obscene, but they would find a little niche for him
because real loyalty is not that common in this day and age. And
there were two gentlemen in burberries, who said they were
recruiting a hand-picked team to deal with a special category of
criminals. I said I would regard it as an honour to work in such a

special field on behalf of the best employers in the world. I only
had one regret, which was that at our parting I couldn't tell my
dear guvnor what a slice of luck I'd had, and as he and his family
went across the tarmac to their plane, I couldn't help thinking
he was feeling sorry for me, thinking I was as good as on the
dole. (*Pause of fifteen seconds.* LILY *still reading, bursts out
singing, the first line of the song,* 'Hungry for Love' *by Johnny
Kidd and the Pirates.*)

LILY: 'Hungry, so hungry for lo — o — o — o — ve!' (*A
silence as they read. Pause.*)

LUSBY: See Lulu last night?

LILY: I did not.

LUSBY: Brilliant. (*Long pause*)

LILY: Used to be a prostitute.

LUSBY (*looks up*): How do you know?

LILY: Common knowledge.

LUSBY: First I've heard of it.

LILY: I can't help the vast gaps in your knowledge —

LUSBY: First I've heard of it. (LILY *doesn't look up.* LUSBY
pauses, then goes back to his paper.)

LILY: So was Mick Jagger.

LUSBY: What?

LILY: A bumboy.

LUSBY: I can believe that. But not Lulu.

LILY: Please yerself. (*Long pause.* LILY *bursts out his one
phrase.*) 'Hungry, so hungry for lo — o — o — o — ve!'
(*Pause*) All the Stones were queers. It was common knowledge.

LUSBY: I'm not denying that. (*Pause*)

LILY: And drug addicts.

LUSBY: Anyone can see that.

LILY: Purple hearts. Hashish. Cocaine. Brian Jones died of
heroin. (*Pause*)

LUSBY (*looking up from paper*): I thought he drowned.

LILY: That is the commonly accepted theory. In actual fact he
died from an armful of Big H. During a homosexual orgy at his
house. They dropped him in the swimming pool to divert attention from the sordid goings-on within.

LUSBY: You are a mine of information. (*Pause. They read.*)

LILY: Marianne Faithfull also was a prostitute.

LUSBY: That may be so.

LILY: It is so.

LUSBY: I don't think Lulu was that type. (*Pause. They read.*)

LILY: Tom Jones also has had considerable homosexual experience.

LUSBY: Is this a hobby of yours?

LILY: I wouldn't call it a hobby. I didn't go to any lengths to uncover this information. I came across it in the normal course of daily life.

LUSBY: I'm not a Lulu fan, but I think you may be wrong there. (*Long pause*)

LILY: Cilla Black also was a street-walker. (*Suddenly, under a strain he can no longer bear,* NOEL *cries out.*)

NOEL: Are you going to kill me! (*They ignore him.*) Because if you are . . . I want to know! (*Pause. Then* LUSBY *walks out left.*)

LILY: Do you know how many illegitimate children the Beatles have between them?

NOEL: Tell me, please . . .

LILY: Eighteen.

NOEL: Tell me . . . please tell me . . .

LILY: You want to know everything.

LUSBY *returns with coffee and biscuits on a tray. He places the tray on the table and begins pouring.*

NOEL: Where am I then? (LUSBY *returns to his chair. Picks up the paper.*)

LUSBY: To come back to Lulu. Why I don't think she is.

LILY: What you think is neither here nor there.

LUSBY: Let me finish.

LILY: In any case, I said she was, what she is now I could not say.

LUSBY: For one thing, her eyes. Whores do not have sparkling eyes.

LILY: What's your evidence for that?

LUSBY: Coroners' reports.

LILY: And have you not heard of contact lenses? (NOEL *suddenly knocks the tray, onto the floor.*)

NOEL: Help me, God! (*Pause, then, putting his paper down,* LILY *goes off left.*)

LILY: 'Hungry, so hungry for lo — o — o — o — ve!' (*He returns almost at once with a broom and begins sweeping up.*)

NOEL: Biledew! You knew the inside of a gaol! Guide me! You did nothing for me, help me now! (*Pause*) Don't leave me! (*Pause*) Dad!

Slowly, BILEDEW *materializes in pyjamas and a dressing-gown, very old, very weary.* NOEL *stares at him.*

BILEDEW: I am in St. Francis's Hospital, forty of us, in the stench of urine and terminal flesh . . . and sometimes, over the sound of clattering pans . . . we hear children in the park . . .
NOEL: I'm scared . . . help me . . .
BILEDEW: Noel . . . they're going to murder you . . .
NOEL: I knew! I sensed it! Don't leave me!
BILEDEW: I'm dying, Noel . . .
NOEL: Advise me! Give me the benefit of your experience!
BILEDEW: Biledew's last testament . . .
NOEL: To his son . . . (*Pause*)
BILEDEW: I was alone . . . .always . . . all my life, alone and not expecting anything . . . (*Pause*) No. Start again.
NOEL: I haven't got that long . . . (BILEDEW *thinks, starts again.*)
BILEDEW: I was alone, in the prison of the world. I had suffered the kicks and cuts of what I had assumed was Fate, and followed the circumstances that what I thought was Fate imposed on me. And I was miserable, and a thing blowing in the wind, and thought that was the nature of the world, like all the others I was herded with. And after I had spent my prime, and suffered, and drifted at the calls of nations and prime ministers, being insulted and dealt blows, shrugging my shoulders like an Indian who felt out of favour with the gods, I took time to think, time when I could have worked and numbed myself. But I did not. I did nothing. And it dawned on me.
NOEL: What?
BILEDEW: The truth. Vaguely at first, in the form of rest-lessness, from which developed an inquisitiveness, and from that — a vision, shafting through the layers of my ignorance. And when I had that knowledge, the agonies of my past fell into place, and it was like I was the first man to see a skeleton, or like Harvey seeing the circulation of the blood, I saw it as a whole, I knew the way the world ran wasn't some divine miracle but was a machine, which came to pieces and was com-prehensible. And I saw how I had been used, and shoved from place to place like scrap. And I wanted to tell you, but I hadn't got the language . . .
NOEL: What truth is this? Will it help me get out of here?
BILEDEW: The first truth is, there are no gods. That when a letter telling you to serve the government, to die for it or bow to

it, lands on your doormat, it has not travelled from some distant galaxy but from an individual, from a man, a human being who exists and is no more than you, and maybe less. And the second truth which follows from this is that what is, is not what has to be, but what we have allowed to be. And the consequence that flows from that is that we can change it. All this I have discovered, through the miseries of my rotten life . . .

NOEL: I'd be scrap. I'd be happy to carry out the orders of the lowest reptile that just lets me crawl.

BILEDEW: They won't let you crawl. They will wipe you away, and it won't even leave a smudge.

NOEL: What, then!

BILEDEW: I tried to tell you, keep your anger for your class. They could not have murdered your whole class . . .

NOEL: Biledew . . . I want to die in bed . . .

BILEDEW: It's nothing marvellous . . . the stinking sheets laid on the rubber . . . it's no privilege.

NOEL: Tell me how to die then!

BILEDEW: I've only just begun myself.

NOEL: Well, I won't die!

BILEDEW: Win them, Noel. Win them with your common suffering. Find the eloquence of Lenin, lick their cruelty away.

NOEL: I'm not a speaker. I haven't got the vocabulary.

BILEDEW: Find it. Your brain will work overtime in your extremity.

NOEL: They're thick as shit!

BILEDEW: Don't despise them, win them, Noel!

NOEL: Give me a start —

BILEDEW (*his light fading*):   Be cogent, earn their love —

NOEL: Don't go! Give me a phrase! Biledew! (BILEDEW *is extinguished.* NOEL *stares. Pause of ten seconds.*)

LILY (*who is still reading*):   I have nothing on Roy Orbison. Though his infatuation with leather entitles one to speculate . . . (*Pause.* NOEL *is in desperate thought.* LILY *looks up to* LUSBY.) Do you remember some young men known as the Tornadoes?

LUSBY: No thank you.

LILY (*going back to his paper*):   As you wish.

LILY *continues reading.* NOEL *walks up and down, pondering his opening gambit. Suddenly, shattering the silence,* LILY *sings again.*

LILY: Hungry, so hungry for lo — o — o — o — ve!

LILY *leans back in his chair, then, with a kind of weary routine, slaps his thighs and is about to rise to his feet. At this moment* NOEL *begins to speak. For a few moments* LILY *stands, suspended, then, slowly, sits down again.* NOEL's *speech begins clumsily and brokenly. By the end, it is eloquent and delivered with conviction.*

NOEL: Claw. That was my nickname. I had it on my back, in studs. Studs in a leather jacket. Like a rocker. But not a rocker. Properly speaking. Just a layabout, who would have been a rocker if he could. But really nobody. And Claw was just my way of saying here I am, Noel Biledew, dragged up nowhere but flashy with it, king of the pavement, Claw rules, OK? (*He runs his hand through his hair, still walking up and down.*) Okay. So I thought I was somebody. Well, everybody has to think they're somebody. All over England there were kids like me called Duke and Tiger and Raven and Blade, all of us, shouting it out with our studs, you know, rubbing it in we didn't get off the pavement but the grandmothers did, and we got shoved around by coppers but we took that because after them came us in the animal kingdom. (*Pause*) You know all that. But of all those kids only a handful went anywhere, and the rest are stripping motor cars in breakers' yards or delivering for Tip Top bakeries, going thin on top and none of 'em wearing studs any more, but the names of their employers on their overalls. McAlpine, Acres the Bakers, Dunlop, Royal Engineers. And they don't know it — what they've come down to, or they've stopped trying and they keep their heads down and they have kids and the kids are already calling themselves Battersea Boot Boys or the Streatham Park Crew, and they think they rule, OK? (*Pause*) You know all that. But Claw had set his heart on something big, he had the Kings Road, Chelsea on his mind, he dreamed of pigskin wallets crammed with credit cards and because he would not lie down he squeezed in, not by the entrance but by the greasy kitchen, so his hands were dirty when he sat at their white tablecloths, but I was there! And there were hardly any like me who had done what I had, who hadn't been washed out by Oxford and Cambridge so they had to scratch their heads to remember where they had been spewed up from. And I saw it all at spittle distance what you haven't dreamed of, I saw who ruled, OK! (*Pause*) Who did I think I was, who had

had to trade in filth to sniff their halitosis? I started hating in the
dirty playgrounds when they pushed me on my knees and peed
on me in the lavatories because some people like me invite
punishment. I'm not an angel but I have seen things, and I've
seen things that make the mugging of old ladies unstinted
generosity! Because our little squabbles and our playground
fights and little murders in the entrances of flats are hardly
crimes compared to that crime they are working on us, all of us
driven mad by their brutality and no coppers to protect us
against their claws! Their great claw, slashing us, splitting our
people up, their great claw ripping our faces and tearing up our
streets, their jaguars feeding on our lazy herds! (*Pause*) And we
have nothing except each other. Our common nothingness. And
our caring for each other. And our refusal to do each other
down. Like a class of schoolboys we won't tell who is the thief.
(*Pause*) Defend me. Don't murder me.

NOEL *is drained. There is a long silence, neither* LILY *nor*
LUSBY *moving. They have listened like jurors, still on their chairs,
revealing nothing. They are terrifying in their solidity and expres-
sionlessness. Slowly,* LILY's *hand goes into his pocket. There is a
click. A transistor begins playing the tune* 'Hungry for Love'. *For
some seconds no one moves, then* LILY *removes the radio and
places it on the floor. After some moments, a bath is lowered slowly
onto the stage. Above the music, slowly drowning it out, the sound
of running bath water which continues until the end of the play.*
LILY *and* LUSBY *rise to their feet and roll up their sleeves. After
some time,* NOEL *begins slowly to undress. He goes slowly to the
bath and climbs in. With a sinlge thrust* LILY *and* LUSBY *force his
head beneath the water. Lights fade, and rise on* CLAPCOTT, *in a
posture which suggests he is speaking in Parliament.*

CLAPCOTT: I am happy to be now in a position to reassure the
House that following the publication of the enquiry set up to
investigate the death of the patient Noel Biledew at the Spencer
Park Mental Institution, Hampshire, there appears to be no
question that death was accidental and in no way reflects upon
the capacities or dedication of the staff. I would take this opportunity to remind the House that accidental deaths in mental
insitutions are running currently at slightly under 20 a year, and
that what at first sight may appear a high accidental death rate
at Spencer Park is not in any way exceptional, though I would
hasten to add that no one in the Health Department or Home

Office is in any way complacent about these figures or regards them as at all acceptable. I would however, stress that there are serious staff shortages in a nursing field which quite properly not everyone regards as the most congenial . . .

NO END OF BLAME
Scenes of Overcoming

CHARACTERS

BELA VERACEK	An Artist, eighteen to seventy-five years
GRIGOR GABOR	An Artist, the same
A PEASANT WOMAN	Of Roumania
ILONA	An Hungarian Artist
BILLWITZ	An Artist's Model
STELLA	Director of an Institute, Budapest
A GARDENER	In a Moscow Park
SIR HERBERT STRUBENZEE	A Foreign Office Official
JOHN LOWRY	A Government Official
FRANK DEEDS	A Government Official
BOB STRINGER	The Editor of a Newspaper
DIVER	The Editor of a Newspaper
TEA LADY	
MR. MIK	A Cartoonist
GLASSON	A Junior Woman Doctor
CUSTOMS OFFICERS	
STUDENTS	
AIRMEN AND AIRWOMEN	
COMRADES IN THE COMMITTEE OF THE ARTISTS' UNION, MOSCOW	
SOLDIERS	
MALE NURSES	
POLICEMEN	
GPU MAN	
SECRETARY	

ACT ONE

Scene One

A remote place in the Carpathian Mountains, 1918. A naked woman, her clothes round her ankles, an expression of terror on her face, stands rigid in the centre of the stage. A Hungarian soldier, ragged and unshaven, sits on the ground, a sketchbook open on his knees. Beside him, a rifle. He sketches feverishly.

Drawing: GRIGOR's *'Soldiers Bathing.'*

GRIGOR (*shouts*): Come on! Where are you! Just look at her! Just look at her breasts! I love her breasts, they go — they're like — they're utterly — harmonious — they fall — they sag — not sag — sink — not sag or sink — they — **Concede** — that's what they do — **Concede** — they are completely harmonious with gravity — **Where Are You**? They are in total sympathy with — (*The* WOMAN *grabs her cloths and tries to run away*. GRIGOR *leaps to his feet and grabs his rifle.*) Don't run away! (*She freezes. He drops the rifle, goes back to sketching.*) She keeps trying to run away — I wish I spoke Roumanian, is it — I'd say, look I'm an artist, I don't kill girls — not that she's a girl, she's a woman, thank God — I can't draw girls — I hate girls — there's no concession in their flesh — too much defiance — everything pokes upwards — nipples, tits, bum, — everything goes upwards — all aspiration, ugh — (*She tries to escape again. He grabs the rifle.*) Don't run away! (*She freezes*). Sorry — sorry — (*He throws down the rifle, picks up his sketchpad again.*) Look at her buttocks — Bela, look at them — do look at them — see what I say — (BELA *comes in, holding a sketchbook limply in his hand. He also wears a threadbare tunic.*) the female body accepts — concedes to gravity — is in profoundly intimate relations with the earth — the curve, you see — the curve is the most perfect line — eliminates all ten-

sion — **why don't you draw**! No, I haven't got it — haven't got
it — no — (*He tears off a sheet, starts another.*) I am so sick of
drawing men — soldiers bathing — never again — I have eighteen books of soldiers bathing — eighteen! — in my pack —
(*He scuttles to a new position.*) — there, you see — the essential female line — the curve — does not resist but — (BELA
moves closer to the woman.) Bela — (BELA *is staring at her.*)
Bela — you are in my view — (*He does not move.*) My fucking
view!

BELA: **I want to kiss her.**

GRIGOR: **Draw! Draw!** (BELA *just stares.*) All right, I'll
move — (*He shifts to another angle.*) There was a peasant
woman in the institute — remember her — the model with the
shoulders — oh, what shoulders, the same shoulders — they
went — no, I haven't got it — (*He tosses away another page.*)

BELA: **I don't mean kiss.**

GRIGOR: The shoulders are the most expressive single ele-
ment — in human anatomy — fact! (BELA *is taking off his
tunic.*) Bela! What are you doing, Bela? Be — la! (GRIGOR
leaps to his feet, seizes BELA *as he advances on the* WOMAN.
They struggle.)

BELA: **It's a woman! It's a woman, Isn't it!**

GRIGOR: **You're hurting me** . . .

BELA: **Let go! Let go!** (*The* WOMAN *draws up her clothes and
hobbles away.*) **She's run away!** (GRIGOR *releases* BELA; *goes
to pursue, then turns back, picks up the rifle.*)

GRIGOR: **Hey! Hey! Stop! I'll shoot!** (*He aims it clumsily after
her.*) **Bang! Bang!** (*Pause. He lets the rifle droop. She dis-
appears.* GRIGOR *turns to his friend.*) **Lost my model, fuck
you!**

BELA (*sitting on the ground, nursing his groin*): Beg
pardon . . . .

GRIGOR. **Shouldn't have!**

BELA (*lying back, wearily*): No . . .

GRIGOR: Shouldn't have . . . (*Pause.* BELA *is about to sit
up.*)

BELA: Grigor —

GRIGOR: Don't move — (*He picks up his sketchpad, begins
drawing* BELA *who is naked.*)

BELA: Grigor, we have just butchered two million Russians, a
million Italians, half a million Poles, the same number of
Roumanians, some Greeks, some French, a few thousand
English, a division of Bulgarians by mistake, we have trod on

babies' brains and caught our boots up in the entrails of old women, yesterday we ate our breakfast on a table made of half a man, Grigor, I do not understand a morality which says we have to draw a line at petty theft!

GRIGOR: Theft?

BELA: Theft, yes. Two minutes of herself, perhaps less. I know the argument, of course, the argument goes —

GRIGOR: Keep still!

BELA: Goes — what is the value of an inhibition if it collapses under strain of opportunity? That's the argument. Either it is incumbent on me not to rape women at all, or I should rape women under all circumstances. But that should equally apply to killing, shouldn't it? **What in God's name are we doing here**? (*Pause*) Did I move? (*Pause. He lies back. Distant sounds of an artillery bombardment.*) There is another argument. A rather shoddy argument. But I'll put it all the same, shall I? (GRIGOR *is drawing.*) **Shall I**?

GRIGOR: Please.

BELA: The other argument says, if I hadn't raped her someone else would. Someone less considerate. (*Pause*)

GRIGOR: A considerate rape . . .

BELA: Yes.

GRIGOR: I'm not sure I understand that.

BELA: The shoddiness of this argument lies in the fact that my having raped her considerately does not preclude her being raped inconsiderately by someone else, so the end result is she gets raped twice. It's a terrible argument you did well to ignore, Grigor, I can only say how greatly I approve your action, sticking your knee there, swiftly, expertly, disabling me in such a way as —

GRIGOR: I'm sorry —

BELA: No, no! I mean to say you are a moral hero, in the midst of all this sin and shame and human vileness, where we eat our breakfast off a man's divided trunk, to find an act of selfless purity is like —

GRIGOR: You're mocking me —

BELA: **I'm not mocking you!** (*Pause*)

GRIGOR: You've moved.

BELA: Because I would have done it, even so. (*He stares at him.*) **My Bad Self**. (*Pause.* GRIGOR *closes the book, gets up. There is a loud cry off.*)

FIRST SOLDIER (*off stage*): **Soldier Got No Clothes On!**

A SOLDIER *rushes on, bearing rifle and fixed bayonet. A second* SOLDIER *follows.*

SECOND SOLDIER: **Soldier got no clothes on!** (*They point their weapons at* BELA.)
FIRST SOLDIER: Don't get up!

An OFFICER *enters. The* FIRST SOLDIER *begins rummaging in* GRIGOR's *pack.*

OFFICER: Why are you naked? Are you homosexuals?
SECOND SOLDIER: **Answer! Are you queers?**
OFFICER: A soldier removes his uniform in the presence of the enemy for one of two reasons only. He is going to desert or he is homosexual.
SECOND SOLDIER: **Are you queers!** (BELA *goes to get up.*)
FIRST SOLDIER: **Don't move!**
OFFICER: What is your name and unit?
SECOND SOLDIER: **Quick!**
GRIGOR: Gabor. 77th Regiment. Field Telegraph.
BELA: Veracek. 18th Brigade Telephonists.
OFFICER: Give in your paybooks.
SECOND SOLDIER: **Paybooks! Quick!**
OFFICER: The penalty for homosexuality is death, Field Punishment regulations. Are you guilty?
BELA/GRIGOR: No!
OFFICER: Then you were planning to desert.
BELA: No!
OFFICER: Then why throw your uniform away?
FIRST SOLDIER: Captain! (*He is holding* GRIGOR's *sketch-pad.*) These books are full of naked men. (*He shows them to the officer, who flicks through them cursorily.* FIRST SOLDIER *looks pruriently over his shoulder. The* OFFICER *snaps the last book shut.*)
OFFICER: Thank God.
FIRST SOLDIER: Why?
OFFICER: He has seen fit to furnish us with proof — (*He turns to* BELA *and* GRIGOR.) On the authority invested in me by the Emperor Charles VIII, I sentence Privates — (*Pause, he looks at the* SECOND SOLDIER, *who is flicking through the sketchbooks.*) **On the authority invested in me** — (*The* SOLDIER *tosses down the books.*) by the Emperor Charles VIII, I sentence Privates —

SECOND SOLDIER (*looking at the paybooks*):   Gabor —
OFFICER: Gabor —
SECOND SOLDIER: Veracek —
OFFICER: And Veracek to Field Punishment Class I.
GRIGOR: Bela —
FIRST SOLDIER: **Kneel!**
GRIGOR: **Be — la!**
OFFICER: In view of the present emergency and the threat to
   the territorial integrity of the Empire, the Chief Chaplain to the
   Army has declared all soldiers who die by summary execution
   may pass into the other world unshriven.
FIRST SOLDIER: **Kneel!** (*They kneel.*)
GRIGOR: **Be — la!**
BELA: I took my clothes off because — (*Pause*)
GRIGOR: Tell them!
BELA: Because I saw a woman. (*Pause.*)
OFFICER: You saw a woman. Do you always take your clothes
   off when you see a woman?
BELA: I wanted to rape her.
OFFICER: You undress to rape someone? What are you, a
   poet?
BELA: Yes. (*Pause*)
OFFICER (*to* FIRST SOLDIER):   Tell the poet the penalty for
   rape.
FIRST SOLDIER: **Field Punishment Class 1.**
OFFICER (*to* GRIGOR):   You. Over there. (GRIGOR *scrambles
   away. Leaving* BELA *alone on his knees.*)
GRIGOR: Tell him! Tell him she ran away!
OFFICER: Take aim. (*The* SOLDIERS *rattle their bolts.*)
GRIGOR: **She ran away!**
OFFICER: Aim! (*They aim their rifles at* BELA. *Pause.*)
BELA: Don't shoot me. The war's over.
OFFICER: The war's over? The war's over, he says. What's
   that, then? (*He cups his ear. Distant gunfire rumbles.*)
BELA: We've lost.
OFFICER: **We have not lost! We have not lost as long as we
   resist!** (*Pause.* BELA *hangs his head. An unbearable delay. The*
   SOLDIERS *looks at their* OFFICER.) Make up a poem.
BELA: What?
OFFICER: A poem. Quick.
FIRST SOLDIER: **Poem! Quick!** (*Pause.* BELA *sweats.*)
GRIGOR: Bela . . . Bela . . . a poem . . .
BELA: **All right —**

GRIGOR: Go on . . .

OFFICER: I have impeccable taste. I like above all, the heroic, national style . . .

FIRST SOLDIER: **Poem! Quick!** (*Pause*)

BELA: I drew my finger down his thigh . . .
Laying my brown male hand upon his brown male breast . . .

GRIGOR: **Be — La!** (*Pause*)

BELA: An insect lapped its moisture from his eye . . .
Blood quit his wound, coy as a girl leaving a bed . . .
(*Pause, then with a groan he falls forward onto his hands.*)

OFFICER: Breast and bed are not full rhymes. If you had said — forgive me — the blood in scarlet dressed — you see?

BELA: That's better, yes.

OFFICER: Much better.

BELA: Yes.

OFFICER: That would have rhymed.

BELA: Yes. (*Pause*)

OFFICER: I drew my finger down his thigh . . . you say it . . .

BELA: I drew my finger down his thigh . . .

OFFICER: Laying —

BELA: Laying my brown male hand upon his brown male breast . . . An insect —

OFFICER: Lapped —

BELA: Lapped its moisture from his eye . . . . Blood quit his wound — in scarlet dressed . . . (*Pause*)

OFFICER: It is better.

BELA: Yes.

OFFICER: I like rhyme. Poetry without rhyme is laying bricks without cement. (*There is a fusilade of shots offstage.*)

SECOND SOLDIER: **Comm — unists!** (*He throws away his rifle and rushes off.*)

OFFICER: (*drawing his pistol*):   Walk towards the shooting! (*He goes off in the direction of the firing.*)

FIRST SOLDIER (*to* BELA):   No 'ard feelings mate? (*He throws his weapon away and follows the* SECOND SOLDIER *off.* BELA *remains on his knees. Sporadic shooting.*)

GRIGOR: Bela . . . get up.

BELA: I can't. . . .

GRIGOR(*pulling him*):   Come on! Get up!

BELA: **I can't get up.**

GRIGOR: Bela!

BELA: I shall never write a poem again.

GRIGOR: Never mind that now —

BELA: **Never again** (*As* GRIGOR *tugs at his arm,* RED
SOLDIERS *come in, ragged armbands on their sleeves. They
are mutineers.*)

FIRST RED SOLDIER: War's over, boys. Go 'ome and fuck
your wife. (BELA *falls against the man's knees.*)

GRIGOR: They were going to shoot us!

FIRST SOLDIER: What for?

GRIGOR: Because we —

BELA: Nothing . . . nothing . . . shut up Grigor . . .

FIRST RED SOLDIER (*as the* OFFICER *is brought in*): Shoot
them now. (*He flings a rifle at* GRIGOR. *He catches it. A*
SECOND RED SOLDIER *forces the* OFFICER *to the ground.*
BELA *gets up.*)

OFFICER: I have a widowed mother. I am everything to her.

SECOND RED SOLDIER (*to* GRIGOR): Bang away, mate.

OFFICER: Couldn't you be satisfied with beating me? I ask
because of my mother. She is a gracious lady, you would like
her.

FIRST RED SOLDIER: I got a mother, far from gracious.
When she shouts the crockery spills in every kitchen in the
street.

OFFICER: Really?

FIRST RED SOLDIER: And when she sits, her knees open like
scissors. Most ungracious, she is. You would 'ate her.

OFFICER: Me, I don't think I —

BELA: **Give me the rifle.** (GRIGOR *looks at him in horror.*)
Give me the rifle.

GRIGOR: Bela, you can't blame him!

BELA: **Can't blame him?**

GRIGOR: He was only — he was doing what —

BELA (*turning to the* OFFICER): He says I can't blame you. I
do blame you.

GRIGOR: Bela, listen to me —

BELA: **He hurt me!**

GRIGOR: He hurt me too, but —

SECOND RED SOLDIER: Buck up, will yer, Grig?

GRIGOR: Think, please think — **I can't bear killing! Don't!**
(SECOND RED SOLDIER *tosses* BELA *his rifle.*) **Now, look!**
(*With a yell* BELA *drags the* OFFICER *off his knees and runs
out with him.* GRIGOR *goes to follow but is blocked. Pause.*)

FIRST RED SOLDIER: Listen, Grig, there must be killing in
this world, because we're angry, and we 'ave our rights. Anyone
who tells you killing is just killing tells you lies. There is all the

difference in the world between a rich man's and a poor man's
death. You must know this, Grig, or we will never build a better
world . . .

There is a shot. The RED SOLDIERS *drift off. After a few
moments,* BELA *enters, the rifle limply in his hand.*

GRIGOR: I can't ever be your friend. I'll walk with you, eat
with you, but I shall never be your friend.

BELA: Oh? (*He puts down the rifle, picks up his tunic.*)

GRIGOR: Although we'll talk, I'll tell you nothing. (BELA
puts the tunic on.) Because friendship is nothing if it isn't pure.
We were pure, and now we're not.

BELA: He went on about rhyme. Fuck rhyme. I hate it.

GRIGOR: I would have given anything to stay your friend —

BELA: Balls to rhyme! Balls to the heroic, national style! His
brains were pitiful, the pus of dead imagination on the ground,
all his rhyming couplets running in the mud . . .

GRIGOR: Friendship dies, Bela —

BELA: Fuck your friendship! Take your friendship back! I did
what all my being told me to, cried out for, I was stifling, then I
did it and I breathed! What do I care if your friendship draws its
soft head in, all shocked and simpering? Keep your gift, I piss
on it! (*He picks up his rucksack.* GRIGOR *crawls over the
ground collecting his scattered drawings.* BELA *looks at him.
Pause.*) I didn't shoot him, Grigor. I made him lie down and
fired in the air . . . (*Pause,* GRIGOR *looks joyous.*)

GRIGOR: Bela! Oh, Bela! (*He goes to embrace him.*)

BELA: Don't touch me! (*He stops.*) Don't celebrate the flin-
ching of a coward. Don't kiss me because I drew back from a
decent deed.

GRIGOR: I'm sorry, Bela . . .

BELA: Let's go home. Four years of soldiering, and we never
put a wound in anyone . . . (*They go off.*)

Scene Two

*The life class at the Institute of Fine Art, Budapest. A female model
sitting on a chair, surrounded by students, among them* BELA *and*

GRIGOR. BELA *still wears his army greatcoat. The silence of attentive work. It is 1921.*

Sketch: *'We will Revive the Spirit of Hungary.' Grotesque cartoon of two soldiers beating a man to death.*

STELLA (*at last*):   Christ, I am thin. (*Pause*) Christ, I am. (*Pause*) Before the war — may I speak — my knees — you should have seen 'em. (*Groan from somewhere.*) You groan, you never saw 'em. (Pause) In silk. (*Groan again*) In silk they were! (*Pause*) They bloody were. (*Pause*) Had hands all over 'em. (*Pause.*) Under tables. In the Café Esterhazy. (*Pause*) The toast of Budapest. I quote. (*Pause*) Had lawyers' fingers creeping over 'em. (*Pause*) Tongues of magistrates went lick, lick, lick.
GRIGOR: You moved.
STELLA: Did I? Beg pardon. (*Pause*) No, only saying the scrag was lovely once. Gave aches to princes while you played soldiers in the mud. (*Pause*) Most fondled female in the Empire. (*Groans and laughter.*) Was! Was! Fact!
GRIGOR: Could you just keep your mouth —
STELLA: Look, Grig, I'm talking, darling —
GRIGOR: I know that, Stella —
STELLA: So how can I keep my mouth —
GRIGOR: It makes your head move —
STELLA: It would do, wouldn't it? (*Pause*) Where was I?
GRIGOR: Oh, look —
BELA: Fondled.
STELLA: Fucked in fur, shagged in chiffon —
BELA: Sucked in silk! (*Laughter*)
GRIGOR: Look, this is supposed to be a life class!
STELLA: This is life, darling!
BELA: Sit down, Grigor!
STELLA: I haven't moved. Have I? I have not moved. (*Pause*) Was kept in silk stockings by an army contractor who put paper soles on army boots . . . (*Pause*) I saw 'is body in the street. Flies running down 'is mouth, 'is mouth that used to suck my toes . . . (*Pause.*) You've stopped drawing, Bela. Have you caught the magic of my knees?
BELA: They've lost something, Stella, through being wedged apart so much.
STELLA: They have . . .
BELA: I wouldn't buy you a sausage sandwich for the joy of being there.

STELLA:　Thank you! Likewise your little spurt of pleasure, dear.

GRIGOR (*jumping up again*):　**Can you keep still, please!** You will keep talking and when you talk you get emotional! Emotion makes you move. It animates you, do you see? Why can't you just — it says on the instructions models are requested not to speak!

BELA:　It animates you, Stella —

GRIGOR:　We are here to study human form —

BELA:　Animates you, darling —

GRIGOR:　Oh, look, Bela —

BELA:　We do not want to hear the wreckage of your life, all right? Be a form Stella. Be art. Thank you! (*Pause. GRIGOR looks at BELA coldly, sits again.*) There. Perfect form. No grievance. No sin. No spit. No wit. No shit. (STELLA *bursts out laughing.*)

GRIGOR (*standing again*):　**You are deliberately sabotaging this!**

ILONA:　Grigor, they're laughing at you. Sit down, Grigor. (*Pause, he sits.*)

STELLA:　I've had one good lover in my life. A sailor in the Red Guard. I'll tell you this, and then shut up, all right, Grigor? He never said to me — not once — I worship you. Never once called me 'is goddess. Or 'is angel. Never once. I said why don't you say you worship me? They always did, the racketeers. I was their idol. He said, because I give you dignity, my love . . . (*Pause, suddenly she bursts out crying, covering her face with her hands. The Head of the Institute appears. Looks at her.*)

BILLWITZ:　Stay like that. (*She sobs.*) Why aren't you drawing? Draw! Draw! (*They begin sketching, feverishly. BELA does not move. BILLWITZ moves round them.*) Why are we artists? We are artists because we thrill to beauty. We look for beauty everywhere. In tears. In pain. We need beauty now. Our hearts cry out. Who drew this please? (*He holds out a paper, which is the cartoon 'We will Revive the Spirit of Hungary'.*) When I see beauty mocked I flush with temper. I tremble at the humiliation of my fellow man. Artists are the guardians of beauty, high priests in the temple Art. Who drew it? One of you did. (*No one replies. He walks round.*) We suffer, oh, don't we suffer? Little human creatures spilled and broken on howitzered hills and maimed in gaols? We reconcile, we reconcile! No wonder I feel anguish when my wounds are opened up again. Who did this please? (*Pause*)

BELA:　Me. (*Pause*)

BILLWITZ: I knew you did. I knew my darling would hurt me most, my best give me most pain. Everybody go now, please! Quick! But Bela. God, I wish it had been someone else. (*The students leave,* STELLA *puts on her gown. Goes out behind them.* BELA *stays sitting in his chair.* BILLWITZ *walks up and down.*) It is not art.

BELA: I feel it. So it is.

BILLWITZ: It is not true. It is not half as true as any life drawing you did for me.

BELA: It's more true.

BILLWITZ: It's prejudice!

BELA: It's more true than any painting you did in your life. Though it took me ten minutes, it's better than any canvas you pored over, sweated through, wept for, exhibited, took pride in, anything.

BILLWITZ: **You will never be a great painter if you do not tell the truth!**

BELA: I don't want to be a painter. I hate oils, studios, manipulating colours inches thick. Give me ink, which dries quick, speaks quick, hurts.

BILLWITZ: Heal us, Bela. If there was ever a people needed healing, it is us . . . .(*Pause.* BELA *does not move.*) I have just come from the police.

BELA: **My art speaks, then!** (*He jumps up.*) Did any single picture of yours win you such an accolade? A visit from the police! There is a diploma, there is a prize! Now I know I am a genius, now I hang in the echoing gallery of human art! **I stirred the police, therefore, I touched the truth.** You make my case for me . . . .(*Pause*) Will they beat me? I am terrified of being beaten. Will you keep them off me? You're famous, I'm not . . . (*Pause*)

BILLWITZ: You have a terrible vanity Bela . . .

BELA: Protect me, will you?

BILLWITZ: You are to be expelled. (BELA *looks up at him. A smile spreads over his face.*)

BELA: Expelled? I thought they were going to hit me! (*He laughs again.*) Expelled! (*He laughs.*) Now I shall never learn to paint a nude, shall I? Never discover which corner of a corpse you put the legs! Or if a tit goes on the front or back? (*Pause. He looks at* BILLWITZ.) I leave Hungary. To policemen, bankers, swindlers, whores, English officers, French diplomats . . . and reconcilers painting peasants in the sun. (*He goes near to* BILLWITZ.) Kiss me, you old tragedy . . .

(BILLWITZ *kisses his cheek, goes out.* BELA *closes his eyes, takes deep breaths.* GRIGOR *appears.*)

GRIGOR: Bela? Bela?

BELA (*turning boldly*):   They threw me out!

GRIGOR: Oh, God . . .

BELA: **Me! And I am the best artist of the lot!**

GRIGOR: Yes . . .

BELA: Dead place, Grig! Stink of old corpse coming through national flag! Admiral's piss and papal vomit! The best Hungarians are dead. We have to leave, Grigor.

GRIGOR: What?

BELA: Shove Off. (*Pause.* GRIGOR *seems shaken.*) Do you want to suffocate? Drown on a thimbleful of lies pissed out the bladder of a landscape painter? Death to the national fucking genius! Get your bag packed! Tell them you **Reject!** (*Pause*) What? (*Pause*) Horrid silence. (*Pause*) Horrid, dirtly little silence while the ego ticks. (*He cups his hand to his ear, mockingly.*) His calculator. Click! Brr! Brr! Brr! (*Angrily*) **What! What!**

GRIGOR: I haven't yet completed one year of the course . . .

BELA: Stroke of luck.

GRIGOR: Why?

BELA: Poisoning not yet affected vital parts.

GRIGOR: You see, I —

BELA: **Oh, what?**

GRIGOR: I wanted —

BELA: A Diploma? Shabby bit of paper for performing dog?

GRIGOR: **Let me speak, will you! Let me speak!** (*Pause.* BELA *sits down.*) I have been in a world war, in a civil war, in a revolution, in a counter-revolution, and I only want a little corner where **I can paint.** (*Pause.*) I live for it. Forgive pretentiousness of this, Bela, but actually, I live for it. The human form. Sorry about this. I have a passion for it. Sorry. (*Pause*)

BELA: All the barrages we lay under . . . in our foxholes holding hands . . . digging one another out of human mess . . . pulled seven corpses off you once. Scooped guts out your mouth, wiped viscera out of your bulging eyes . . .

GRIGOR: Yes . . .

BELA: No Russian bombs could blow our promises apart. Takes peace to do that.

GRIGOR: Listen —

BELA: No! War is so childish! One says so many silly things with death next door! With death shoving its mouth against the sandbags, say a lot of babble, not from the head, just speaking from the bowels —

GRIGOR: **All right, I'll come!** (*Pause*)

BELA: Good. Go and tell him you resign. (*He jumps up.*) With sneers. With curling mouth issuing fine spray of contempt. Go on.

GRIGOR: Now?

BELA: Yes! Now, of course! While you're full of **temper**. In his office. Fling your weight about! Shake the vases! Make the typist blush. I know you when you're wild. (*He smiles. GRIGOR starts to go out.*) Grig. (*He stops.*) Grig, I will find you nudes. Get nudes for you, anywhere.

GRIGOR: Yes . . .

BELA (*going to him*):   What is it you like? Their bums, is it? Makes you go — (*He grabs GRIGOR by the crutch.*)

GRIGOR: **You make me very angry.** (*Pause*).

BELA (*walking away*):   Yes . . . (GRIGOR *leaves. The student* ILONA *comes in.*) I'm going, Ilona. No more life class for me. No more pencil and rubber, trying to get the setting of her poor old joints. Never did her justice, anyway . . .

ILONA: Take me. (*Pause*

BELA: No. You smell of Budapest. Rank with blood and coffee, fear and petits-fours . . .

ILONA: Take me. (*He stares at her, then suddenly extends his arm.*)

BELA: That way — Russia! (*He extends the other arm.*) That way — France! (*Pause, then with inspiration, hurries to the blackboard. He takes a piece of chalk and divides the board, writing 'Russia' in one column and 'France' in the other. He extends his arm again.*) That way — (*Pause*)

ILONA: Tolstoy! (BELA *puts one point under 'Russia'. Then extends his arm again.*)

BELA: That way —

ILONA: Flaubert! (BELA *ticks 'France' and so on . . .*)

BELA: That way —

ILONA: Pushkin!

BELA: That way —

ILONA: Baudelaire!

BELA: That way —

ILONA: Mayakovsky!

BELA: That way —

ILONA: Appolinaire!

BELA: That way —

ILONA: Lenin!

BELA: That way — (*Pause.*) That way — (*Pause*) That way —

(ILONA *shrugs. He addes up the figures. Russia wins 4 - 3. He looks at her.*)

ILONA: Marry the future! Divorce the past! (*He smiles.*) I'll pack a bag.

BELA: No. Why pack a bag? A bag says, you came, so you can go back again. We don't go back again.

ILONA: Got no stockings. Bela, Russia's cold. (BELA *goes to a desk, dips a paintbrush in some colour, goes to her. Kneels, and rapidly paints her legs. He stops.*)

BELA: Fuck. Laddered it.

Scene Three

The offices of the Writers' and Artists' Union, Moscow. A single table. People enter with chairs from various directions. Some have briefcases. It is 1925.

Sketch: *'The New Economic Plan'. A capitalist is robbing an old Bolshevik. The figure of Lenin, behind a wall, covers his eyes.*

FIRST COMRADE: 'morning, Anatol.

SECOND COMRADE: I'll have that chair —

FIRST COMRADE: 'morning, I said —

SECOND COMRADE: Sorry, Roy —

FIRST COMRADE: S'all right, s'all right —

THIRD COMRADE: Roy, did you do that paper?

FIRST COMRADE: I did, I have it, I will give it to you —

THIRD COMRADE: Thank you.

FIRST COMRADE: 'ullo, Ludmilla —

THIRD COMRADE: I'll collect it off you afterwards, shall I?

FIRST COMRADE (*sitting, opening his bag*):   I love that skirt (*She ignores him.*) I do. I love that skirt. My wife wears such dismal skirts. Why is it? I dunno. Whenever you see Ludmilla she 'as —

SECOND COMRADE: Is everybody here yet?

FIFTH COMRADE: 'ello, 'ello, 'ello! Anyone got me a chair?

FIRST COMRADE: Certainly not. Get your own chair.

FIFTH COMRADE: The finest poet in the USSR and —

THIRD COMRADE: Opinion —

FIFTH COMRADE: An opinion, obviously — and I am reduced to transporting chairs —

FIRST COMRADE: Only your own chair, Oleg —

FIFTH COMRADE: Roy — no humour, love. (*He goes out again.*)

THIRD COMRADE: Will somebody remind me, there is a meeting of the entertainments committee this afternoon? Everyone invited, needless to say.

FIRST COMRADE: Drinks?

THIRD COMRADE: Yes.

FIRST COMRADE: On the fund, though?

THIRD COMRADE: Yes, out the funds of course.

SECOND COMRADE (*at the table*):   I'd like to push on please, everyone.

FOURTH COMRADE: Yes, let's please.

FIFTH COMRADE: I wanted to sit next to Ludmilla.

FOURTH COMRADE: Why?

FIFTH COMRADE: Why, she says!

FIRST COMRADE: Oleg's a poet, that's why.

FOURTH COMRADE: I still don't see —

SECOND COMRADE: I take it everybody's read the papers on this one? Have they? Everybody?

THIRD COMRADE: On the train.

FIRST COMRADE: I have.

SECOND COMRADE: Shall we get him in, then? I take it he's here.

FIRST COMRADE: Who's introducing it?

FIFTH COMRADE: You are.

FIRST COMRADE: Get stuffed.

FOURTH COMRADE: Why not you?

FIRST COMRADE: Why not me?

FOURTH COMRADE: Yes, why not?

SECOND COMRADE: Because he always does it.

FIRST COMRADE: Thank you, Anatol. Someone notices. Someone appreciates.

SECOND COMRADE: What about you, Vasily?

THIRD COMRADE: Rather not.

FOURTH COMRADE: He never does, do you?

FIRST COMRADE: Well, have a go.

THIRD COMRADE: I'd rather not.

FIRST COMRADE: Well, I'm not doing it again! You do it, Anatol.

FOURTH COMRADE: Anatol is addressing the foreign correspondents this afternoon.

FIRST COMRADE: Of course, of course! And what about you, Oleg?

FIFTH COMRADE (*shakes his head*): Sorry.

FIRST COMRADE: Not well enough briefed, I suppose?

FIFTH COMRADE: Exactly —

FIRST COMRADE: Oh, 'ere we go, all right, all right. Give in now, I may as well — I don't suppose you — (*He looks at* FOURTH COMRADE, *who shakes her head.*) No, I didn't think you would. All right.

FIFTH COMRADE: Hooray!

FIRST COMRADE: Lord High Executioner.

SECOND COMRADE: I don't think we should look at it like that.

FIRST COMRADE: Joke, Anatol.

FOURTH COMRADE: Jokes reveal attitudes.

FIRST COMRADE: Bloody 'ell —

FOURTH COMRADE: They do.

FIFTH COMRADE: Get on, shall we?

SECOND COMRADE: Ask him in, then. (FIFTH COMRADE *goes out of the room. The others read their papers.* FIRST COMRADE *lights a cigarette.*)

FIRST COMRADE: Sorry, Ludmilla. Got to smoke.

SECOND COMRADE: Vasily, would you fetch in another chair?

FOURTH COMRADE: Have you had your child yet, Anatol?

SECOND COMRADE: No. (THIRD COMRADE *goes out, returns with a chair.*)

FOURTH COMRADE: You want a boy I suppose?

SECOND COMRADE: Not at all, Ludmilla, no.

THIRD COMRADE (*putting it in the middle*): There?

SECOND COMRADE: That's fine. (*They read on.* FIFTH COMRADE *appears with* BELA *smiling and still wearing his army greatcoat.*)

BELA: Good morning.

ALL COMRADES: Good morning — How do you do — (BELA *shakes hands with them all.*)

FIRST COMRADE: I know that coat.

SECOND COMRADE: Would you care to take a chair?

BELA: Here?

SECOND COMRADE: Thank you, yes.

FIRST COMRADE (*still standing*): I know that coat.

BELA: It's a little bit the worse for wear. All the best wool went to make the officers' bed rolls.

FIRST COMRADE: Infantry. Hungarian Infantry.

BELA: Telegraphy.

FIRST COMRADE (*sitting*):   I knew it. Had a brush with you at
   Przemysl.
BELA: Not me, I think.
FIRST COMRADE: You weren't at Przemysl?
BELA (*affably*):   No, and even if I had been, I shouldn't have
   brushed with you. I never brushed with anyone.
FIRST COMRADE: Me neither. Figure of speech. We love
   your work, comrade.
BELA: Thank you.
FIFTH COMRADE: The best.
BELA: Thank you.
FIRST COMRADE: So I'll begin by saying no one here — or
   anywhere else for that matter — disputes your talent.
FIFTH COMRADE: You are a master.
BELA: Oh . . . .(FIRST COMRADE *flicks through sheaf of
   drawings.*)
FIRST COMRADE: Incredible. (*And on.*) Lovely.(*He shows it
   to* FOURTH COMRADE.) Look at that. (*He shakes his head.*)
FOURTH COMRADE (*leaning over*):   Yes . . .
FIRST COMRADE: Wonderful. I'll tell you something about
   that one — (*He holds it up.*)
SECOND COMRADE: Yes, do tell him.
FIRST COMRADE: No, you tell him, Anatol. I wasn't there.
SECOND COMRADE: Lenin was Guest of Honour at the
   annual conference of the Union of Printing and Graphic Trades
   in August, and he drew attention to your work.
FIRST COMRADE: Well, go on.
SECOND COMRADE: Praised it very highly.
FIRST COMRADE: No, Anatol will put things in the baldest
   manner possible — what Lenin said was —
SECOND COMRADE: You tell it —
FIRST COMRADE: He said why is there no one in the whole of
   the Soviet Union can draw half as well as this Hungarian chap?
   That's what he said.
SECOND COMRADE: Half as well.
FOURTH COMRADE: Lenin holds cartoons in the highest
   regard.
THIRD COMRADE: Yes.
FIRST COMRADE: So there we are. You can't do better than
   that. So anything we have to say, you interpret in the light of
   that, all right? Do you smoke? (FIRST COMRADE *chucks the
   packet.*) No, we're all fans here. To a man. Or to a woman. All
   right, Ludmilla? To a woman. (*She grimaces.*) I think I'd like to

start by saying — as is my wont — that we are struggling —
(*He stops.*) I 'ate struggling — we are trying, quite simply,
trying — to evolve a different sort of art here. All right? An art
which is not bourgeois. That is why you came here. Correct me
if I'm wrong. That is why you came to Russia in the first place.
Because although we have no shoe laces for our boots and no
lenses for our spectacles, our art is free. By free I mean free of
bourgeois constraints. By bourgeois constraints I mean the tying
of the creative act to the demands of private ego. Individualism,
I mean, all right? How am I doing?

BELA: All right.

FIRST COMRADE: Good. And it's not been easy, you know
that. Everyone in this room has suffered in some way from
trying, this particular type of trying. It has cost us, hasn't it?
Given us trouble, and pain. A great deal of pain. But we believe
it's worth it. And one of the ways we have continued, have kept
up the struggle — why do I keep saying struggle, Anatol? I
must get shot of struggle — one of the ways we have — sustained our effort — is through meetings like this, in which —
sometimes happy, sometimes sad — we have exerted our com-
munal will to rescue artists from their bourgeois habit. There.
Have I put it fairly? Vasily?

THIRD COMRADE: I think so, yes.

SECOND COMRADE: Good, Roy.

FIFTH COMRADE: Thank you. I get so much experience, you
see. None of this lot will make the opening speech. Terrible,
ain't it? I shall end up smooth and oily.

FIFTH COMRADE: That'll be the day.

FIRST COMRADE: So we ask you along, as a member of the
Cultural Union because — why? Because — there is a feeling — a more or less unanimous feeling — that you — might
benefit from a session of his sort. (*Pause*) Voila! Now you say
something. Fuck off, if you like. (*He takes a drink of water from
the table. BELA is silent.*)

FOURTH COMRADE: Some people, you see, resist this very
strongly. They think we are taking a liberty with their God-
given right to speak their minds. They feel affronted. That is a
negative response. We're not bureaucrats. You know Anatol.
Vasily is a painter. Roy's a first rate critic. I'm a graphic artist.
Oleg's a poet and a sculptor. You know that, you know that
artists grow enormously when they exchange ideas. Take in-
sights from each other. That's very good. A lonely artist withers,
rots, dries up. We want to stimulate you. We are not bourgeois

critics who see their role as destruction in the interests of maintaining existing cultural values. We attack existing cultural values. Am I going on too much?

FIRST COMRADE: No, that's all good stuff, Ludmilla.

FOURTH COMRADE: Yes, but does he understand it? (*Pause*) I know a lot of artists have gone away from these meetings arguing with themselves, forced to confront things they had been hiding from. On your own, you can hide from anything can't you? And they became better artists. Even artists who were very good in the first place.

SECOND COMRADE: I did.

FOURTH COMRADE: Anatol is one.

SECOND COMRADE: I was outraged. Everything in me prickled. I remember feeling terribly hot, and ashamed. But that was silly. Because I am an artist does not mean I'm not human, that I'm above criticism. But it must be the right criticism. With the right criticism I could benefit.

FIRST COMRADE: Anatol's work has improved ten fold.

SECOND COMRADE: Well, I don't know about ten fold —

FIRST COMRADE: Ten fold. (*Pause*)

FOURTH COMRADE: Do you want to speak? (*Pause*)

BELA: Are you telling me I've done wrong?

FIRST COMRADE: No. Let's get the word wrong disposed of, shall we? Chuck wrong out. The word wrong is —

FIFTH COMRADE: Wrong.

FIRST COMRADE: Thank you. In a sense, Bela, no artist can be wrong. I will be accused of residual bourgeois thinking — lovely phrase —

FOURTH COMRADE: You will —

FIRST COMRADE: Here we go — if I say no artist can be wrong — in the most fundamental sense — because he is obeying an impulse from somewhere within —

FOURTH COMRADE: I don't go along with this —

THIRD COMRADE: Me neither —

FIRST COMRADE: They don't go along with it —

FOURTH COMRADE: Absolutely not —

FIRST COMRADE: There you are, residual bourgeois habit —

FOURTH COMRADE: Of course an artist can be wrong —

FIFTH COMRADE: Scrap it, Roy —

FIRST COMRADE: No. I won't entirely scrap it, I'll refine it —

FIFTH COMRADE: Scrap it!

FOURTH COMRADE: It's confusing him.

FIFTH COMRADE: It's confusing us —

FOURTH COMRADE: Yes.

FIRST COMRADE: Beg pardon, beg pardon, see I can't always be right —

FOURTH COMRADE: You damn well can't.

FIRST COMRADE: No artist does wrong knowingly. Or else he's not an artist. (*Pause. He cups his ear.*) Anyone?

FOURTH COMRADE: I don't understand it.

FIRST COMRADE: Oh, come one —

FOURTH COMRADE: I do not understand it.

FIRST COMRADE: Tell you later. You know what I mean, Bela, do you?

BELA: Yes.

FIRST COMRADE: But he can do wrong unknowingly. Because he has power. Artists are very dangerous people. That is why they go to prison, that is why they have gags stuck on their mouths. They are more dangerous than tanks and planes. It's a terrible power, this power of addressing hearts and minds, articulating the unspoken will of peoples. What a treasure that is, Bela, a gift of the most massive kind, a power which in the case of the very greatest artists, may be beyond even the control of genius itself . . . (*Silence. He takes a drink.*) So. To this cartoon. (*He shuffles his papers. The others do the same. Noise of papers.*) Where is it? (*Rustling papers.*) Too much bloody paperwork.

FOURTH COMRADE: You are just untidy.

FIRST COMRADE: I am untidy, but there's still too much paperwork. Really, Anatol, can we cut down on this? (*He finds what he wants, stands, hands a copy to* BELA.) Do you want to comment on that cartoon? (*Pause. They all look at him.*)

BELA: It's a very good example of my work.

FIRST COMRADE: Yes. (*Pause*)

BELA: It's a superb piece of draughtsmanship.

FIRST COMRADE: Yes. It is. (FOURTH COMRADE *looks at* THIRD. *Pause.*)

BELA: It's a bit too heavily shaded.

FIRST COMRADE: Well, that's a matter of opinion.

BELA: Quite. (*Pause.* FIRST COMRADE *takes his glasses off, rubs his eyes, replaces them.*)

FIRST COMRADE: Anything else? (*Pause*) Oh, dear . . .

SECOND COMRADE: I don't think it will help much if you adopt a posture — if you — on principle resist what we are saying. Because it isn't really a very worthy principle, is it? If you think about it.

BELA: I'm sorry —

SECOND COMRADE: I think there's only one principle that we ought to be rigid about, and that is — do we, as artists, serve the people? That's the only one, I think.

BELA: Yes.

SECOND COMRADE: You agree with that?

BELA: Yes. (FIRST COMRADE *lets out a sigh of relief.*)

FOURTH COMRADE (*turning to him angrily*): It's quite obvious he believes that! Don't insult him! Would he be here if he didn't believe that?

SECOND COMRADE: I just wanted to clarify —

FOURTH COMRADE: He doesn't need to clarify it. All these pictures clarify it.

SECOND COMRADE: Obviously. (*Pause*)

FIRST COMRADE: Yes. Which brings us to the tricky question, doesn't it? (*He draws breath.*) Is this cartoon saying — no — start again — Is what the cartoon says — in the service of the people? In other words, with reference to the criteria we have established and agreed upon — is it a good cartoon? (*He looks around.*)

FOURTH COMRADE: No.

SECOND COMRADE: No.

FIFTH COMRADE: Absolutely not.

BELA: What is this? Are we counting heads?

FIRST COMRADE: No, it was a rhetorical question. Give us a fag. (BELA *tosses him the packet.*) Anybody else want to speak? I've done a lengthy introduction. (*Pause*) Anyone?

SECOND COMRADE: You go on.

FOURTH COMRADE: You're doing very well.

FIRST COMRADE: Never have the gift of the gab. Have you got the gift of the gab, Bela?

BELA: No.

FIRST COMRADE: Lucky feller. It's an almighty handicap.

FOURTH COMRADE: Just go on. (*Pause.* FIRST COMRADE *drinks again.*)

FIRST COMRADE: In this cartoon — and others — there is a tendency — a critical tendency —

BELA: It's a cartoon —

FIRST COMRADE: Quite, it's a cartoon —

BELA: Isn't a cartoon meant to be —

FOURTH COMRADE: Let Roy finish —

FIRST COMRADE: A tendency to criticize the line that Comrade Lenin is advancing. Which is — which is — unhelpful —
BELA: Unhelpful?
FIRST COMRADE: Let me go on a minute — not because Lenin is a god, not because he is infallible but because the experiment we are undertaking here, which drew you here in the beginning, which brought you and many others scuttling across the border, without a suitcase even I believe — this great experiment — must be endorsed by all the people, and not undermined. I mean, there is a case for criticism, but it's not now. (*Pause*)
SECOND COMRADE: Would you care to reply to that?
BELA: I did not scuttle across the border, I walked.
FIRST COMRADE: Beg pardon.
BELA: I did not bring a suitcase because I came to make Russia my home. And I came to make it my home because it's free.
FIFTH COMRADE: Quite.
FOURTH COMRADE: Good.
BELA: Because to an artist, freedom of expression matters even more than nationality. I say that as a patriotic person, a person who loves his country and his people. Not as a licker of governments. I say it as a person who loves socialism and materialism. As a person who admires Lenin more than any other man alive. But to an artist freedom comes above all things, above —
SECOND COMRADE: Wait a minute, wait a minute. Not above justice, surely? (*Pause. BELA is silent.*) You see, this is what we mean when we say we are against the bourgeois definition of an artist. We say an artist is only free if his society is free. He cannot be free **against** the freedom of his society. Can he? That is intellectual sickness. (*Pause.*) Isn't it? (*Pause. BELA stares ahead.*)
BELA: I am not a good intellectual.
FOURTH COMRADE: You mustn't say that.
BELA: I don't think I —
FOURTH COMRADE: You mustn't shelter behind a fog of anti-intellectualism. That is a posture, a calamitous affectation, isn't it?
FIFTH COMRADE: Carry on, Bela. (*Pause. He seems unable to speak.*)
BELA: It's oppressive in here, all this —
SECOND COMRADE: It can seem oppressive, I agree —
FOURTH COMRADE: It's not oppressive. It is not a persecu-

tion. We aren't the Inquisition, are we? This is not the Middle Ages. Argue with us, please. (*Pause*)

SECOND COMRADE: Yes. Defend your cartoon, please. (BELA *shuts his eyes.*)

BELA: There's something wrong somewhere.

SECOND COMRADE: Where? Tell us where. (*Pause*) Fight for your work. It won't speak for itself.

BELA: It should do!

SECOND COMRADE: But it won't

FIRST COMRADE: Shall I get us all a cup of tea?

FOURTH COMRADE: No, Roy, don't lighten the atmosphere. Bela is not a child, is he? He is a great artist. (FIRST COMRADE *gets up, walks a little.*)

BELA: I disagree with Lenin.

FIFTH COMRADE: That is a supremely arrogant statement.

FOURTH COMRADE: Of course it's not!

FIFTH COMRADE: She says it's not.

FOURTH COMRADE: He is entitled to disagree with anyone he wants. That's freedom, isn't it? But he must be able to restrain his criticism in the wider interests of the people. That's responsibility, isn't it? (*Pause*)

BELA: So you are saying —

FIRST COMRADE: Lenin sees much further than we do.

BELA: Ah.

FIRST COMRADE: And even if he didn't we should have to follow him, because to resist him is to resist the revolution, isn't it? **At this time.** (*Pause*) Later on, yes, let's all squeal at once.

BELA: **But I want to protest!**

FIRST COMRADE: Tomorrow. (*Pause*)

BELA: You have created a most terrible effect, quite unintentionally, the terrible effect of making me, who is so small and insignificant, a hero, a colossus towering over you, you who are so much better men than me, you shovel earth beneath my feet, and raise me up and up, aren't I vain enough already but you want to make me a saint, I who did so little, who have so little honour, **am much greater than you!** (*Pause*) You should not do that. It makes me ashamed . . . (*Pause*)

FOURTH COMRADE: Bela, we stretch our little fingers out, to try to catch the swinging boot of history, treading generation after generation into blood, help us catch it, bend it, make it our tame thing . . . (*Pause. He tears up his cartoon, drops it on the floor.* FIFTH COMRADE *goes to him, embraces him. Scraping of chairs as the meeting breaks up.*)

FIRST COMRADE: Anybody going my way?
THIRD COMRADE: I better take that paper, Roy, while I remember.
FIRST COMRADE: Anyone getting a bus? Oh, good —
FIFTH COMRADE (*calling as he leaves*):   Ludmilla, Ludmilla!

Scene Four

A garden in a suburb of Moscow. A massive bed of flowers featuring a hammer and sickle. A GARDENER *is at work with a trowel. It is 1934.* ILONA *enters pushing a pram.*

Drawing: GRIGOR's '*Naked Woman Looking at her Feet.*'

GARDENER (*springing up, pointing with trowel*): Geraniums — the blood of Russia — Chrysanthemums — the future of mankind — Lobelia — The solidarity of the party — Lily — Comrade Stalin's favourite plant. (*He stands to attention.*) Floral tribute of the 9th District Workers' Flats! (*He smiles, looks at the baby, kneels down again to work.* BELA *comes in, overcoated though it's a summer's day, with* GRIGOR. *The* GARDENER *leaps to his feet again.*) Geraniums — the blood of Russia — Chrysanthemums — the future of mankind — Lobelia — the solidarity of the party — Lily — Comrade Stalin's favourite plant. (*He stands to attention.*) Floral tribute of 9th District Workers' Flats! (*He kneels down again.*)
ILONA: I am perfectly prepared to have a child by each of you.
BELA: Grigor isn't. Grigor doesn't fancy that.
GRIGOR: I love her.
BELA: So you keep saying.
ILONA: It's been done before.
BELA: Grigor thinks passion is exclusive. Grigor thinks passion's got rights.
GRIGOR: It has got rights!
BELA: There you are. The gospel according to Saint Grigor. Flesh and babies. Babies and flesh.
GRIGOR: Can I speak for myself?
BELA: Go ahead! (*Pause*)

GRIGOR: We should go away. We have had twelve years of Moscow. We should live in the forest.

BELA: Oh, my God . . .

GRIGOR: We should expose ourselves unhesitatingly to our human essence.

BELA: Eat berries. Wipe our bums on leaves.

GRIGOR: **Don't laugh at me! Why do you have to laugh at me!**

ILONA: I can't live in the woods.

GRIGOR: You love me. I love you.

ILONA: Yes, but I can't live in the woods.

BELA: Grigor thinks, because he is in love, that puts a stop to the argument. You are in love — ergo — the woods!

GRIGOR: Yes.

ILONA: Grigor, I am secretary of the Works Committee.

GRIGOR: That's not a reason for, or against, doing anything.

ILONA: Of course it is.

BELA: The truth about human nature, Grigor, is not lying underneath an oak tree. I have sat under oak trees, and it isn't there.

GRIGOR: Nobody wants to listen to me! Everybody wants to talk and nobody wants to listen! Everybody wants to be clever and nobody wants to be wise! (A MAN *enters. He is a member of the GPU.*)

GARDENER (*leaping up*):   Geranums — the blood of Russia — Chrysanthemums — the future of mankind — Lobelia — the solidarity of —

GPU MAN: Shut up. (*He shows briefly, a very small card. The* GARDENER *goes back to his work.*)

BELA (*deliberately*):   I believe, historically speaking, the option of the woods — the woods option, we'll call it — has been tried before. I believe from time to time, at moments of crisis, at moments of doubt, persons of a philosophic disposition have retreated to the relatively unspoiled regions of the earth in search of wisdom, invariably in the company of women with big tits —

GRIGOR: Look, Bela, will you —

BELA: But I don't believe, in all honesty, given the complexity of the present social and industrial machine, the woods option is a wholly satisfactory response, since the deliberate rejection of experience contributes nothing to the alleviation of human pain, nor relieves you from its consequences, or to put it brutally — (*He goes up to the* GPU MAN.) You don't miss the bullets by

shutting your eyes! (*Pause, smiles*) Good morning. I thought
we'd lost you on the underground.

ILONA: Grigor, what are you looking for? (GRIGOR *shrugs.*)

BELA: I must say, Grigor's deceit is practically insupportable.
All these years he has been consuming — ostensibly for artistic
reasons — the nakedness of — dare I say, my wife? — his char-
coal scratching white paper which his fantasy converted into
bedroom sheets —

ILONA: Shut up —

BELA: When all the time, his intentions, conscious or uncon-
scious, have been — I can hardly bring myself to say it!

ILONA: Shut up —

BELA: As if Moscow wasn't full of models! Splendid Russian
women perfectly buttocked, gorgeous hipped! And he — in
twelve years — has not attempted one! I should have seen it, a
man with half my sensitivity would have known.

ILONA: You do not love me. So you didn't know.

BELA: She says I do not love her! And what's her evidence?
That I trust her with my friend!

ILONA: You know you don't.

BELA: The absence of jealousy is perfect proof! God help us!

ILONA: **I said you know you don't**. (*Pause*)

BELA: No. You're quite right. I'm not in love with you. (*Pause*)
Strange, how those words set you free . . . (*Pause*) Go to the
woods if you want to. If they'll let you. Go.

GRIGOR: You don't mind?

BELA: Mind? Why should I mind? You exercise your will to
oblivion, if it's oblivion you want. If the world hurts you, do it,
bend your knee to mystery, drink dirty water, worship funny
little forest gods, dig out a religion for yourself.

GRIGOR: I don't want a religion!

BELA: You will have to have one! Go backwards and you must
take the backwardness that goes with it. Make her your idol if
you like. Her parts, her fecund this, her fertile that. Go down
on your knees and lick her, offer up dead lambs on the altar of
her magic cunt, carve women with huge bellies and tiny, rudi-
mentary heads —

GRIGOR: You don't know what —

BELA: I do know! I know where the real fight is! It is against
worship, it's against the surrender of your self! (*Pause*) Will you
wear clothes, or not? I see you in a tutu, sewn together from
pigs' ears . . .

ILONA: Nobody asks me what I want. (*Pause*) **Nobody asks me what I want.**

BELA: Ilona is getting emotional. (*Suddenly she weeps, covers her face bitterly.*) You see?

GRIGOR: Don't cry. I cannot bear to see you cry.

BELA: Let her.

GRIGOR: I love you! Don't cry!

BELA (*shakes his head*): Oh, Grigor . . . as if that could make her stop! Your little sticky thing of love! Your glue! Her head splits and he offers his smelly little tube of glue.

GRIGOR: **You don't know how I hate you sometimes!**

BELA: You don't know how I hate myself. (*Pause*)

ILONA: Sometimes, I really want to be myself. Want utter hardness. Be like a pebble, round and safe, and walk along a street, not going from anybody, nor to anybody. Whole. (*Pause*) And then, when I feel most like that, stop dead suddenly, go cold and hot, and crumble, and pray somebody wants me, for anything, a fuck, a fingering, because it wants my milk or is afraid of the dark. (*Pause*) And I go from one to the other, being ashamed or angry. I want to go to the woods, and I don't. I like being Grigor's goddess, and I don't . . . (*Pause*)

GPU MAN: Women . . . don't know what they do want . . .

BELA: And do you, comrade?

GPU MAN: Me, comrade?

BELA: Yes, comrade. Tell us what you want, comrade.

GPU MAN: Think you caught me?

BELA: No.

GPU MAN: Yes, you do. (*Pause.*) I want Comrade Stalin to enjoy another forty years of health. (*Pause. BELA turns to ILONA.*)

BELA: It's my child in the pram, I believe . . .

ILONA: She stays with me. (BELA *goes. Looks in the pram.*)

GRIGOR: Come with us, Bela . . .

BELA (*shakes his head*): The quiet would kill me. Since they built it, I've done nothing but ride around the underground . . . (*He picks the baby out, holds it up.*) Oh, Judith, don't let them fool you with their gods . . .

GRIGOR: **What about your gods! Aren't these gods!** (*He looks at the GPU MAN.*)

BELA (*putting the baby back*): Send me drawings, will you? Of her growing up? (*Pause. GRIGOR hugs him tightly, then leaves with ILONA. BELA watches them disappear. Pause. The GPU MAN comes forward.*)

GPU MAN: Intellectuals . . . ! What does it matter what they say? (*Pause*) Ask me, has industrial production risen much? (*Pause.*) Go on, ask me. (*Pause*) **Ask me, then!**

BELA: Has industrial production risen much?

GPU MAN: Rolled steel bars, seven hundred and fifty-eight per cent. Railway wagons, four hundred and twenty-six per cent. Chemicals, not including fertilizers, two hundred and seventeen per cent. Fertilizers, four hundred and one per cent. (*Pause*) Ask me about housing now. (*Pause*)

BELA: Housing, please.

GPU MAN: Units of accommodation, six hundred and ninety-two per cent (*Pause*) Imagine all that happiness.

BELA: Yes.

GPU MAN: Comrade Stalin. People will talk about him for thousands of years. At night, I read those figures before I go to bed. That's how I live with pain, comrade. (*Pause, BELA moves away to leave. The GARDENER jumps up, eagerly.*)

GARDENER: Geraniums — the blood of Russia — Chrysanthemums — the future of mankind — Lobelia — the solidarity of the party — Lily — Comrade Stalin's favourite plant. (*He stands to attention.*) Floral tribute of the 9th District Workers' Flats! (BELA *stares at the flowers. Suddenly he lets out a cry and plunges into the middle of the flower bed.*)

BELA (*lying and writhing*):   **Idol — atory! Idol — atory!**

GARDENER (*in disbelief*):   Hey, you bugger! Out of there!

BELA: **Idol — atory! Idol — atory!**

GARDENER: That's art! That's my art you're rollin' on! (*The GPU MAN puts a whistle to his lips and blows loudly.*)

Scene Five

BELA *is standing holding a suitcase. He faces* FOURTH COMRADE *across the stage.*

FOURTH COMRADE: I put eye-shadow on. I put lip-colour on. I shopped for underwear. I found some which made me feel bridal, do you know what I mean? And new stockings, which I rolled up my smooth legs, and in the car kept looking at them, at my perfect untouched knees, and they were shaking . . .

(*Pause.*) And in the Kremlin, going down the corridors, was thinking all the time, are my seams straight . . . will someone tell me if my legs look nice, and from the way they looked, the men who took my papers, who smelled me, caught my scent of fear and roses, watched my trembling body pass them, yes, knew I was nice, luscious with nerves and moistened lips, and when the door behind the door after the door was opened, stood there, saw him and —

BELA: **What about me!** (*She shuts her eyes. Pause.*)

FOURTH COMRADE: Pissed myself . . . (*She shudders.*)

BELA: Please, Ludmilla, what about me?

FOURTH COMRADE: I said you had a momentary onset of dementia, brought on by your wife's desertion. I think I said that. I may not have done. To which he said, socialism had not yet discovered the answer to domestic incompatability. I think he said that. I may have imagined it. I wonder if he is immune to the stealthy smell of urine?

BELA: But I am —

FOURTH COMRADE: He wants you to have a holiday.

BELA (*horrified*):   A holiday . . . ! (*Pause*)

FOURTH COMRADE: Visit relatives abroad. (*Pause. He holds out the suitcase.*)

BELA: I shan't be wanting this —

FOURTH COMRADE: Take it. It means you may come back again. (*His hand drops. He goes to take a step towards her.*) No, don't kiss me goodbye. It will look as though I defended you for personal reasons.

BELA: Would you like to kiss me?

FOURTH COMRADE: Ideally, yes.

BELA: May I imagine it?

FOURTH COMRADE: Yes.

BELA: Where?

FOURTH COMRADE: On your lips.

BELA: And you'll imagine mine, will you?

FOURTH COMRADE: I will imagine yours.

BELA: On your breasts?

FOURTH COMRADE: If you say so. (*Pause. He smiles.*) Quick! Hurry up!

Scene Six

Dover, the Customs shed. A woman's voice over a tannoy announces a train departure. Two CUSTOMS OFFICERS *stand in a posture of lethargy against a desk.* BELA *enters, with suitcase. He kneels, kisses the ground.*

Sketch: 'The Dark Ages.' *A Hitlerine bat, its wings outspread, casts a shadow over the European portion of the globe.*

FIRST OFFICER: Oi! (BELA *kisses on.*) Oi! Cut that out. (*He walks over, lazily.*)

BELA: I kiss this soil, I kiss this ground. I kiss. I kiss.

SECOND OFFICER: 'ave that bag over 'ere, please!

BELA (*grasping the officer's ankles*):   Kiss this trouser! Kiss this feet!

FIRST OFFICER: Mind my creases!

SECOND OFFICER: That bag over 'ere, please!

FIRST OFFICER: **Get your fingers off my crease!**(*Pointing to the suitcase.*) On the desk.

BELA: (*standing, holding out his suitcase*):   Nothing!

SECOND OFFICER: That's what you say.

BELA: Emptiness!

SECOND OFFICER: That's what you say, is it? (BELA *puts it down. The* SECOND OFFICER *snaps open the locks.*)

SECOND OFFICER: Fuckin' is, an' all.

BELA: I got nothin'! Only freeness! Breathe it, see? No magic here!

FIRST OFFICER: Got nothing, eh?

BELA: Nothin'! (*He grins.*)

FIRST OFFICER: You may not enter the territories of His Britannic Majesty without the equivalent in currency of ten pounds —

BELA: It rains on me, I don't care! I lie under hedges and the rain piss on me, who cares? I am empty belly, **I do not care,** I am rich, see, I am dressed in freeness, I am eating freeness, see?

FIRST OFFICER: Dom.

BELA: Beg pardon?

FIRST OFFICER: Dom. Not ness.

SECOND OFFICER: Have you the equivalent of ten pounds?

BELA: No money.

FIRST OFFICER: Right.

BELA: Got this — (*He takes out a pencil.*) Draw your picture.
Beautiful English face —
FIRST OFFICER: Come on —
BELA (*inhaling*):   I breathe, see, breathe deep of English wind!
FIRST OFFICER (*to* SECOND OFFICER):   Michael! Get this
silly bugger out of here! (*A man enters from the opposite direc-
tion. He greets* BELA.)
STRUBENZEE: Mr. Veracek? I'm Sir Herbert Strubenzee,
(*He holds out a hand.* BELA *grasps it. Falls to his knees.*) No,
no, you don't kneel to me, I am a knight but you still don't have
to . . . We pride ourselves on being rather casual about things
like rank — (*He turns angrily to* OFFICERS.) **Don't laugh at
him, please!** (*Turns back to* BELA *who gets up.*) Welcome to
Great Britain, (*To* FIRST OFFICER.) Take his case.
BELA: No, no, I take my —
STRUBENZEE: He likes taking cases. I say, what a spiffing
coat!

BELA *stops, looks down at the ancient greatcoat, then unbuttons
it, and takes it off. He looks at it, drops it on the floor. They go out.*
SECOND OFFICER, *with studied casualness, walks over, a clip-
board in one hand. With the other, using two fingers, he plucks it
up. Suddenly, the violent interruption of sound effects: the mono-
tonous firing of a light gun,* ILONA's *voice desperately calling for*
GRIGOR. *The* SECOND OFFICER *strides off.*

ACT TWO

Scene One

A hut on an airfield. A group of RAF *personnel, sitting, standing, talking, reading. An* AIRMAN *enters, followed by* BELA *in a dark overcoat. It is 1943.*

Drawing: GRIGOR's *'Dead Woman after a Raid.'*

FIRST AIRMAN: Ladies and Gentlemen —
SECOND AIRMAN: Boys and girls —
FIRST AIRWOMAN: Comrades, surely?
FIRST AIRMAN: As you wish —
FIRST AIRWOMAN: What's wrong with comrades?
FIRST AIRMAN: Sorry to keep you waiting. We couldn't find the hut. The hut had vanished.
THIRD AIRMAN: It is always the same hut, Roger.
FIRST AIRMAN: Thank you, Don.
FIRST AIRWOMAN: Hut 48C.
FIRST AIRMAN: I'm indebted to you, Dorothy. (*He ushers* BELA *forward. Chairs shift, people sit.*) I would like most cordially, on behalf of the Brave New World Club, RAF Basingbourne, to welcome our most distinguished visitor, Mr. Bela Veracek, better known to most of us as Vera of the *Daily Mirror* — er — (*He looks round.*) Where is the Distinguished Visitor's Chair, please? (*Everyone looks round.*) The DVC? (*He looks to* BELA.) Sorry about this. Has anyone seen the —
FIRST AIRWOMAN: Chopped it up. (*Pause*)
FIRST AIRMAN: Chopped it up?
FIRST AIRWOMAN: For firewood, yes.
FIRST AIRMAN: You did **what**!
FIRST AIRWOMAN: Oh, come on, Roger —
THIRD AIRWOMAN: We had a bit of a discussion about it, and then we —

FIRST AIRWOMAN: Chopped it up.

BELA: It's perfectly all right, I'll sit down here —

FIRST AIRMAN: No, it's not that, it's —

FIRST AIRWOMAN (*to* BELA):   It's not that we don't want you to have a chair.

FIRST AIRMAN: Of course it's not —

FIRST AIRWOMAN: It's just that some of us — the hardliners in the struggle for cultural democracy — have always challenged the notion that distinguished visitors needed distinguished chairs —

FIRST AIRMAN: That's all very well —

FIRST AIRWOMAN: It burned very well, Roger. All the genius soaked in the wood. The sweaty palms of greatness. Went like paraffin. **Woof!** (*Pause*)

FIRST AIRMAN: Discuss this later.

THIRD AIRMAN: Put it on the agenda, Michael!

FIRST AIRWOMAN: Inquest on the DVC.

FIRST AIRMAN: It isn't funny, Dorothy.

SECOND/THIRD AIRMEN (*shaking heads*) No — no — no —

FIRST AIRMAN: We are self-governing, but we must have rules!

THIRD AIRMAN: Yipee!

FIRST AIRMAN: Rules, Don, yes —

SECOND AIRMAN: Can't do nothink without yer rules —

FIRST AIRMAN: That happens to be absolutely true, like it or not —

SECOND AIRWOMAN: Look, we are being very bloody rude! (*Pause*)

FIRST AIRMAN: Quite.

FIRST AIRWOMAN (*standing*):   We welcome Vera. We feel very honoured. Could I offer you a rather ordinary chair?

BELA (*taking the chair from her*):   Thank you, I am happy with any chair. (*He puts his hat on it.*) Beastly weather. (*He takes his coat off.*) No flying today. (*He folds his coat over the back of the chair, leans on it, clears his throat.*) I was born in Budapest on January 15th, 1898. I lived in Hungary until 1922. I lived in the Soviet Union until 1936. I am a cartoonist. I believe the cartoon to be the lowest form of art. I also believe it to be the most important form of art. I decided in my twenty-fourth year I would rather be important that great. I decided this because I have always preferred shouting to whispering and humanity more than myself. The cartoon is a weapon in the struggle of peoples. It is a liberating instrument. It is brief like life. It is not

about me. It is about us. Important art is about us. Great art is
about me. I am not interested in me. I do not like me. I am not
sure if I like us either, but that is private and the cartoon is not
private. We share the cartoon as we cannot share the painting.
We plunder painting for the private meaning. The cartoon has
only one meaning. When the cartoon lies it shows at once.
When the painting lies it can deceive for centuries. The cartoon
is celebrated in a million homes. The painting is worshipped in a
gallery. The cartoon changes the world. The painting changes
the artist. I long to change the world. I hate the world. Thank
you. (*Pause. He sits, blows his nose.*)

FIRST AIRMAN (*standing*):   There we are, then. Plenty to
chew on there. Mr. Veracek has said he'll answer questions, so
the meeting is open to the floor. First question, please. (*He
sits.*) Or statement. Whatever you like . . . (*Pause*) I'm sure
we're all bursting with suggestions. (*Pause*) Anyone? (*Pause*)
Margaret, I'm sure you — (SECOND AIRWOMAN *shakes
her head curtly.*) All right, I'll kick off, then. (*He turns to
BELA.*) Mr. Veracek, I've always wondered why the papers
are —

FOURTH AIRMAN: **I don't like this fucking world either.**
(*Pause*)

FIRST AIRMAN: I don't think that's a question, Kenny, is
it —

FOURTH AIRMAN: **I don't like it any more than you.**

SECOND AIRMAN: Got a question, put yer hand up —

FOURTH AIRMAN: **Question.**

FIRST AIRMAN: I think I was asking something, wasn't I?

FOURTH AIRMAN (*standing*):   **Why are we dropping phosphorous bombs on kids?**

THIRD AIRMAN: Come on, Kenny —

FOURTH AIRMAN: I was doing Aachen last night, wasn't I?

FIRST AIRWOMAN: Sit down, Kenny —

FOURTH AIRMAN: **Asked a question!**

SECOND AIRMAN: Always ask that question —

THIRD AIRMAN: Every bloody meeting, Kenny says —

FOURTH AIRMAN: **Because I haven't got a fucking answer
yet!**

FIRST AIRWOMAN: We will hold a special meeting on the
subject of civilian bombing —

THIRD AIRMAN: Just for Kenny —

FIRST AIRWOMAN: Can we have that in the Suggestion
Book?

FOURTH AIRWOMAN: **Don't want it in the fucking Suggestion Book! Don't want you to answer it! Want him to Answer It!** (*Pause*) Want genius to answer it, see? (*Pause*)

BELA: This is a very good question.

FOURTH AIRMAN: Cheers. He says it's a good question. (*He sits.*)

FIRST AIRWOMAN: It is not a good question. It is a confusing, inaccurate question.

FOURTH AIRMAN: It's a question, ain't it?

FIRST AIRWOMAN: It is a stifling, suffocating question. It's a bog question. I hate bog questions. I don't want to be sucked down in Kenny's bog.

FOURTH AIRMAN: Well, answer it!

FIRST AIRWOMAN: Hitler has been gassing kids since 1938.

THIRD AIRMAN: 's' not the answer, Dorothy . . .

FIRST AIRMAN (*to* BELA): Kenny is a tail-end gunner. Did his bit in setting light to Rotterdam . . .

FOURTH AIRMAN: I'm sorry I can't draw. You do the cartoon for me.

FIRST AIRMAN: I don't think we asked Mr. Veracek here in order that he should —

SECOND AIRWOMAN: Why not?

FIRST AIRWOMAN: Kenny is trying to drag pacifist slogans into this discussion —

SECOND AIRMAN: What discussion?

FIRST AIRWOMAN: Correction. Kenny is trying to initiate a pacifist discussion —

SECOND AIRWOMAN: He is asking for a practical demonstration of the cartoonist's art —

FIRST AIRWOMAN: He is trying to annexe the meeting —

FIRST AIRMAN: Can we get a bit of order here? We obviously can't ask Mr. Veracek to take a pencil and just go —

SECOND AIRWOMAN: He has just said the cartoon is the people's art. We are people, aren't we?

FIRST AIRMAN: This is worse than when we had Bertrand Russell —

THIRD AIRMAN: Bertrand Russell couldn't draw —

FOURTH AIRMAN (*stands, tosses a pencil*): Here —

FIRST AIRWOMAN: All right, if the cartoon represents the people it'll have to represent me too. It will have to include my view, which is the opposite of Kenny's. If they took female aircrew I would drop phosphorous.

THIRD AIRMAN: On children?

FIRST AIRWOMAN: Yes.

BELA: I do not actually see how in a single cartoon I can reconcile such contrasting points of view. I do not see how in one drawing I can show both pacifism and support the war. I can only say I have to draw what speaks to me —

SECOND AIRWOMAN: No. (*She stands.*) No. You see, you are talking about private art again. You are talking about painting. What you think. What strikes you. Artist stuff. Somewhere in the contradictions, there is the proper point of view. There is a correct one.

FIRST AIRWOMAN: Absolutely.

SECOND AIRWOMAN: It's a matter of finding it. (*Pause. BELA gets up, picks up his coat.*)

FIRST AIRWOMAN: Don't go!

BELA: I have to, because you see —

FIRST AIRWOMAN: **No, don't.** (*Pause*)

BELA: What you are saying I know will drive me mad! (*Pause, then he turns to leave.*)

FIRST AIRMAN: I'd like to thank Mr. Veracek on behalf of everyone —

FOURTH AIRMAN: **I could be killed tonight.** (BELA *stops.*) Don't want it to be for nothing, see? (BELA *shakes his head, closing his eyes.*) Must have a little bit of truth to go with, please. . .

SECOND AIRWOMAN: Draw the real war. Not Hitler. Easy hating Hitler. Too easy for a man like you. Draw the real war, will you? The war which goes on underneath the war? The long war of the English people. Draw that, please. . .

BELA *hesitates, then turns back, tossing down his hat. The room is full of cheering. Sound of slamming doors and echoing footsteps on corridors.*

Scene Two

STRINGER, *an editor, comes in, looks at* BELA, *shakes his head.*

Sketch: BELA's *cartoon 'There always was a Second Front'. An*

English Soldier is struggling with Hitler. A profiteer is trying to strangle the soldier from behind.

STRINGER: I will do the talking, all right? Me. (*He crosses the room.*) You — you look small and intellectual. You look insignificant. Be a sort of bewildered academic rat. Got any spectacles? (BELA *takes out a pair, puts them on.*) No. Terrible. Smelly Bolshevik. (*He takes them off again.*) If they speak to you at all, what you say is things like this. 'This is a country I've admired all my life.' Okay? 'The King is a gentleman.' All right? 'Parliament is a national asset.' **Nothing critical and do not defend yourself.** You have done wrong, all right? I want a sort of atmosphere of shame. I want this room to feel tacky with humility, I want tangible regret. I ask you to do this, Bela, because they do not like me and they want to shut the paper down. They have this act, this thing called the Defence of the Realm Act and it means they can shut papers down and stick the editors in gaol, all right? It's very like what Hitler's got. Only they had it long before Hitler. And it means we can end up in a concentration camp. And they had that long before Hitler, too. I don't want to end up on a draughty Scottish island nibbling sheep shit off the barbed wire, see? Highland cack for breakfast and galloping TB? No thank you. I don't want that and nor do you.
BELA: Nope.
STRINGER: Good. So be small. Be error incarnate.

There are voices off, loud and braying. STRINGER *prepares himself for his ordeal.* STRUBENZEE *enters with two officials.*

STRUBENZEE: Good morning.
STRINGER (*offering his hand*): Sir Herbert —
STRUBENZEE: Hello, Bob — this is — Frank Deeds —
STRINGER: How d'ye do?
STRUBENZEE: And John Lowry —
STRINGER: Good morning —
STRUBENZEE: Hello, Bela!
LOWRY/DEEDS: Good morning.
STRUBENZEE: Bela Veracek.
LOWRY (*sitting at the desk*): Sit down, will you?
STRINGER: Here, okay?
LOWRY: Thank you. (*He clicks open his case.*) And you, Mr.

Veracek. (BELA *sits*. STRUBENZEE *looks out the window*.)
Cik, is it? Or cek?

STRINGER: Cek.

LOWRY (*ignoring* STRINGER):   Cik is it, or cek?

BELA: Cek.

LOWRY: Thank you.

DEEDS: Look, don't want to lose the entire morning over this,
so get to the point swiftly, shall we? Winston doesn't like this.

STRINGER: Ah.

DEEDS: He doesn't at all. In fact he hates it. And I don't like it
either.

STRINGER: I see.

DEEDS: It's you-know-what, isn't it? Pure you-know-what.

STRINGER: I suppose it is.

DEEDS: Very much so. And we feel we want to crack down on
it, don't we, John? Crack down on it very hard.

LOWRY: Anybody smoke, do they? (*He vaguely offers a
packet. No one accepts.*)

DEEDS: We agree about that, don't we?

LOWRY: Absolutely.

STRINGER: Yes, of course.

DEEDS: Coming back to Winston, I can assure you first thing
this morning he was practically pissing blood. That's no exaggeration, is it, John?

LOWRY: No.

DEEDS: He was that cross.

STRINGER: I see.

LOWRY: Did the papers in bed, as usual.

DEEDS: As he always does, picks up the first one and there's
this — this drawing, by this gentleman — and really, I can see
his point. It is crude and ugly and utterly you-know-what.

STRINGER: Agreed.

DEEDS: Go on, John, will you?

LOWRY: He wants to shut your shop . . .

STRINGER: Ah.

LOWRY: That was his first reaction. Shut the shop.

STRINGER: Ah.

DEEDS: What do you say, Mr. Veracek?

BELA (*with a shrug*):   King George is a gentleman.

DEEDS: Sorry?

BELA: I am very fond of King George.

STRINGER: I think you know the *Mirror* has backed Winston
solidly since Munich.

LOWRY: Yup.

STRINGER: Uncritically.

LOWRY: Yup.

STRINGER: Has not wavered in its backing for the war effort.

LOWRY: Yes.

STRINGER: Supported every change in military command.

LOWRY: Yes.

STRINGER: Has been a wholly loyal and patriotic paper.

LOWRY: Yes, and Winston recognizes this. Doesn't he, Frank? In his better moments recognizes it.

DEEDS: Winston is thoroughly cognisant about the press. But feels you have abused his trust.

STRINGER: I don't think so.

DEEDS: Well, I say you have. And I am minded to close you down. What do you say, Mr. Veracek?

BELA: Parliament is the highest stage of human consciousness —

LOWRY: I don't think Mr. Veracek is being wholly —

STRINGER: Bela is rather bewildered by all this —

DEEDS: Is he so! Is he bewildered! Well, indeed! Perhaps you would inform him I am an officer of the King, that I have his warrant in my pocket here! King George VI of England, with all his many and diverse dominions, I am his voice, all right? (*Pause*)

STRINGER: Yes.

DEEDS: Good. I don't know about you, John, but I am minded to shut them down. (*He leans back in his chair.*)

LOWRY: You see, even if we were persuaded by you, and at this moment I must tell you I am not, we have an uphill struggle on our hands, a momentous task before us. We shall have to go from this room to Chequers and we shall get a rather rough ride, shan't we?

DEEDS: Very rough.

LOWRY: And I'm not prepared to do that if I don't feel wholly and completely satisfied. And I'm not. (*Pause*)

STRINGER: You can't shut all the papers down.

DEEDS: Oh, I can, I can! I have the warrant, yes I can!

STRINGER: All right, you can —

DEEDS: Oh, I can, Bob.

STRINGER: All the banned papers are small papers. The *Mirror* has one and a half million.

LOWRY: Slightly more, I think.

STRINGER: All right, yes. A growing circulation, and you can't just —

DEEDS: Do not keep telling me what I can and cannot do —

STRINGER: All right, I'm sorry, you have the power, obviously, but does it look good?

DEEDS: Well, I'm not sure we're all that bothered what it looks like, are we, John? Winston isn't.

STRINGER: Well, I'll put it another way —

DEEDS: Is anybody bringing tea? (*He looks round at* STRUBENZEE.) I did ask for tea, didn't I? I find it very peculiar to have to ask for it, but I did ask for it, all the same —

STRUBENZEE (*going to the door*):   I'll look —

DEEDS: Thank you — No, I'm perfectly clear-minded on the —

STRINGER: I was saying —

DEEDS: Sorry —

LOWRY: He was saying —

STRINGER: This is supposed to be a war for democracy. At least I believe that is the common comprehension of the people, and an expression of democracy, as I understand it, is a plurality of political opinion within the —

DEEDS: Quite. (*Pause*)

LOWRY: Within, you see.

DEEDS: Within.

STRINGER: Yes. Within an accepted frame of reference.

LOWRY: That's it. I don't think Mr. Veracek, for all his love of parliament, is quite within. Are you, Mr. Veracek? Within? (BELA *shrugs, looks at* STRINGER.) I mean, what are your politics, Mr. Veracek?

STRINGER: I think that's Mr. Veracek's own —

DEEDS: What are your politics?

LOWRY: I think his politics are you-know-what, aren't they? Going by the cartoon?

BELA: My politics are to look for the truth, and when you find it, shout it. That's my politics.

LOWRY: Very good. But what are your politics?

DEEDS: I don't want to bring up the point about Mr. Veracek being an alien — not specifically at this point — but — well, I seem to have brought it up, don't I?

LOWRY: You have, I think —

DEEDS: Yes, I have brought it up now, so I may as well go on with it —

LOWRY: Yes —

DEEDS: Mr. Veracek, you are only too aware, I'm sure, that you enjoy the status of an alien as far as King George and the Government's concerned, and what is more, an alien originating from a country with whom King George and the Government regard themselves as in a state of war, the so-called Magyar Republic — do you want to come in here, Herbert?

STRUBENZEE: Tea's on its way, I can see the trolley . . .

DEEDS: Do you?

STRUBENZEE (*returning*):   Yes, you see Bela, we are under no very special obligations to you, coming here as you did from the territory of a country with whom we are at war —

BELA: The Soviet Union? We are not at war with the Soviet Union!

LOWRY: We are. (*He looks to the others.*) We are.

STRUBENZEE: It's a tricky one —

BELA: Someone should tell the English people! They are under the impression they are at war with Hitler!

STRUBENZEE: Well, so they are —

BELA: They are under the cruel misapprehension that it is Nazi bombers that are blowing their limbs off and killing children in their beds! How has this wicked deception been permitted?

STRINGER: Bela —

BELA: How is it Herr Hitler has been so cruelly discredited?

STRUBENZEE: The point is this —

LOWRY: Don't let him make a fool of you, Herbert, please.

STRUBENZEE: No — the point is this — that in a sense we are at war with the USSR, even though we are on the same side —

LOWRY: Dear, oh, dear —

STRUBENZEE: Under the Aliens Act, the authorities have special powers to place you in detention if it is deemed you represent a threat to national security —

LOWRY: Thank you.

DEEDS: And God knows, we may well deem it. Where is the tea?

BELA (*to* STRINGER):   I am being threatened with imprisonment.

STRUBENZEE: That is a very —

BELA: **I am being threatened with gaol!**

STRUBENZEE: No — no — not at all —

BELA: **Why are you telling me this, then?**

STRINGER: Bela, why don't you sit down?

BELA: **Why is he telling me?**

DEEDS (*as if a catechism*): Tempra — mental — central — Euro — pean — intell — ectual — bore . . .

STRUBENZEE: You are not helping, Frank —

BELA: I ask you why this conversation was begun!

STRUBENZEE: It was begun because Frank asked me to explain the provision of the Special Powers Act —

STRINGER: Bela, I will tell you what they're saying shall I? They are saying there is a very draughty, damp and disease-infected place where they stick foreign communists, all right? (*He looks at* DEEDS.) Now shut the paper down! We'll go out with a dirty great red-edged edition, banner headline seven inches high!

LOWRY: Now, Bob, that's silly, isn't it?

DEEDS: Bob's blown.

LOWRY: It is particularly silly because of course we won't allow it —

DEEDS: Never —

LOWRY: We will shut you down from six o'clock tonight.

DEEDS: Or now.

LOWRY: Or now, even.

DEEDS: I only have to pin this notice to the doors, and you can send the printers home.

LOWRY: All right?

DEEDS: This is a mighty piece of paper, Bob. (*He waves it.*) This paper says troops with bayonets on all the doors and lock the printers out. Now, where were we? Here's the tea.

A WOMAN *enters with a trolley. She pours a number of cups in silence, then turns to go.*

BELA: What do you think?

WOMAN (*stops*): Wha'? Me?

BELA: **What do you think of this!**

LOWRY: Herbert — (*He sips.*)

BELA: **This is your country! Look what they do behind closed doors!**

WOMAN: Er —

STRUBENZEE: Thank you. Just go.

BELA: You're a human being, aren't you? Shout out you won't stick this.

DEEDS: Just go out, please.

BELA: Don't just push the trolley, darling, fight! (*She goes out. Pause.*)

DEEDS: That is —
STRINGER: I'm very sorry —
DEEDS: No, listen, that is **absolutely not done here**.
STRINGER: I'm very sorry —
DEEDS: **It makes me absolutely certain that I want to shut you down!**
STRINGER: I can see that —
STRUBENZEE: Sugar, John?
DEEDS: **Certain of it.**
LOWRY: All right, Frank . . . (*Pause. They drink.* STRINGER *beckons to* BELA, *takes him aside, to the window.*)
STRUBENZEE: Biscuit?
DEEDS: Drink the tea and close him.
LOWRY: Have the tea first.
STRUBENZEE: Biscuit?
STRINGER: Look out of the window, look at the street. What do you see?
BELA: People, of course!
STRINGER: Good. And in those people, somewhere, is the one **who thinks**. Who, by a miracle, or accident, or because his brain is kinked **will see through the flannel**. Who, by blinking at a lucky moment, sees through the great pouring curtain of piss. Let's not desert him. Eh? Let's do our tiny little bit. (*Pause.* BELA *looks at him, shakes his head in weary resignation.* STRINGER *goes back to the others.*) I beg pardon for the divisive cartoon. On bended knee I acknowledge the error of sowing seeds of dissension in the British people, of undermining the national effort and breeding an atmosphere of doubt. I will publish a rebuke of Vera in the first edition. I will vet all future submissions by this artist. I will arrange regular meetings at which we can discuss the paper's line. (*Pause*) Can I carry on, or not? (*Pause*)
LOWRY: I think Bob's offer goes a long way towards —
DEEDS: I am very upset.
STRINGER: Yes.
DEEDS: I am very upset. You understand that, Bob?
LOWRY: Yes, we know you are, but this is virtually what we wanted, isn't it? This way we retain a plurality of papers. I could go to Chequers with an offer of that sort.
STRUBENZEE: It's voluntary, that's what's good about it, surely? Why use compulsion when people are toppling over backwards?
DEEDS: Bert, you have your department, I have mine.

STRUBENZEE: Yes. (DEEDS *gets up, walks around.*)
DEEDS: Say it again.
STRINGER: Well, I can't remember the exact phrasing —
LOWRY: Apologize. Rebuke. And vet.
STRINGER: Yes. (*Pause*)
DEEDS: All right. Did I bring a coat?
LOWRY: Downstairs in the lobby.
STRINGER: Thank you.
LOWRY: Good-bye.
STRINGER: Thank you. Good-bye.
DEEDS: Cheerio, Bob. (*He picks up his bag.*)
LOWRY (*to* BELA):   Cheerio. (*They depart. Pause.*)
STRUBENZEE: Anybody want a drink?
STRINGER: Urgently.
STRUBENZEE: Good. Bela? (BELA *shakes his head.*)
STRINGER: Why not? (BELA *shakes his head again.*)
STRUBENZEE: Oh, come on!
STRINGER: No . . . (*They go out.* BELA *stands there. The* WOMAN *comes back for the tea.*)
WOMAN: Left you, have they? On your own — ee — o? Never mind. (*She puts the teacups on the trolley.*)
BELA: Supposing freedom's not the truth? Have you ever thought of that? Suppose the truth's somewhere else after all? (*She looks at him.*) I go about, I shove the thermometer of freedom in the great wet gob of humanity and I go, good, we're healthy, when the mercury goes up, and bad, we're ill, when the mercury goes down. The fever of truth. Suppose freedom's nothing to do with it? Suppose it's just a virus? Suppose the truth is love?
WOMAN: You never know.
BELA: You don't. (*She goes to move away.*) I mean, you've only got one life, haven't you?
WOMAN: That's for sure.
BELA: Got to use it properly. Haven't you? No good being on your deathbed and saying, fuck, I got it wrong, I was up the wrong tree. That would be silly.
WOMAN: Bloody silly.
BELA: Got to use it, haven't you? Use it all up, like toothpaste, to the bottom of the tube. Squeeze! Squeeze!
WOMAN: That's it! (*She starts to go again.*)
BELA: Are you using yours up?
WOMAN: Good question. (*Pause*)
BELA: Got children, have you? Got a man somewhere?

WOMAN: Two kids in Clapham. Old man in the infantry.

BELA: Give us a kiss. (*Pause*)

WOMAN: Better not.

BELA: Better not, she says. Why better not? What's better about it?

WOMAN: You know what kissing leads to.

BELA: No . . . where does it lead? (*Pause. She goes to move off.*) I used to draw women.

WOMAN: Oh?

BELA: Drawn lots of women in my time. You have a lovely back.

WOMAN: Do I?

BELA: It's very strong and beautiful, your back. (*She doesn't move, but stands still, looking away from him. He runs his hands across her shoulder. Pause. He turns away again.*)

WOMAN: What's the matter?

BELA: I'm sorry. I'm not a good man.

WOMAN: I don't mind that.

BELA: Talk drivel just to get you — just to — lies and stuff —

WOMAN: Don't matter. Got to, haven't you? Got to go through that. For what we want. Never mind that. (*She turns, looks at him.*) No more going down the underground.

BELA: Can't keep the bombs off. With my little drop of love.

WOMAN: No? Why not?

Scene Three

A solitary figure is sweeping a path in a London Park. He has a systematic movement, eyes on the ground. BELA appears. He watches him. It is 1960.

Drawing: GRIGOR's *last drawing. A horribly emaciated female figure in a posture of rejection. As the last phase of* GRIGOR's *nude drawing it is violently distorted and pained.*

BELA: Did you do much queuing, friend? (GRIGOR *ignores him.*) Your feet look like feet that have shuffled down endless corridors . . . (*Pause*) And your head is like a head bowed down by the drizzle of futile interviews . . . (*Pause*) And the way you hold that broom, like it's a rock and you'd be swept away if someone took it from you. (*He goes towards him.*) Grigor, I shan't take your broom away — (*Suddenly* GRIGOR *lifts the dustbin out of the little cart, raises it above his head and flings it down. Beer cans roll across the stage. Pause.*) Glad to see me, I can tell. (*Pause*)

GRIGOR: Council given me a flat, okay!

BELA: That's good.

GRIGOR: Given me overalls, okay!

BELA: Very smart —

GRIGOR: **Six pound a week!**

BELA: Yes —

GRIGOR: **Okay!** (*He stares at the ground. Pause.*)

BELA: Buy paint with that?

GRIGOR: Buy paint.

BELA: Oils?

GRIGOR: Oils.

BELA: Good.

GRIGOR: By numbers.

BELA: What?

GRIGOR: By numbers! (*Pause*)

BELA: Paint by numbers?

GRIGOR: Done good. Done flower garden. Difficult. Done Good Queen Bess. Difficult, oh, fucking difficult.

BELA: Go on.

GRIGOR: Done cat. Done dog.

BELA: Lecture me, Grigor. Lecture me on the point of art.

GRIGOR: Done Windsor Castle.

BELA: On the function of a line. What the line does, Grigor. Line does not exist in nature. Line is an invention of mankind. Go on, Grigor . . . (*Pause.* GRIGOR *doesn't move.*) Line is the means by which we venture into the formlessness of nature, which guides us through the labyrinth. (GRIGOR *is motionless.*) He who draws a line puts form on formlessness. The line describes unconsciousness. Draw me a little picture, Grigor. Draw me a picture of your mind . . . (*Pause*)

GRIGOR: Done Yankee Windjammer. Oh, fucking difficult! Tricky little sails — and —

BELA: What happened in the wood, Grigor?

GRIGOR: Rigging — difficult.

BELA: **What happened in the wood!** (*Pause.* GRIGOR *doesn't react. After a few moments, he begins picking up the beers cans, tossing them in the bin.* BELA *watches, then joins him, kneeling* *on the ground, filling up his arms. Suddenly he stops.*) Got to keep sane! Got to keep my lovely head! Last decent brain in Europe! Oh, mind my head! Don't cross the road! Look out for bricks and bottles falling off of flats! Got the truth there! Oh, look after it! (*He drops the cans, staggers to his feet, his arms wrapped round his head to protect it.*) Mind out! My precious head! My head! (*He careers offstage, clasping his head awkwardly.*)

Scene Four

The office of the manager of a daily paper. He sits in a Swedish chair. A figure enters in a suit.

Sketch: BELA's *'They Grew Tired of Thought'. A spectacular panorama of Europe in a nuclear fire. Heaped with corpses, and above it a monstrous deformity in mask and goggles.*

MIK (*shaking DIVER's hand*):   I brought my folder. For your delectation.
DIVER: Do you drink?
MIK: All day long.
DIVER: For inspiration?
MIK: No. Intoxication. Shall I sit?
DIVER (*reaching for a bottle*):   We love your work.
MIK: Thank you. I'm rather fond of it myself. (*Pause. DIVER's hand remains on the bottle.*)
DIVER: Can I just say, before we go any further, you need not feel under any obligation to be witty talking to me. Of course we know you're funny, that's why you're here, so you don't have to prove anything, all right?
MIK: Sorry.
DIVER: If you talk like that all the time, all well and good, but don't put yourself out, okay?
MIK: Sorry. Nerves.
DIVER: Of course. Whisky?
MIK: Thank you. (*Pause, while DIVER squirts the syphon.*)
DIVER: We have a very fine cartoonist on this paper.
MIK: Vera.

DIVER: Vera, yes. I say a cartoonist, but he's more than a cartoonist. He's a visionary.

MIK: Absolutely.

DIVER: He is a genius. But Lord Slater feels — correctly if you take that point of view — that there is not a lot of comedy there. Lord Slater says he hasn't actually laughed at Vera now for fifteen years.

MIK: He's not a barrel of laughs.

DIVER: That is exactly what Lord Slater said. He is not a barrel of laughs. As you know, Lord Slater has owned nearly every paper in the world at some time or the other, excluding *Pravda* and the *Peking People's Daily,* and he has come to the conclusion, in his wisdom, that human beings need to laugh.

MIK: Absolutely.

DIVER: You agree with Lord Slater then?

MIK: I do.

DIVER: Good. Because this is where you come in. Lord Slater isn't looking for a genius.

MIK: No problem.

DIVER: No problem with you, no.

MIK: No one's ever called me a genius.

DIVER: Nor likely to?

MIK: I shouldn't think so.

DIVER: Have another drink.

MIK: Thank you. (DIVER *refills.*)

DIVER: Lord Slater's sense of humour — and he admits this — is altogether basic. He can actually laugh — I do mean laugh —

MIK: Ha, ha —

DIVER: Quite — actually laugh at postcards which show bald Englishmen at the seaside who have lost their dicks — (MIK *laughs loudly.*) Can choke himself at pictures of fat women who are manifestly sexually deprived — (MIK *laughs loudly again.*) He finds that genuinely funny.

MIK (*shaking his head*): Terrific . . .

DIVER: Well, I think you're just the man he's looking for. What shall I call you? Do you like to be called Mik?

MIK: Suits me.

DIVER: Yes, I think it does.

MIK: My real name's Michael, but at art school I cut it down to Mik.

DIVER: You have been trained, have you?

MIK: Doesn't it show?

DIVER: I'm no expert, Mr. Mik. Just one other thing. As well as being terribly funny, Lord Slater is very keen for you to have a point of view. Do you have a point of view?

MIK: I think life's a non-stop comedy show.

DIVER: Yes, quite, but I think Lord Slater was thinking more along the lines of — well, to take his own example, do you like trade unions?

MIK: Well, to be quite —

DIVER: Lord Slater doesn't madly, you see.

MIK: Me neither.

DIVER: There we are, then. Would you like to see yourself out?

MIK (*draining his drink*): Thank you very much for seeing me. (*He picks up his folder, starts to go.*) Is Vera going, then?

DIVER: Vera is seventy-five. (MIK *goes out.* DIVER *walks a little way round the room,* BELA *comes in, arms entwined about his head. He sits without ceremony in* DIVER's *chair.*) Ah, Bela —

BELA: Oh, this is a dirty place. Have to wear my old coat here, see? Got my old mac on. Great dirty place this Fleet Street. How do you stick it? Don't your wife say when you come in, don't bring that muck in here! Better be a coalminer, it comes off with a bit of soap, but you, in bed with your soft white Mrs., carry in the sheets your little smears . . .

DIVER: We always have to go through this . . .

BELA: That's why you change your secretary every week. Never got the same one has he? Think you lose your dirt by going through all this knicker, but you don't, if anything gets worse. Try to block your nostrils with girl smells and the Johnny Walker! No, Anthony, this stink comes from inside, rotting brain . . .

DIVER: Thank you, Bela . . .

BELA: No, don't thank me, I say this because I look at you and I have to say, is this a way to live?

DIVER (*looking at* BELA's *absurd posture*): Ah . . .

BELA: Now you think I envy you, you think I'm spiteful because I'm old, you think I want to suck your secretary, no, I don't, believe me I don't, I only say go and stand in a bit of daylight, there ain't no daylight here, look at these lights, you live in soft mad places, all girls and carpets, see yourself for what you are, another man's thing, you got no freedom, only Johnny Walker.

DIVER: Thank you.

BELA: That's all right, I want to help. It's what they used to give the natives, see? Liquor and cunt? You a native, are you?

DIVER: I suppose I am.

BELA: Poor old English native. (*He pretends to call someone.*) 'ere, give the man another crate!

DIVER: How are you, Bela? How's your head?

BELA: It's okay as long as I take care of it. I don't know why I come here, though, I don't like towns, so fucking dangerous, all scaffolding and them great cranes, I don't like nothing above my head but sky. Only safe place, Salisbury Plain.

DIVER: I'm very grateful to you, coming up like this.

BELA: Of course that ain't safe either. There's no safe place, there never was one. Look at that ceiling, smooth, ain't it, looks fine, looks perfect, but underneath the plaster, how many little parasites? Them great steel joists, how much metal strain? You go down the escalator, lovely shiny tiles and all them clean girls with the tits and bras, but just behind it, mud and clay, pressing, pressing to get in, wanting to burst through and stuff your mouth with earth.

DIVER: You can never be sure —

BELA: Always, you make something, and from that moment, from that second, everything works to its destruction, everything racing to decay. I talk so much because I haven't seen no one for five days. What did you ask me here for?

DIVER: I think absolutely everything you say is absolutely true.

BELA: It is true, 'course it's true, but it's a truth you can't do nothing about. When you're old you think of all the things that can't be done, and when you're young you think of all the things that can. The young are best. Give us a fact you can grasp in your fingers, and all the rest, in the bin with it. I am a materialist. I always was a materialist, God bless it. There, I contradict myself, but then I always have. What am I here for, Anthony?

DIVER: Well, to talk.

BELA: Obviously.

DIVER: So I can sip a little at the well of wisdom. My little sparrow brain. My little hungry beak.

BELA: That's good . . .

DIVER: Goes dip, dip, dip . . .

BELA: Dip, dip, dip . . .

DIVER: Bela, I've got the job of murdering you. (*Pause*) My seedy little business. My calm and dirty duty. (*Pause*) Going home to bed, as you say, caked. (*Pause*) The black bits in between my toes —

BELA: **Never mind my fucking metaphors**. (*Pause*)

DIVER: Yes. (*Pause*) I wonder if you'll hear me out? (*Pause*) You see, the feeling exists —

BELA: **The Feeling Exists!**

DIVER: No, I didn't think you would —

BELA: **The Feeling Exists!**

DIVER: Yes —

BELA: **No such fucking thing**. Feelings don't exist. What do you think they are? Floating around in the air? Pluck 'em do you, whizzing past like wasps? Who feels the feeling, Anthony?

DIVER: Well, all right —

BELA: If it stinks, if it rots your little conscience, in the passive tense it goes! Nuclear devices were dropped — shots were fired — feelings exist — No! Say it in your person, **I dropped, I fired, I feel!**

DIVER: Very well —

BELA: I was a poet, but I got to hate words, do you see why? There is a great wide river flowing out the bottom of this building, a river of words, newsprint pouring over the waterfalls of inking machines and streaming through the city, washing men away with lies, the great flood of dirtiness, hold your heads up in the swell! Where is the ark? **I am. I am Noah, get on board!**

DIVER: Very good, very like one of your drawings, but this is precisely where the board —

BELA: Why don't you say it?

DIVER: Say it? Say what?

BELA: **You hate me**.

DIVER (*bewildered*): Hate —

BELA: Hate me because I see! Like a great snake of blindmen tapping sticks, heading for the cliff edge, **Hate the man who sees. I see, I got the vision and you hate me!**

DIVER: Bela!

BELA: You do! You do!

DIVER: Will you let me —

BELA: Rather fall off than hear the **Man Who Sees!**

DIVER: Let me finish, will you please?

BELA: Finish? Finish what?

DIVER: **I prepared this fucking speech**. (*Pause. BELA shrugs contemptuously*.) Because it hurts me, too. You aren't the only one with pain. You aren't the only well of suffering. Dip my bucket just as deep . . .

BELA: You call that pain? That's not pain. Just a little leak of guilt. Just a damp patch on your Y-Fronts . . . (*Pause*)

DIVER: You are so arrogant. So terribly arrogant. (*Pause*) It is the board's feeling that there is a quality of — depression — in your work — of nihilism — which makes it inappropriate — I summarize, of course, to a national, family newspaper. (*Pause*) And anyway, you're seventy-five. (*He goes to pick up the whisky bottle and pour a drink.* BELA *knocks it flying.*)

BELA: Liquor don't give me the sack!

DIVER (*seeing the liquid on his suit*):   You're going a little bit —

BELA: Not Johnny fucking Walker kicking Bela Veracek downstairs! You do it. Don't get Johnny in. (*Pause.* DIVER *wipes his fingers on a handkerchief.*)

DIVER: The Corporation want to publish a collection of your work . . . In hard and paperback.

BELA: Never.

DIVER: Bela —

BELA: Never! I ain't for putting on girl's laps and kissing over. I ain't art!

DIVER: Think about it —

BELA: Anthony, don't you see? They want to make me into art, do you know why? 'cos art don't hurt. Look at Goya. His firing squad — I seen it on stockbrokers' walls! But I still hurt, see? I touch their little pink nerve with my needle, like the frog's legs on the bench. I shock their muscle and they **Twitch!** They don't want to twitch, see? They're so much happier lying dead! But I twitch 'em! **I shock the bastards into life!** (*Pause*)

DIVER: Yes . . . (*Pause*) Yes . . . (*He goes to the intercom.*) Jane! (*Pause*) Bring in a cloth, will you? (*Pause, then a* SECRETARY *enters, holding an old towel.* DIVER *indicates the spilt whisky. She kneels, rubs the carpet. They watch her.*)

BELA: Oh, darling, all your sweet bits . . . I've not touched you so much with all my genius as one groove of a loud boy's disc . . .

Scene Five

The sound of Big Ben. It is a dark night in the pool of London. Two officers of the River Police are seen observing the figure of an old man silhouetted on the parapet of Tower Bridge. PC DOCKERILL *holds a loud hailer.*

DOCKERILL: **You are not allowed to jump in the water. Can you hear me? You are not allowed to jump in the water.**

BELA: I wish to die.

DOCKERILL: **This river is full of germs.**

BELA: I am not afraid of germs. I am a germ. You are a germ. The human race is a germ.

DOCKERILL: **Who are you calling a germ?**

HOOGSTRATEN: I'll do the talking, Michael.

DOCKERILL: **Who's 'e calling a fuckin' germ?**

HOOGSTRATEN: Michael — (*He takes the hailer.*) Good-evening. This is John here.

BELA: John who. (*Pause*)

HOOGSTRATEN: PC John. Metropolitan River Police.

BELA: Look, John, get your boat away.

HOOGSTRATEN: Why don't we talk this over eh?

BELA: No.

HOOGSTRATEN: You see, I don't think you want to die at all. You just want a bit of attention.

BELA: Thank you, I have had all the attention I want.

HOOGSTRATEN: Tell us about it.

BELA: I don't want to discuss my life, I want to finish it! So kindly shift your motorboat.

HOOGSTRATEN: Now listen — (*The hailer goes off.*) What's the matter with this — (*It comes on.*) Now listen. I've done a course in psychology —

BELA: **I hate psychology.**

HOOGSTRATEN: You what?

BELA: **I hate psychology! I hate magic!**

HOOGSTRATEN: All right, you don't like it —

BELA: Why can't you just let a man —

DOCKERILL: **'Cos it's an offence, all right? That's why!**

HOOGSTRATEN: Michael —

DOCKERILL: **Bin up all fucking night fishing buggers out the water!**

HOOGSTRATEN: Michael —

DOCKERILL: What is it about Saturdays?

HOOGSTRATEN: You see — no one really wants to die.

BELA: I do.

HOOGSTRATEN: No. You only think you do.

BELA: Of course I think I do.

HOOGSTRATEN: That's it, you see.

BELA: What is?

HOOGSTRATEN (*desperately*):   How old are you?

BELA: Seventy-five.

HOOGSTRATEN (*delighted*): Seventy-five! How about that? Seventy-five, Michael!

DOCKERILL: **What is it, yer gas bill?**

HOOGSTRATEN: Seventy-five! A wonderful age!

DOCKERILL: **Look, go an' lay yer 'ead across a railway track, all right? Just don't jump in my river —**

HOOGSTRATEN: Michael —

DOCKERILL: **Cos I ain't pullin' yer out.**

BELA: Thank Christ for a good man.

HOOGSTRATEN: Michael, that is just about the — (BELA *jumps*.)

BELA: Thank you, thank you!

HOOGSTRATEN: Fuck. Fuck. (*The engine revs up.*)

Scene Six

The grounds of a hospital. A group of MALE NURSES *are grouped round a patient in a wheelchair. The patient is staring with intense concentration at a bedpan some yards away on the grass.*

Sketch: BELA's '*They Grew Tired of Thought*'.

FIRST NURSE: Come on! Come on!

SECOND NURSE: Lift it! Lift it!

THIRD NURSE: Make it a fiver, Barry?

FIRST NURSE: Doing it! Doing it!

THIRD NURSE: Where?

FIRST NURSE: Doing it!

THIRD NURSE: Where?

FOURTH NURSE: **Moved! I saw it!**

THIRD NURSE: Where?

SECOND NURSE: Lift it! Lift it!

FIRST NURSE (*pointing*): **Whassat!**

THIRD NURSE: Fuckin' ain't, yer know —

FIRST NURSE: **Whassat!**

THIRD NURSE (*kneeling by the bedpan*): Nothing . . .

FIRST NURSE: Bloody did — it sort of —

THIRD NURSE: Nothing!

FIRST NURSE: Shuddered — (*The patient is showing signs of stress.*)

THIRD NURSE (*contemptuously*):   Shuddered. . . .

SECOND NURSE: Lift it!

FIRST NURSE: It's gonna go! It's gonna go!

THIRD NURSE: Gotta be off the ground, Roy . . .

SECOND NURSE: Come on! Come on!

THIRD NURSE: See daylight underneath it . . .

SECOND NURSE: Come on!

THIRD NURSE: No daylight no payout . . .

FIRST/FOURTH: **Move it! Move it! Move it!**

THIRD NURSE: Who's fuckin' doin' it? 'im or you?

SECOND NURSE: 's 'going! (*With a cry of despair the patient falls back in his chair.*)

FIRST NURSE: 'e did it! 'e did it!

THIRD NURSE: Bollocks —

FIRST NURSE: Did it!

THIRD NURSE: Daylight, Roger . . .

GRIGOR: **Can't concentrate! Can't concentrate!**

FIRST NURSE: It moved mate . . .

THIRD NURSE: I am not accepting cheques . . .

FIRST NURSE (*taking out his wallet*):   It moved, Don . . .

GRIGOR: Air got . . . too heavy, see?

THIRD NURSE (*taking money all round*):   Thank you . . .

GRIGOR: Started to . . . air got heavy . . .

THIRD NURSE: I can change a fiver, Clive . . .

GRIGOR: First, the object's got to chuck off all its habits, see? Got to stop being a piss pan, see? Think of itself like something else.

THIRD NURSE: Three pounds, change.

GRIGOR: Got to be God's will —

SECOND NURSE: That's it, mate —

THIRD NURSE: Thank you —

GRIGOR (*seized as if from beyond*):   **Do it again! Coming again!**

FOURTH NURSE: 'ello, 'ello!

GRIGOR (*rigid in his chair*):   **Coming again!**

THIRD NURSE: Gentlemen, lay your bets!

GRIGOR: I feels His spirit over me! God's body floating over London! Hold tight, please!

FIRST NURSE: Ding! Ding!

THIRD NURSE: Two pound, Barry? Two pounds anyone?

SECOND NURSE: Okay —

THIRD NURSE: Two pounds!

GRIGOR: I draw Him in! He comes! I am the vessel of His will!

THIRD NURSE: Roger? A sheet?

GRIGOR: My ol' skin, my ol' bones, got God in 'em!

FOURTH NURSE: Fifty pence.

THIRD NURSE: Clive, living dangerously . . .

GRIGOR: **Ready, God!**

THIRD NURSE: Daylight! Daylight pays!

SECOND NURSE: Shuddup!

FIRST NURSE: Shh! (GRIGOR's *face assumes maximum tension. They stare at the bedpan.*)

GRIGOR: Neck . . . Neck! (SECOND NURSE *hurries to massage his neck.*)

FIRST NURSE: Lift — lift — (*They stare. Suddenly* FOURTH NURSE *drops to his knees.*)

FOURTH NURSE: Somethin'! Somethin'! (GRIGOR *groans.*)

THIRD NURSE: Daylight . . .

FOURTH NURSE: **'s comin!**

THIRD NURSE: Daylight only . . .

FOURTH NURSE: Yes! Yes! (THIRD NURSE *hurries over, kneels to look.*)

THIRD NURSE: What?

FOURTH NURSE: Yes!

THIRD NURSE: What? What? (GRIGOR *shudders violently, lets out a cry.*)

SECOND/FIRST/FOURTH: Ye — Es! (*They begin clapping. The bedpan has not moved.*)

THIRD NURSE: What, fuck it, what! (*Amidst this feverish applause,* BELA *enters in a wheelchair, pushed by* DOCTOR GLASSON.*)

GLASSON (*gazing, shaking her head*):   Oh, Jesus bloody Christ . . . (GRIGOR *lets out a long wail, his head falls back. Sheepishly, the* NURSES *withdraw.*) Whatcha trying to do? Drive the ol' boy barmy?

GRIGOR: God says —

GLASSON (*of the bedpan*):   That's for pissing in, not praying to.

GRIGOR: God says —

GLASSON: Shuddup, I'm taking yer temperature! (*She shoves a thermometer in his mouth.*) If I was going to drown myself, I'd do it up at Henley. It's cleaner. Yer don't get contraceptives stuck in yer throat. Or Cliveden. All those lovely beech trees and conspiring aristocrats. Might catch a glimpse of you out the library windows . . . People are so boring when they die. Tiny little deaths in rooms, not making a nuisance. Same way as they were conceived, I suppose . . . quietly, on a sofa . . . Come and go without a trace. Why don't we scratch our little mark, I wonder? Claw some little protest on the granite ball? (*She looks offstage.*) Look at 'em, peering through the railings . . . **It's all right, we're all barmy in 'ere!** Schoolgirls bunking off lessons . . . wait till yer married and the old man beats yer up, the kids' ave got the whooping cough and the rent goes up — **Keep a bed warm for yer!** (*She turns back to* GRIGOR. *She removes the thermometer.*) I declare you normal. I declare you fit to proceed with your extraordinary life, with all its richness, colour, vigour, thrills. I'm getting a cup of tea. Don't run away. (*She turns to* BELA.) And don't talk! (*She goes off. Pause.*)

GRIGOR: Hern the Hunter has been seen at Windsor Castle. (*Pause*) Oi. (*Pause*) Hern the Hunter. (*Pause*) Fuckin' Hern, see? **Ain't been seen since 1931.** (*Pause*) Oi. (*Pause*) Two comets crossed tails over Peking. You listening? (*Pause*) Oi. Got a message for yer. Oi. **Doncha wanna message?** (*Pause*) We don't live alone. All right? Always these happenings, see? Spirit world like an overcoat. Invisible overcoat. They tell us, you born naked. **Bollocks. Balls.** You born in garments of **other spheres**. Oi. (*Pause*) Oi. Ain't gotta be what you are, see? That's the message. (*Pause*) **What's the matter? You deaf?** Pisspan. Don't 'ave to be a pisspan, see? (*He stares at the bedpan. Slowly, it rises off the floor, remains suspended about ten feet up.*) Wants to be a bird, see? Wants to be a bird! (BELA *looks. Suddenly he lets out a scream.*)

BELA: Help! Help! (*The pan drops with a clatter.* FIRST *and* SECOND NURSES *rush in.*) Get him away from me! Bloody madman, get him off me!

GRIGOR: I am Grigor Gabor, I got God with me!

BELA: There ain't no God! There ain't no Grigor!

SECOND NURSE: Shuddup, the pair of yer!

BELA: Gotta fight him! Fight barminess!

GRIGOR: Got Christ in my ol' body, peace, He says! Peace, He says!

SECOND NURSE: Get him out, Roger —

BELA: He hurts my earholes, get him out! He gives me pains here. (*He touches his head.*) Gives me murder, get him out! (SECOND NURSE *wheels* GRIGOR *away.* GLASSON *enters.*)

GLASSON: 'e does speak!

BELA: **Get him away from me!**

GLASSON: All right, darling, he's gone.

BELA: I knew him! I knew him! Always 'is fucking spirit! I don't want 'is spirit! Gets me here! (GLASSON *takes his hand.*)

GLASSON: Come on sweetheart, give us yer hand, — (BELA *is weeping. She cradles his head.* SECOND NURSE *watches, uncomfortable.*) The tears, the tears! This place is floating on tears! Slippery stairs and slippery ceilings, I go 'ome wet to my bra, like a nursing mother, soddened with the milk of old men's weeping! Straight to the bath I go, down the plug 'ole with your misery . . . !

SECOND NURSE: Take 'im back, shall I?

GLASSON: No!

SECOND NURSE: Time for 'is —

GLASSON: Barry, fuck off, please! (*He goes out. Pause.* GLASSON *wipes* BELA's *eyes, sits on the grass, draws up her knees, looks at him. Pause.*)

BELA (*in disbelief*): The piss pan . . . Pisspan went up in the air . . .

GLASSON: Yup.

BELA: **Did it?** (*She nods.*) Christ . . .

GLASSON: 'e does . . . I'm afraid 'e does . . . (BELA *sobs again, bitterly.*) Shall I kill you? Because I can, you see. I do it all the time. The people who won't go on swallowing the daily dose of pain and gibberish. It's there, see? The lying, the barmy, the savage, all swimming in the spoon. If you can't swallow it, I'll do it. If we 'urt your brain to much . . . (*Pause*)

BELA: All gone mad . . .

GLASSON: No. That isn't it.

BELA: **Gone mad.**

GLASSON: That isn't it. Don't give into that. (*Pause*) You build your little temple, somewhere in the bottom of your brain, put brass doors on it, and great big hinges, burn your little flame of truth and genius and worship it, **What about us?** (*She points to the cartoon.*) **That don't 'elp us!** (*Pause*) Assign the blame. (*Pause*) It's madness if yer don't. 'Cos that's how we go on, blame this, blame that, get it wrong sometimes, of course, but never say we're barmy, or we will be . . . (*Pause*) Tea's cold . . . (*She gets up, leaves. Pause.*)

BELA: Give us a pencil . . . somebody . . . (*He staggers out of the chair, advances towards audience.*) Give us a pencil . . . give us a pencil give us a pencil . . .

VICTORY
Choices in Reaction

CHARACTERS

BRADSHAW	The Widow of a Polemicist
SCROPE	A Secretary
CHARLES STUART	A Monarch
NODD	His Intimate Friend
DEVONSHIRE	A Mistress
BALL	A Cavalier
McCONOCHIE	A Surgeon
CROPPER	Daughter of Bradshaw
BOOT	A Soldier
SHADE	A Soldier
WICKER	A Soldier
GAUKROGER	A Captain
ROAST	A Civil Servant
CLEGG	The Poet Laureate
SOUTHWARK	A Male Landowner
CLEVELAND	A Female Landowner
PONTING	A Court Official
HAMSPHIRE	A Male Landowner
BRIGHTON	A Female Landowner
SOMERSET	A Male Landowner
DEBYSHIRE	A Male Landowner
GLOUCESTERSHIRE	A Male Landowner
FEAK	A Republican
PYLE	A Republican Woman
EDGBASTON	A Radical Preacher
HAMBRO	A Banker
MOBBERLEY	A Builder
PARRY	A Stockbroker
UNDY	An Exporter
STREET	A Lawyer
MONCRIEFF	A Minister
GWYNN	A Prostitute
FOOTMAN	To Devonshire
MILTON	A Genius
BEGGARS	

ACT ONE

Scene One

A field. A man enters.

SCROPE: I know I swore. I know I promised. On the Bible. And because I can take or leave the Bible, got your child in and told me put my two hands on her cheeks and looking in her eyes say I would not disclose this place. No matter what the madness, what the torture, leave you underneath the nettles, safe. I did. I know I did. (*He points to a place.* SOLDIERS *enter with spades.*)

BOOT: A scythe, John!

SHADE: Oh, the cunning of 'im, oh, the artfulness, sneakin' is bits under the lush at night . . .

BOOT: Mind the thistles.

WICKER: Now tell us 'e is twelve foot deep.

SCROPE: Twelve feet at least . . .

WICKER: Twelve foot, Michael! And the sun like the bald baker's bollocks!

BOOT (*to* DARLING): No, a scythe, you know a scythe, do you? (DARLING *goes out.*)

WICKER: Ow! Thistle got me!

SHADE: This is nothin' to what we 'ave 'ad, is it? Draycott was under fifteen ton a rock.

BOOT: At low water.

SHADE: At low water. We was in and out like the mad vicar's dick.

BOOT (*to* DARLING): Thank you. That is a scythe.

SHADE: An' Rouse, who 'ad 'imself stuck in the street, 'alf in the pavement, 'alf in a shop —

BOOT (*scything*): Mind yer legs!

GAUKROGER: I wonder if one of you cunts would condescend to fetch my stool? In your own time, of course, at your very own cunt leisure?

BOOT: Captain's stool, John! (DARLING *hurries out*.)

GAUKROGER: I hate to trouble you cunts, I honestly do.

SHADE: This draper says,'What! The corpse of a rebel under my shop! Well, I never! 'ow did that come about!' So we go through 'is bedrooms, an' is trunks, an' 'is girls. And there it is. Milton. Latin dirt.

GAUKROGER (*as* DARLING *brings in a stool*): Thank you. I have commanded some cunts, but you take the cunt biscuit.

SHADE: So we slit it, this draper's long nose. For misuse of the highway. 'Well I never! Well, I never!' 'e says . . .

BOOT (*scything*): Mind yer legs.

GAUKROGER: A stool, Mr. Scrope? These cunts will be at it all day. (SCROPE *shakes his head*.) Who had my sunshade? (*They are digging*.) My sunshade? (*The clash of shovels*.) I do love the way they pretend to be deaf. They really are such extraordinary cunts.

BOOT: Captain's sunshade! (DARLING *goes out*.)

GAUKROGER: We never had one out of a field. Under the whispering cow shit and adulterous hips. Gob open to clay and the milkmaid's hot little puddle. But in sight of church steeple, I notice. How picturesque he was and diligent. Was he, Mr. Scrope? Cunt picturesque your master? (SCROPE *bursts into tears*.) The files are such cunts here. Would one of you run for a whisk?

Scene Two

A room. A WOMAN *and two* OFFICERS *of the crown*.

BRADSHAW: I am not asking you to sit. If I ask you to sit you will think at least she has good manners, at least she does things properly, she keeps things clean. I do not wish to do things properly or keep them clean. What do you want?

ROAST: I have to inform you —

BALL: Oh, the pontificating shitbag —

ROAST: I am instructed by His Majesty's —

BALL: Oh, the pontificating shitbag —

ROAST: May I just get this —

BALL: No, she is though, isn't she, a most pontificating bag of shit, Brian —

ROAST: If I could just —

BALL: Laying aside the instructing and informing for a minute, you have to marvel at her poopy aspect. I do. I have to marvel at it, all her straight back and white linen, her simple dignity and so on, it makes me want to kick the table through the window —

ROAST: I cannot see the point of making this —

BALL: I haven't finished yet! (*He goes to her.*) Brian is for being nice. Brian is ice cold and happy. But Brian never swagged his hours with the bints of Calais. I will be rude because I have lost fifteen years! Oh, my breath smells, my breath smells and she winces! Yours does not, does it, breathe on me, breathe on me —

ROAST: Andrew —

BALL: Oh, breathe on me your English breath, sweeter than roses, but then you have had English gardens to wipe your rump against, I have not but I am not angry, no, I'm not, I have licked Frenchmen's bums for nourishment and Spaniards' crotches! Breathe on me, breathe on me, do, when you stand there icy in your purity I could really dagger you with my old cavalier dick, that or murder, carry on informing, Billy. (*He walks away.*) Carry on!

ROAST: Mrs. Bradshaw, the Government is in possession of your husband's body.

BALL: Oh, Brian is so poop official! We have the rat-gnawed, stinking thing you clutched in bed once. That is what we have. What stuck up you when the cold mood took him, when God commanded fuck thy spouse or what you Bible-suckers term it, him who made you buck or whimper, is a nest of worms now and in our possession. Did you see the bollocks, Brian? I did, I thought them very mean and shrivelled little blobs, no parasite would touch them **I wish I could be more offensive I really do**. (*She is rigid.*) Oh, don't stand there like a mask of honour, I shall slap you. Did you swallow him or is that against the scriptures? I shall slap her if she looks like that!

BRADSHAW: How would you have me look?

BALL: Not like that!

ROAST: His body is to be hung in London. His head spiked and exhibited.

BRADSHAW: Why?

ROAST: It was in the King's conditions. He would not return
without his father's murderers be on display.

BALL: There is a hole in your stocking, you slag.

BRADSHAW: How long before I can collect and bury him?

ROAST: There is no possibility of burial.

BRADSHAW: What?

ROAST: The pieces must be left to freely disintegrate.

BRADSHAW: What!

BALL: There is a hole in your stocking, I said.

BRADSHAW: That is so disgusting! What?

BALL: No, it is the hole that is disgusting, with its sixpence of
white flesh —

ROAST: **I think we ought to cut this out**. (*He stares at* BALL.
BALL *shrugs*.)

BALL: All right.

BRADSHAW: Let me bury him. When the public's done with
him.

ROAST: I can't.

BRADSHAW: Come on, when they have spat their mouths dry,
surely?

ROAST: The orders are the pieces be —

BRADSHAW: Yes, but when they drop, the limbs, they can —

ROAST: I only repeat —

BRADSHAW: I know, but then, when they are in the gutter,
then I —

ROAST: You would need to petition —

BRADSHAW: Oh, come on, can I pick his bits or not! (*Pause*)
They knew this. Which is why they laid in such strange places.
On the seashore and so on. Knew their bits would be
hunted . . .

ROAST: This is a new world, Mrs. I was at Worcester for the
Parliament. But in the end it had to stop.

BRADSHAW: Why?

ROAST: Why, because —

BRADSHAW: Yes, why!

ROAST: Because what was needed had been done. And all the
rest was chaos.

BRADSHAW: I disagree.

ROAST: You disagree, but people cannot swallow all the
change you and your husband wanted —

BRADSHAW: I disagree.

ROAST (*going to leave*):   Thank you for your hospitality.

BRADSHAW: What hospitality! There was none!

BALL: One night, I shan't say when, someone, I shan't say who, may toss a flaming haybale through your glass, and up will go your smart, dark privilege, the spotless boards and so discreet few flowers in the oh-so-very-unostentatious bowl . . . there has been burning up and down the country, singeing rebels' widows in their empty beds, the odour of the stale old crutch and knicker . . .

BRADSHAW: There is a sort of cleanliness in you. A sort of honour in your vileness I can understand. But you — (*She looks to* ROAST.)

BALL: Ugh, she flatters me! Ugh! Off! Flattery! (*He pretends to wipe himself.* ROAST *goes out.*) I will fuck you, shall I? Say and I will. (*She looks away.*) They say you killed old love in England. You never! (*He goes to the door.*) I shall come back. And give you a poem. (*He leaves. A young man enters, warily.*)

McCONOCHIE: I would have come down, but what help would I have been? It might have made them worse. I don't like foul language. Nor do you, of course. Are you crying? So I listened with the door half open, and my book on my knees. It was about blood. I would have come down in the event of violence. Blood has coloured pieces in it. It is actually not red beneath a microscope. **I don't see how I can be educated if there is no peace and quiet!**

BRADSHAW: I'm sorry.

McCONOCHIE: I have wished — if only you knew how I wished — my father had been a grocer. You cannot know how I envy the children of grocers.

BRADSHAW: Yes.

McCONOCHIE: There is no prospect of progress in science or art without complete and utter stability. The universities are utterly disorganized! I may not get a place!

BRADSHAW: I know.

McCONOCHIE: I am not a political person and it is most unjust! (*Pause*) Did they frighten you? I would have come down but I hate bad language and anyway you are so very strong. I do admire you. The things you can take and cry hardly ever. When I am blown haywire by interruptions. You are so resilent.

BRADSHAW: They are sticking his head on a spike.

McCONOCHIE: Does that hurt you?

BRADSHAW: No, no it's only a head, it's only my husband's rotten old head, I often wanted to put it on a spike myself, what does it matter if your father is hung on a gate?

McCONOCHIE: You are getting emotional, aren't you? I can tell.

BRADSHAW: What's a gate? What's a spike?

McCONOCHIE: You are.

BRADSHAW: It's his head.

McCONOCHIE: Yes. Yes. But when you love someone — I don't know this — I have not actually loved — but when you love — it is not the flesh, is it, that one loves? Am I being indelicate?

BRADSHAW: I loved his head.

McCONOCHIE: Yes, but I think one needs to examine what we mean by —

BRADSHAW: I do not —

McCONOCHIE: All right, you do not, but —

BRADSHAW: Your dad's head. (*Pause*)

McCONOCHIE: Please, you mustn't be angry with me.

BRADSHAW: No.

McCONOCHIE: Or shout. I do not see the point of shouting. Things are difficult enough without recourse to shouting.

BRADSHAW: Yes, I'm sorry.

McCONOCHIE: I could shout as well. There are plenty of things I would like to shout about. I could lie down on the floor and cry. But I don't, do I?

BRADSHAW: No. You don't.

McCONOCHIE: I have my problems too. I want to be a doctor. How am I going to be a doctor? You must help me, please. I am only eighteen. I do think you might give me some advice. (*Pause*)

BRADSHAW: We knew this would happen one day. We knew, while we argued in his little room, the ground was going from under our feet, on late summer evenings crossing the lawn, felt the threat in the shadows under the trees, and the mockery of the placid fountain. So he made me swear to bury him in an unmarked spot, in a field where he'd sat, very deep where nothing would come to abuse him. And you, I created like this, to spare you pain. What more can a mother do for her child? No ardour to be bruised, no passion to be beaten for. A cold armouring of the eyes, the slowest of heart beats, and a tongue whose habit is to lie low in the mouth, dark as a bottomfish, not red or roaring and at the end, ripped out. I think you will survive, my dear little blue-eyed boy . . . (*He turns away. Pause.*)

McCONOCHIE: I am thinking of changing my name.

BRADSHAW: Good.

McCONOCHIE: And leaving. (*Pause*) I am sorry to bring this up now —

BRADSHAW: No, bring it up now —

McCONOCHIE: I think it would be hypocritical if I spared your feelings today only to wound them tomorrow. I do think that would be hypocritical, don't you?

BRADSHAW: I hate tact and wariness . . .

McCONOCHIE: I do, too.

BRADSHAW: Idiot kindliness.

McCONOCHIE: Yes, yes!

BRADSHAW: Off with that now. Ditch pity! Ditch fuss.

McCONOCHIE: I do like you. (*Pause*) I am going to Scotland and calling myself McConochie.

BRADSHAW: A very good name. Ideal for a surgeon.

McCONOCHIE: That's what I thought.

BRADSHAW: I am very proud of you. I mean that. Now pack your bag and go.

McCONOCHIE: Now?

BRADSHAW: Yes now. I have done my best by you. Please go.

McCONOCHIE: What — just —

BRADSHAW: Go. (*Pause. Then he turns and leaves. He passes* CROPPER, *who enters*.) They have found him. And stuck his head on a pole. (CROPPER *goes to her, embraces her*.) Through his brain. His poor brain. An old spike. (*She parts from her*.) Or not, do you think? I say brain, but that's silly, that really is silly, the brain I'd have thought, being soft —

CROPPER: Shh —

BRADSHAW: The very first thing to rot, I expect, I imagine would —

CROPPER: Don't imagine —

BRADSHAW: I want to imagine! Would go liquid or possibly — I have not seen a brain — dry up like a nut — a rattling nut —

CROPPER: Shh!

BRADSHAW: . . . in the skull — a pebble — or imagine —

CROPPER: Don't imagine —

BRADSHAW: I will imagine! Stop telling me not to imagine! Alternatively, a skull full of muck, which if tipped, or tilted, would drip through the eyes, would weep its own brains out, cry muck down your skirt, splash dirty intellect on stockings and shoes —

CROPPER: We want you to move in with us.

BRADSHAW: His scrotum, though shrivelled, evidently was intact —

CROPPER: The spare room —

BRADSHAW: . . . His scrotum —

CROPPER: Please —

BRADSHAW: . . . After how many years? Did you see it? I saw it occasionally, though not in the light, his ardour was strictly nocturnal and grew rare with the strain, they will see it more clearly than I did, see it in hot sun and white light, his thing on some gate, his thing there for pelting and pecking, no, I shan't move in with you, your piety really makes me sick. But thank you. Thank you, and thank you again.

CROPPER: Mother —

BRADSHAW: Oh, didn't I say thank you enough? My manners are in disarray —

CROPPER: I only want to help.

BRADSHAW: Yes . . . (*Pause*) He would have had you study Latin. Was all for giving you a tutor. I stopped that. Leave her dark, I said, bovine, religious and clean. Then she will survive and fuck with a farmer. I cannot tell you how glad I am so many of my children died. I should have had to do this six times. Six times indeed!

CROPPER: That is very hurtful. But I shall always love you.

BRADSHAW: Yes, you would do. The more hurtful I am the more you love me. It is all part of being bovine, religious and clean.

CROPPER: I am not bovine!

BRADSHAW: You are bovine. You are breasts and milk and belly, moist and passionate as stables and wet fields. No Latin, but red, oh red inside!

CROPPER: I think you have gone mad.

BRADSHAW: Yes. Now blot me out with pigs and children. And when the boots come up the pathway, give them your own bread and beer and jam, and they will see in your eyes your harmlessness. They will!

CROPPER (*bitterly*): I will visit you tomorrow.

BRADSHAW: **He had such a horror of being dug!** (CROPPER *turns away, in tears, goes out.*) Oh, sob, run away and sob! The one will never cry and the other never stops! **I should not have been given children!** (*Pause*) I will bring you back. I will get your bits, your chops and scrag, your offal and your lean cuts, I will collect them. I will bring your poor bald head away that hurt me so much with its arguments . . .

Scene Three

The KING OF ENGLAND *enters a room.*

CLEGG: Oh, see the shadows flee the land!
  The dark hour gone, and the dread hand,
  The envy of the world our situation,
  Ecstasy and coronation!
SOUTHWARK: I'm pissed on pomp, look at me, I'm pig hot in
  this ponce stuff! It's all right for you, your knockers hang out in
  the breezes . . .
CLEGG: Our star, our moon, our radiant sun
  Like orbs of wisdom, lo, he comes!
  And through our joyous, ringing city
  Rides his chariot of divinity!
CLEVELAND: I never saw more dug, more boob out, like a
  market of fresh tit, I thought, the Abbey was a tit market, pew
  after pew, I never felt more like a nibble at the fruit, blew my
  eyes hither and thither, screwed in squint I was . . .
HAMBRO: His father hovered, saw him hovering, I thought,
  behind the altar, Charles the martyr, noble Stuart . . .
CLEGG: With fountain and with firework write his name,
  In flower scented of his honour do the same,
  Bird chants, the infant gurgles and bee hums
  Oh, Charles in all his glory comes!
CHARLES: I did not actually like my dad. My dad who kept his
  cock dry for my mother, my mother who was a bint in essence
  but would shag monsignors only with her eyes, all the silliness of
  confession-boxes and monsignors' knobs. I adore my mother, I
  revere my mother, but she was an unfulfilled bint actually. And
  my father was in any case a sod. So there. You cannot wonder at
  the revolution. I never wondered at it. I think any nation
  governed by a bint and a sod will rise in protest, I said so at the
  time.
CLEGG: Rejoice, rejoice, this is our day,
  Leave labour, toil, depart, the fray,
  Both God and Reason annointeth us
  Carolingus noble, Carolingus just!
CHARLES: But my father would complicate matters by being a
  saint as well as a sod. A most peculiar combination. Peculiar
  and incomprehensible. I am neither peculiar nor incomprehensible. I am a male bint pure and simple. I assure you, there is
  no better stimulus to loyalty than for an apprentice to be molly

shagging only minutes after I have left her off. He grasps your flesh, he shares your monarchy. (*He turns to* HAMBRO.) Is that the head?

HAMBRO: (*looking out the window*). It's Bradshaw, yes.

CHARLES: There is shagall left of it.

PONTING: He is three years dead and the field was wet.

CHARLES: I will chuck skittles at it. Lower the window. I will head shy.

PONTING (*calling*): **Skittles!**

CLEVELAND: Oh, what's Charlie up to, and with the annointment still damp on his forehead! Shall we come?

CLEGG: Now grows my voice thin —

HAMPSHIRE: Good, I have a skinful of yer poetry —

CLEGG: . . . Imagination sheer amaze,
My lyre expires from excess of praise,
The hours tarry, drag their feet for fun,
Delay your journey they plead of the sun!

SOMERSET: Shall we come there?

CHARLES: I head shy! I head shy!

CLEVELAND: Oh, look, a bonze all rotten underneath the window . . .

BRIGHTON: Where? (*They crowd at the window*).

CLEVELAND: You are leaning on me.

BRIGHTON: Ugh! (*They peer in silence*.)

CHARLES: Is it true he wore an iron hat at my father's trial, for fear of murder?

DERBYSHIRE: And a chain vest, certainly.

GLOUCESTERSHIRE: I think you have in that one picture all the vanity and squirming terror of a man who dares to kill his master. Probably a puddle of his poop lay on the usurper's bench at the adjournment.

HAMBRO: Yet we should not resent him.

CHARLES: How's that, Hambro? How not resent him?

HAMBRO: To kill the king is no bad thing provided there follows restoration. It honours monarchy. Is proof of indispensibility.

CHARLES (*coldly*): Where is my duchess? I must grasp her arse.

NODD: Oh, Pam, dear, hither and bring your bum!

PONTING: Lady Devonshire!

NODD: Charlie, what is Hambro?

CHARLES: Billy? Billy is the banker.

NODD: I'd not go chase the clap with him, would you, love?

CHARLES: Not on your belly.

PONTING: The skittles come! The skittles!

CLEGG: The evening falls, by obligation,
Spoils the humour of our situation —

HAMPSHIRE: Oh, fuck this chanting!

CLEGG: Come night or storm we shall not move
Out of the sunlight of our monarch's love!

DEVONSHIRE: I'm here.

CHARLES: Oh, Nodd, am I not a poor male bint, wiping my
knob on swan and cockatoo, draping the silk over my rump?

NODD: Now, now, this is the time of your life, silly!

CHARLES: Bradshaw cropped his hair and wore no wig, and
when he pissed did not wince, I dare say, no tart came near his
thing —

PONTING (*offering a tray*): Skittles?

CHARLES: . . . Did it — (*He takes one.*) near — your —
thing? (*He chucks one.*)

DEVONSHIRE: I'm here.

CHARLES: You may all chuck now, and my hag, let her fling at
the regicide's bonze! (*They begin throwing in earnest.*)

DEVONSHIRE (*to* SOUTHWARK): What are we doing?

SOUTHWARK: Pelting.

CHARLES: The trunk's on Blackfriars, the legs on the Strand.
Come on, chuck!

NODD: Oh, I 'it 'im!

GLOUCESTERSHIRE: He spun! I touched him, he spun!

CLEVELAND: The eyeballs! The eyeballs are watching us,
ugh!

HAMPSHIRE: Knock him round, then, knock him round!

DEVONSHIRE: What are we doing, exactly?

NODD: Jaw dropped! Did yer see it?

DEVONSHIRE: I think I'll lie down.

CHARLES: Oh, no, my duchess, my duchess will chuck like a
man —

DEVONSHIRE: Oh, must I?

CHARLES (*propelling her forward to the window*): Must I,
must I, she says . . .

PONTING: **More skittles!** (*The* SERVANT *runs out.*)

DERBYSHIRE: Oh, Teddy —

NODD: Oh, bad chucking, Ted —

HAMPSHIRE: My arm is rheumatic —

DERBYSHIRE: His arm is rheumatic —

NODD: Terrible chucking —

CLEGG: Genius lay down thy arrogance here,
    Martial ardour undo thy mask of fear,
    Virgins, youths, pale from celebration
    Mock thy stern countenance across the nation!
DEVONSHIRE: Charlie, you are hurting my arse . . .
CHARLES: Get me then, get me in your hand —
HAMPSHIRE: I struck! I did, see! Shook on its spike!
DEVONSHIRE: Look, do you want me to throw or not?
GLOUCESTERSHIRE: Clipped him! Clipped him on the ear!
BRIGHTON: Oh, the ear drops off!
DEVONSHIRE: Because I cannot if —
CHARLES: Oh, tight in your hand!
DEVONSHIRE: I am —
CHARLES: Tighter!
NODD: Oh, poor little ear! 'is little ear, look!
CHARLES: Tighter yet!
DEVONSHIRE: Ouch!
GLOUCESTERSHIRE: Cracked him! He's down!
NODD: 'e 's down!
CLEGG: Come nymphs, come satyrs to our court,
    Old Thames thy hoary locks disport,
    And Time delay thy pouring glass,
    This gilded hour wastes too fast!
CLEVELAND: Horrible dust stuff flew away . . .
BRIGHTON: Dust stuff, Harry —
PONTING (*hanging out the window*): It's down in the yard . . .
HAMSPHIRE: Down, Charlie . . .
NODD: Bob done it.
CHARLES: I done too, quicker than I wanted . . .
PONTING (*peering*): Still in one bit, I'll be buggered . . . !
CHARLES: Out now, all of you . . .
CLEGG: Monarchy, our ancient treasure,
    Restores our joy in lavish measure —
BRIGHTON: Did you see that, Harry, grey stuff fly out the head?
SOUTHWARK: I been listening to Sam's bum-ache, ain't I?
CLEGG: And spreading dazzling luminosity,
    Irradiates our curiosity!
CHARLES: Out now! Did you hear me?
NODD: Out?
CHARLES: Yes, even you, Nodd —
CLEVELAND: Out?

CHARLES: Yes, you know the word, madam, meaning the contrary of in —

PONTING: We are due on the river in fifteen —

CHARLES: Oh, listen, who is the monarch here? Who wears the ermine bum-fluff, me! I have been down, ain't I, in sight of the tit of England, got the oil of Christ on me, out then when I say it, Out! (*They depart.*) Not you! (*He grabs* DEVON- SHIRE's *wrist. They are alone.*)

DEVONSHIRE: Charlie, I must wash my hand —

CHARLES: No.

DEVONSHIRE: I am sticky —

CHARLES: Lick it, then, cats do — (*She turns away.*) **I am a clown!**

DEVONSHIRE: Oh, dear . . .

CHARLES: **A clown, madam!** (*He walks up and down.*) Why do I? My little sprig, my little green shoot, poor little flower of my dignity, piss on it, why? It will wither, won't it? Go a monkey to my grave!

DEVONSHIRE: I hope you aren't going to be deep . . .

CHARLES: This prancing wig and whatnot, garters and the royal etcetera, why!

DEVONSHIRE: Do up your fly.

CHARLES: No, let it out!

DEVONSHIRE: Oh, God he is going to tear his raiment . . .

CHARLES: Garments down! Out bum ! Out all the old flesh, grey and bedroom stale the human meat! (*He flings off his wig and trousers.*)

DEVONSHIRE: I am not looking. (*She turns resolutely away.*)

CHARLES: Hear me, please!

DEVONSHIRE: You are always like this when you've come.

CHARLES: Yes, it is the only time I see things.

DEVONSHIRE: It is a great burden to everyone else. This is your coronation.

CHARLES: A burden! A burden, she says! Truth is such a nuisance, better tuck it down somewhere, put some swan down on it, stuff it under cockatoo, a sash, a ribbon on it, quick! Madam, I have frigged my way through Europe, banging in the gardens, banging in the maze, how long can I — this — I am forty-seven — this — this — I am a red-bummed monkey!

DEVONSHIRE: Blue-bummed.

CHARLES: Blue-bummed, is it?

DEVONSHIRE: Their bums are blue.

CHARLES: Exotic-bummed in any case, to catch the glance of

weary English eyes, and antic, very antic up my bars. **For whom!**

DEVONSHIRE: I am going to wash my hands.

CHARLES: I do not wonder the Emperor of Madagascar sent me baboons. I thought him at the time just black and savage sending me baboons to augment my coronation. But now I see it, now I see his wisdom in their coloured arses! He mocks me! I meant to send a fleet to bomb is palace but parliament would not have voted it, what kind of monarchy is this? Where did they go? Some zoological place, I hope to God no one dissected them, I would see them, where are my baboons? **Rob!** (*He calls off for* NODD.) I shall wear baboon skin, on the river, by the light of firework, the royal barge shall be babooned! **Rob!** And bum paint, blue-arsed I shall be!

DEVONSHIRE: I must say I prefer you with your fist up me to this, the foul thing on your lips, altogether prefer it, do you see? Dragged out of dinners and humped in the passage before the eyes of servants, much prefer it —

NODD (*entering*): Charlie, you got yer trousers —

CHARLES: Where are my baboons?

NODD (*bewildered*): Baboons?

CHARLES: My blue-bums, from the great and absolute of Madagascar, him who rules by word and not by paper, the wit of Africa, almighty black arse, find them, quick!

NODD: The barge is waitin' Charlie —

CHARLES: **Find them, tavern yob!** (NODD *goes out.*)

DEVONSHIRE: Your knob I understand, your knob I will bow down to, but not sentiment, not this yellow thing from underneath your tongue you dribble —

CHARLES: **Rob! And bum paint! I will droop my glistening arse for London out the prow!**

DEVONSHIRE: Oh, Charlie, come here, catch me underneath now, quick, not in my fingers, do look, look now, see I have no knicker, look . . . (*Long pause, as she poses with her skirts flung up.*)

CHARLES (*all passion spent*): Please tuck your cunt away. When you are not after them, they do look hideous . . .

NODD (*entering as she recovers herself*): Did you say bum-paint? (*Pause*) What's that, exactly? (*Pause*)

CHARLES: Pull up my trousers, Rob . . . (NODD *kneels.*)

DEVONSHIRE: I think you are the most insulting man.

CHARLES: Yes.

DEVONSHIRE: And loathsome.

CHARLES: Yes.

DEVONSHIRE: To the spunk, to the fart in you.

CHARLES (*to* NODD): The wig is over there, somewhere . . .

DEVONSHIRE: To your little, weak come.

CHARLES: Yes. Now I think it's time you visited one of your estates.

DEVONSHIRE (*horrified*): Go out of London?

CHARLES: How else? Do you have estates in London? Get to your tin-mines.

DEVONSHIRE: No, Charlie . . .

CHARLES. Get down to Essex, then, and count your lobster-pots . . .

DEVONSHIRE: Charlie, no thank you.

CHARLES: Oh, do. Do, yes. (*Pause, then she tears out.* NODD *adjusts his wig.*) Thank you, Rob. Now go down to the yard and fetch me Mr. Bradshaw's head.

NODD: Do wha' —

CHARLES: Oh, now, don't quarrel! And see it washed, and the sparse hairs parted, as he would have wished, no mockery. (NODD *shrugs, starts to go.*) Rob. (*He stops.*) We shall go drinking, soon. In dirty jerkins over Brixton.

NODD: Yup. (*He goes out.* HAMBRO *enters.*)

CHARLES: And Rob! (*He reappears.*) I think, ask Lady Devonshire postpone her coach. I do not now, but a time will come I'll want her. I guarantee no sooner will she pass the toll than my knob will be up and barking for her. (NODD *goes out.* CHARLES *walks a little, adjusts his sash.*) What, Billy?

HAMBRO: It's time.

CHARLES: Oh, it is, is it?

HAMBRO: Time, yes, and such a shame to spoil the day. The people line the river.

CHARLES: Oh, let 'em wait. I'm king, ain't I?

HAMBRO: Indeed, but —

CHARLES: No, no, I'm the bloody monarch —

HAMBRO: Quite, but —

CHARLES: **Monarch, Monarch!** (HAMBRO *is silent, looks at the floor.* CHARLES *beckons him with a finger.*) Billy, what if I am barmy? I think the dad had it, you see, suppose I'm barmy?

HAMBRO: What if you're —

CHARLES: Sister-fucking — up nieces — down nephews — bad blood and funny bones — Stuart eggs all broken in the saucepan — what then, Billy? Would yer have me quietly butchered?

HAMBRO: I prefer not to imagine —

CHARLES: Billy won't imagine! Billy won't! (*He goes close to him.*) Or don't it really matter any more? (*Pause*) Billy, I do not like you awfully. You have such cold grey eyes and never fuck nobody. I wish I was cleverer, I would follow your tricks like the dog to the bitch's arse. I think you entertain some sort of treason.

HAMBRO: Treason?

CHARLES (*mocking*): What! Treason! What! (*He smiles.*) No, Billy, darling, I mean I don't think you love me, do you, my flesh, the bone and blood of Charlie? Do you ? Really love me?

HAMBRO: I was prime-mover in your —

CHARLES: Prime mover, oh, prime mover, yes, you would be, I never saw a man more purely prime moving, a prince among prime movers, it clings like shit to the instep the prime mobility of you, Billy, did you not get this day for me, you did and thank you, I am well primed though not exactly moved, but never mind, you primed the day, oh, thank you, Billy, but — (*He looks closely at him.*) I wish you fucked more . . . (*Pause*) Off now. I come.

Scene Four

BRADSHAW's *house at dusk.* SCROPE *enters.*

SCROPE: I sinned.

BRADSHAW: I was afraid you would appear.

SCROPE (*flinging himself down*): I sinned! I sinned!

BRADSHAW: Just at the moment I wanted to be alone, at the very moment I most needed to collect my thoughts, I knew you would appear —

SCROPE: I sinned!

BRADSHAW: And be very abject.

SCROPE: One blow!

BRADSHAW: Will you not shout, please?

SCROPE: One blow and I gave away the place! One blow and I led them to his grave!

BRADSHAW: How many blows did you want? (*Pause*)

SCROPE: It wasn't a blow . . .

BRADSHAW: What was it, then?

SCROPE: A flick.

BRADSHAW: A flick?

SCROPE: A flick of a glove . . .

BRADSHAW: What sort of glove? A mailed glove?

SCROPE: **A calf glove.**

BRADSHAW: Well, flicks can be painful.

SCROPE: You mock me! You mock my cowardice!

BRADSHAW: Mr. Scrope, I have pain, too —

SCROPE: **My cowardice!**

BRADSHAW: What of my pain, Mr. Scrope! (*He looks at her, sobs.*)

SCROPE: I have no courage . . . I have no dignity . . .

BRADSHAW: No, but you have your teeth. After the glove comes the fist, and after the fist comes the boot, and after the boot —

SCROPE: What I would not give for courage!

BRADSHAW: No. Let us chuck courage and hang on to our teeth.

SCROPE: I betrayed him!

BRADSHAW: Mr. Scope, I am beginning to think you overdo the abject rather —

SCROPE: **I betrayed him!**

BRADSHAW: You did not, then! He betrayed himself. (*Pause*)

SCROPE: How?

BRADSHAW: By sharing his secret with a man who, in the last resort, preferred to keep his teeth.

SCROPE: There! You mock me!

BRADSHAW: Not at all. He was an appalling judge of character.

SCROPE: Well, you accuse me, then!

BRADSHAW: I accuse no one. I am done with accusing. I am done with shame, and conscience, duty, guilt, and power, all of it! All of your words, chuck out! (*Pause*) Now, shake hands with me, I'm leaving.

SCROPE (*amazed out of crying*):   Leaving?

BRADSHAW: Yes. Now. In the dead of night. In what I stand up in. (*Pause*) Scrope, your lip is quivvering. Do stop, you look an old man suddenly . . . (*She turns away.*)

SCROPE: Where? Where to?

BRADSHAW: London, to collect his pieces. And nowhere after that.

SCROPE: Why?

BRADSHAW: Why? Because we must crawl now, go down on

all fours, be a dog or rabbit, no more standing up now, standing is over, standing up's for men with sin and dignity. No, got to be a dog now, and keep our teeth. I am crawling and barking, stalking, fawning, stealing breakfast, running when I see a stick, taken when I'm taken, pupping under hedges, being a proper four-legged bitch. (*Pause. He stares at her.*) Well, of course I shall have to learn it! Can't be be a dog overnight!

SCROPE (*as she turns to go*):   I think my master's wife is ill . . .

BRADSHAW: I'll, me? I am weller than I ever was!

SCROPE: How can I see you, who was wife to the President of the Council, and walked with him in honour and in —

BRADSHAW: Oh, down I go! See! (*She goes down on all fours.*) Bow! Ow! Ow!

SCROPE: Oh, you shame him!

BRADSHAW: I shame him? What about him shaming me? Getting his ugly reason out, his great moral purpose, showing it in public, and his wisdom! Could not walk with him five minutes but he had his wisdom out, forever exhibiting his mind, was ever a mind hung out so much in public, dirty thing it was, great monster of a mind so flashed and brazenly dangled? Ugh! No, I was shamed if anybody was!

SCROPE: I think you should see a doctor.

BRADSHAW: A doctor? Don't you mean a vet?

SCROPE: You have gone mad with grief!

BRADSHAW: No, sane with it. Now, stand away from the window, I am leaving by it. There is a spy watches the door —

SCROPE: I refuse —

BRADSHAW: Now, be a good secretary and —

SCROPE: I must refuse —

BRADSHAW: Don't be silly, Scrope —

SCROPE: **I will be honourable in this at least**.

BRADSHAW: Scrope, I will push you over . . . (*Pause. Then he stands aside, bitterly. She goes to climb through the window.*)

SCROPE: I must come, then, mustn't I? (*She looks at him.*) It is my duty.

BRADSHAW: I really do not want —

SCROPE: **I must.** (*Pause*)

BRADSHAW: Then throw away your satchel. You won't need pen and paper on four legs.

SCROPE (*taking out a book*):   Mr. Bradshaw's 'Harmonia' I will not part with. Read it every night beneath the hedge.

BRADSHAW: Idiot.

SCROPE: Bring comfort to us in our —

BRADSHAW: Chew it, suck the moisture out the ink —
SCROPE (*stuffing the book in a pocket*):   It's gaol to have in your possession —
BRADSHAW: Quick! Someone's coming! Quick! (*They climb out of the window.* McCONOCHIE *comes in holding a book.*)
McCONOCHIE (*rehearsing*):   Guid morning to ye . . . is it noo a fine sky o'er the Firth of Forth . . . (*He stops.*) The capital of Scotland is Edinburgh. The Highlands are high. The Lowlands are low . . . (*He walks a little, stops.*) The sheep are in the heather . . . the coos are in the burn . . . (*He goes as if to shake hands.*) I am McConochie, surgeon of Leith . . . (*and again*) McConochie at your service, Bachelor of Medicine, Physician of Dundee . . . (*He ruminates.*) Dun-dee . . . Dun-dee . . . no, Leith. (*He procedes to a rocking chair, sits and reads.* BALL *appears at the window, climbs in.*)
BALL: Across the lawn I come, left off my boots, and sockless like a cavalier. But you will dry my poor wet feet in your lap, in your hot place, oh, excuse the cavalier in me, I know it offends but I have thought a lot of you in your cold puritan shift and come to master you like taking England back. I looked at England through a telescope from Calais thinking of your starched under-things and uncoloured face, and the smell of you, a little musty, I expect, the musty hair of a sad-eyed puritan, oh, I shall have you shuddering with love, do reply, but very sweetly, and with dignity, no cock and cunt talk, you are not a cavalier tart, are you? Oh, the modesty of a real woman it does wonders to me, I am hard as rock . . .
McCONOCHIE (*in terror*):   I think you have come to the wrong house, sir . . .
BALL: What.
McCONOCHIE: I think you have, sir —
BALL: **What!**
McCONOCHIE (*jumping up*):   Don't hit me, please, I am only a surgeon!
BALL (*drawing a dagger*):   Oh, I stab you, I kill the rebel filth!
McCONOCHIE (*on the ground*):   Mercy!
BALL: What do you do in this stinking house? In this disgusting cleanliness? I burn it! I burn it ! What do you do?
McCONOCHIE: Surgeon, sir!
BALL (*releasing him*):   I shall burn it, I shall! All this polish and this timber, I was a pig in Calais while they lorded it. Lorded it, I say lorded it, whatever they do in their stiff-gobbed manner! Who do you examine? In her starchy knicker with your prod?

Where is the woman? Where is the widow of the king's assassin, the murdered saint's accuser, where's his pale wife? I did not prattle all my knob talk for your dirty doctor's ear.

McCONOCHIE: Ow!

BALL: Where is she?

McCONOCHIE: Don't know sir!

BALL: Get her, then, and quick about it, in her shift or naked off her pot, for all I care! (McCONOCHIE *hurtles out the room*.) Oh, after I shall write a sonnet, when the fire has gone, a melancholy piece on how her sad face was like a pearl, and her hair like silvered weed flowing o'er the pillow . . . (McCONOCHIE *enters with a sheet of paper*.)

McCONOCHIE: She's gone . . .

BALL: Gone! Oh, shit and piss! Then I have lost the cunt I wanted! (*He snatches the paper from* McCONOCHIE. *Reads*) 'Have gone to be an animal' — what is this — 'in time of animals' — what's this!

McCONOCHIE: Don't know sir.

BALL: Oh, yes, I think you do —

McCONOCHIE: No —

BALL: In time of animals ! You have had her!

McCONOCHIE: Never!

BRADSHAW (*grabbing him*): Oh, I'll stick my dagger in your crack if you dirty doctor got in there before me!

McCONOCHIE: Never! Never!

BALL: Dog-wise, yes, you did, I know it from your simper!

(McCONOCHIE *sobs*.) I never knew a doctor not share the sickbed of his patient had she got half a tit was healthy . . .

McCONOCHIE: No . . . no . . .

BALL (*his dagger out*): Deny once more, I'll slit your carotids — there — I know a surgeon's patter — and see your gore across the shiny boards, I swear it! (McCONOCHIE *freezes*.) So, was she hot for you? You being animal? Oh, was she, hot and clinging?

McCONOCHIE: Yes . . .

BALL: And whispered you were wonder to her, being animal, sheer wonder, did she?

McCONOCHIE: Yes . . .

BALL (*throwing him down*): Oh, God and Christ, I do want a puritan woman! They know what they do with their eyes cast down and starchy collars! They do know it! 'Gone to an animal!' Well, mistress, I shall find you in your den! (*He turns to go, stops.*) Can you cure me of what I've got? It stings me something awful.

McCONOCHIE: I don't know what you —

BALL: I'll sit and unbutton. And if it rises thinking of the Bradshaw woman, tap it with some cold instrument. And blunt, mind you . . . (*He sits, unbuttons.* McCONOCHIE *looks.*) Why are you snivelling? Am I so ill you cannot keep your tears back?

McCONOCHIE: No, I . . .

BALL: Touch it, then, it won't bite you . . . (McCONOCHIE *feigns an examination.*) I have been on my own soil for six months now, hounding communists and antichrists, doing the midnight knock on the doors of old republicans. It is my treat. I have been on an eight-year holiday. How is it?

McCONOCHIE: Mild, mild, I think . . .

BALL: Eight years, watching the cliffs of England from a whore's back on the continent, jostling Louis le this and Monsignor that, purple vicars and slag duchesses. I did not think I should get back, let alone rip down the lanes and burn the manors of this lot. How mild? No other quack could shift it.

McCONOCHIE: Mild . . . and yet . . . tenacious . . .

BALL: Where's the sense in History? I came here to a feast of bonfire and applauding. Who would have flung shit in my eye once were all bow and scraping, and me with not a clean whole garment! I don't pretend to know no history. How is the knob, then? Can you cure him?

McCONOCHIE (*bluffing*):   It is a somewhat rare infection . . .

BALL: Rare, is it? It would be.

McCONOCHIE: Rare, definitely, rare, yes . . .

BALL: What became of all the roundhead troopers? Is their armour up behind the door? Or rusting in the cabbages? I seen none since I came here, prance in their cottages and get only silence, muddy silence, and they used to yell so much, chivvied the world's guts once — ow! Don't pluck it, quack, examine it!

McCONOCHIE: I am very sorry . . . I am not a pox specialist . . .

BALL: What are you, then!

McCONOCHIE (*shaking*):   It is not my speciality . . .

BALL: Listen quack, I get no fuck here, very well, but I shall have a cure for my trouble!

McCONOCHIE: Yes —

BALL: Get down your pox book —

McCONOCHIE: Yes —

BALL: And study it —

McCONOCHIE: Yes —

BALL: Fast! In Jesus' name, I shall leave here healthy!
(McCONOCHIE *rises and hurries to the door*.) Quack! (*He
stops*.) Listen. Now the puritans are done for you will make a
living as a cock specialist, if you're so minded. We bring from
Europe every boil and sore now, it's the restoration of old
lewdness and the reign of fucking. Specialize in troubles of the
mucus and you will live in posh, if posh you fancy.
(McCONOCHIE *perceives*.) Christ knows why I favour you
like this. Do you angle after posh? I never knew a doctor didn't.

McCONOCHIE: Yes.

BALL: Start here, then. On my ailing foreskin.(*Pause. Then
filled with inspiration,* McCONOCHIE *turns to leave. He stops
at the door*.)

McCONOCHIE: Perhaps a little essence of saltpetre?

BALL: Why not? Fling the contents of the pharmacy at it.

McCONOCHIE (*his mind racing*):   Or sulphur in suspension of
boracic . . .

BALL: You mix, I'll do the swallowing. (McCONOCHIE
leaves.) And I spend the night here! Among her things, run my
fingers through her garments, slip her knicker on my haunches
and dream in her bed. Tomorrow I'll pursue her.

Scene Five

A field. A man digging, a woman watching, and a preacher.

FEAK: I done enough. Bring out the dead, Mrs.

EDGBASTON: In certain knowledge of thy resurrection, in
confidence thy mouth will speak again, sleeping only till the call
come, we plant thee like a seed to rise when anger warms the
ground!

PYLE (*taking a rifle from a cloth*):   Anybody looking?

FEAK: Give us it.

EDGBASTON: Oh, Lord of Battles, bless thy son, and keep his
silence brief!

FEAK (*handling it fondly, offering the muzzle*):   Give 'im a kiss,

eh? (PYLE *kisses the muzzle.*) And you, Bob . . .
(EDGBASTON *kisses it.*) Bye bye, pal . . .

EDGBASTON: Oh, death and mutilation to thy enemies! He
shall return to us in blood and smoke, I vow!

FEAK: Where ain't I carted that bloody gun . . .

PYLE: Where ain't I cleaned it . . .

EDGBASTON: A crop of armour and a field of bullets from thy
temper shall be harvested!

PYLE: Scotland, Ireland, Flanders, Jamaica . . .

FEAK: All for nothing.

PYLE: Good times . . .

FEAK: Ta ta, pal, it won't be Sue's fault you get dirt up yer
spout now . . .

PYLE: Good times . . .

EDGBASTON: Oh, let his sleep be brief before our wrath
return to boil, in blood and terror drive the stinking Stuart from
our soil!

FEAK (*to* EDGBASTON): All right, Bob, you done? (*He
nods.*) Cover it up, ducks. (PYLE *begins filling the grave.*) We
was the champions. Now look at us. Time's a cunt.

PYLE: So's God.

EDGBASTON: Now, sister, you are letting your grief run away
with you . . .

PYLE: Am I? I said he's a cunt, didn't I? He is a cunt.

EDGBASTON: And did He not guide the parliament to raise
the standards of revolt? Did he not steer the Lord Protector in
his —

PYLE: Oh, fuck the Protector, Bob . . .

EDGBASTON: I will not hear this scandal of Almighty God!

FEAK: Yer can't tell Sue, Bob, she's defaced too many monu-
ments. Always first up cathedral aisles, our Sue, 'ammer flyin',
trail a' broken glass an' angels' 'eads . . .

PYLE: Good times . . .

FEAK: Must end . . .

EDGBASTON: It is one thing to wreck the graven image, but
another to attack His dwelling place inside our hearts.

PYLE (*patting down the earth with the flat of the shovel*): Show a
bloke a good thing . . . (*She notices* BRADSHAW *and*
SCROPE *are watching them. Pause.*)

BRADSHAW: I must say I have some trouble following the
Lord myself. His ways and so on. I expect we got too proud,
don't you? He really has a passion about proudness. One day
you're prancing and the next day you are in the trough. And

Howard Barker

vice versa, I expect, well, look at Charles Stuart, have you got a bun or something, we are starving. (*They look at her.*) Well, if not a bun, a —

FEAK: We are fuckin' ragbags as it is —

BRADSHAW: Yes, I can see that, I wasn't asking for your life-blood, only —

EDGBASTON: We live very frugal here —

BRADSHAW: Oh, come on, where's your charity?

PYLE: Charity's for comrades.

BRADSHAW: With all respect, I don't think you have quite grasped the principle of charity, have you? The point, I think, is that it's undiscriminating, am I right? (*She looks at* EDGBASTON. SCROPE *mutters to her.*)

SCROPE: Come on, we'll get nothing here —

BRADSHAW (*hissing*): **I want a bun.** (*She turns back to* EDGBASTON.) You're a preacher, aren't you? What is charity, isn't there a character of moral obligation in the word?

FEAK: You get none 'ere —

BRADSHAW (*turning on him*): **You get none 'ere!** Well, what does the meaning matter, the offence is clear enough **I see you kill the old republic** here and quite right, bury old equality, **who said that!** Shh! All these old dirty words, under the sod and stamp on them, come on — (*She turns to* SCROPE.)

EDGBASTON: We are wary of strangers —

BRADSHAW: No, no, don't be kind now, you will only suffer for it, keep your bun, a man must watch his bun nowadays, don't feed a stranger, what is this, the Commonwealth, **who said that,** not me!

SCROPE (*desperate*): Take it!

BRADSHAW: Shut up! We can have the lot off them! (*She turns back to them.*) I do respect your narrow eyes, your tight lip, very wise now, hands in pockets, there are bun thieves about! (*She makes as if to go.*)

FEAK: What were you, Mrs.? With the Republic? (*She stops, looks down at her garments.*)

BRADSHAW: Do I look a duchess? My husband gave the king his death. Trembling somewhat. Well, wouldn't you? He expected God to strike him dead. Sat on a ring of rubber in case lightning struck his head. (*Pause. Then* PYLE *flings herself at* BRADSHAW's *feet and kisses her hand.*)

FEAK: Get buns!

BRADSHAW (*as* PYLE *hurries off*): With butter!

FEAK: An' beer!

BRADSHAW: Two bottles!

FEAK: Bring all the beer we got!

SCROPE (*in joy*): Oh, Christ, I hurt with hunger!

EDGBASTON: Our great rebels brought to this . . . there is mud to your knees, sister . . .

BRADSHAW: So there is! You do see life without a carriage! Has she any bacon?

EDGBASTON (*shouting off*): Bacon, sis!

FEAK: We saw 'im, we was beside 'im when they axed the bugger Stuart, weren't us, Bob?

BRADSHAW: Ask her to wrap a dinner up, in cloth or something —

EDGBASTON (*shouts*): Make a dinner up! A dinner! Make one up!

FEAK: Where you are standin', that's where we was, 12th Footguard, battle-dress in case a' bother, trailin' pikes —

EDGBASTON (*shouting*): In a cloth! A dinner! Yes!

FEAK: I said, that is the President a' Council, that is Bradshaw, 'e was like from 'ere to there — remember, Bob? An' 'e was pale, dead pale 'e was —

BRADSHAW: He had a very fair skin —

FEAK: Fuckin' right 'e did, an' when the blood spilt, did 'e jump!

EDGBASTON: We all jumped —

FEAK: I jumped, you jumped, every bugger jumped!

EDGBASTON: **King's blood!**

FEAK: An' I thought, Christ Almighty, it's the same as any other, it's the same red stuff . . .

EDGBASTON: Off came his shoe —

FEAK: An' the foot —

EDGBASTON: The foot without the shoe was going —

FEAK: On the wooden boards —

EDGBASTON: Bang — bang —

FEAK: On this frosty mornin' —

EDGBASTON: Bang — bang, the Stuart foot . . . (PYLE *returns with a small parcel of food. They look at it disparagingly.*)

FEAK: What's this?

PYLE: It's little. Because they gave us little.

EDGBASTON: Sue —

PYLE: You give what you get —

EDGBASTON: Sue —

PYLE: **Don't yer, though? That's life!** (*Pause*) I thought, crossin' this field, this bloody field which is runnin' in our sweat an' our dad's sweat before us, what are yer doin', Sue, you silly bitch, why fetch for them?

BRADSHAW: Give us a bite.

PYLE: I thought, you are forgettin' something, girl, in your excitement you ain't thinking right.

BRADSHAW: Give us a bite.

PYLE: Because we came from 'ere, 'alf starved as usual out this bloody field to chuck the bastard Stuart over an' get Oliver an' Mr. Bradshaw in, ten years of killin' Spaniards, Scots an' Irish, an' for what?

EDGBASTON: You are being most —

PYLE: To come back to this soddin' field again! This field of bloody clay, only this time it was buggered with the horses ridin' over it an' wouldn't take a crop —

FEAK: It was, Bob —

PYLE: But did they let us off the rent? Did they? I ask yer, did they give us one bloody little quarter off the rent?

FEAK: They never, Bob . . .

PYLE: An' we are still tryin' to wring a dinner out this mud! Commonwealth? Whose commonwealth? Give them dinner, I thought, fuck! (*Pause. Then she holds out the food to* BRADSHAW. *She takes it, sits at once and starts eating.* SCROPE *watches anxiously.*)

SCROPE: I do think . . . with all respect . . . you are not being entirely fair . . . Mr. Bradshaw . . . you may know . . . was highly critical . . . of the . . . slow progress . . . of agrarian . . . reform . . . the tenant question . . . very . . . memoranda . . . to . . . and . . . (*He drops to his knees and grabs at the food, stuffing it in his mouth in ecstasy.*) Oh! Oh! (*The others watch them a few moments, then drift off.* BRADSHAW *stops eating, stares after them.*)

BRADSHAW: Listen —

SCROPE: Mm — mmm —

BRADSHAW: Oh, listen. I did something.

SCROPE: Mm — mmm —

BRADSHAW: Will you listen to me.

SCROPE: Mm —

BRADSHAW: Scrope, I did it. When he kissed me. **I took his wallet.** Get on your feet!

SCROPE: Wha'?

BRADSHAW (*showing it*): **I took his wallet!** Oh, my lovely quick hands, look! (*He stares at her in horror.*) Congratulate me. (*He just stares.*) **Congratulate me, then**.

SCROPE: But they — they were our people —

BRADSHAW: **Congratulate me, then!** (*Pause. He stares at her.*)

SCROPE: You cannot do it to them . . .

BRADSHAW: I did, you see, I did!

SCROPE: Listen —

BRADSHAW: Look at my fingers! Aren't they wonderful, and swift? They tremble in their little ecstasy, do look!

SCROPE: Please, listen —

BRADSHAW (*collecting the remaining bread*):   Hurry up, or they'll discover it, and then it's noses slit and ears off, do be quick!

SCROPE: I refuse to move until you hear me!

BRADSHAW (*stares*):   What, then? What? (*Pause*)

SCROPE: You must not injure people in their faith.

BRADSHAW: Why not? What's so precious about faith? Why can't it take a kicking like anything else? I do them a favour. They get an education, and I get a wallet. Cheap at the price, there is fuckall in it —

SCROPE: You swear, I hate to hear you —

BRADSHAW: Ask a rat about his faith! (*She starts to go.*)

SCROPE: Wait!

BRADSHAW: Scrope, your ears!

SCROPE: A man may be beaten, and his wife violated, and his house burned, and his children murdered by his enemies, and yet stay whole. But to be so treated by his friends . . . you encourage madness.

BRADSHAW: **I do know that**. Do you think I found it easy? It wasn't easy. But that's my triumph. Any fool can rob his enemy. Where's the victory in that?

SCROPE: Mr. Bradshaw would suffer if he could see this . . .

BRADSHAW: It's a long time since he lost his eyes, if he ever had any. What colour were they? I forget . . . (SCROPE *begins to sob.*) Oh, Scrope, you are a wet little sparrow of a man . . .

FEAK (*off, distantly*):   **Oi!**

SCROPE (*grabbing his satchel*):   Oh, Christ!

BRADSHAW: Oh, Scrope, the argument . . .

FEAK: **Oi!**

BRADSHAW (*grinning as he tears offstage*):   What about the argument?

Interlude

The vaults of the Bank of England. GAUKROGER *beats a staff.*
HAMBRO *appears.*

GAUKROGER: Oh — King — Charles — our — rightful —
chief!
HAMBRO: I am the Governor.
GAUKROGER: I am the Officer.
HAMBRO: Give me the keys.
GAUKROGER: What is the password?
HAMBRO: The password is orange.
GAUKROGER (*holds out a bunch of keys*):   God save the
monarch!
HAMBRO: His honour and his might! (GAUKROGER
marches out.) Where are you, Frank? (*He jangles the keys.*) Oh,
don't be a silly bugger.
MOBBERLEY (*from hiding*):   'is honour and 'is might . . .
HAMBRO: Quite.
MOBBERLEY: 'is bollocks and 'is conk . . .
HAMBRO: Very funny. Now, when you're ready, perhaps you'd
help me get a table out.
MOBBERLEY (*stepping out the darkness*):   Gimme the
keys . . .
HAMBRO: Because I'm not doing this all by myself . . .
MOBBERLEY: Give us 'em.
HAMBRO (*shifting a table*):   Frank, you are supposed to be the
Minister for Public Works, I wish you'd —
MOBBERLEY: **I wanna look at me gold.**
HAMBRO: You can't. Bring over those chairs.
MOBBERLEY: **Show us me gold.**
HAMBRO: I keep trying to explain to you, it is not your gold,
it's everybody's gold.
MOBBERLEY: **I wanna see my bit, then**.
HAMBRO (*pausing*):   Frank, one of these days you will have to
come to grips with the principles of banking —
MOBBERLEY (*snatching the keys*):   **Got 'em! Ha, ha! Got 'em!**
HAMBRO: Sooner or later focus the great beams of your intel-
lect on the mobility of money — (*He attempts to recover the
keys.*) **Give them back**.
MOBBERLEY: **I don't trust yer!**
HAMBRO: This is precisely why we have a bank. (*Pause.*
MOBBERLEY *leans on the table.*)

MOBBERLEY: Billy, I am a brickman with paws so clumsy I can 'ardly scratch my name. All the juice in the royal 'ores' cunts will never make my fingers soft. I 'ad one kiln I fired with my own furniture, an' one cart, which when the army took the 'orse off me, I stood in the shafts myself. I now 'ave fifty carts an' fifty drivers, an' there ain't one night my wagon lights ain't bumpin' down the London road, come snow or flood. Show us me gold and don't fog my 'ead with science. (*He goes off to the vault. A man enters.*)

PARRY: I said velvet. Velvet, I said. Velvet, you silly arse. He thought the word was orange. I don't know about orange, I said, I only know velvet.

HAMBRO (*laying out glasses*):   Velvet was last night.

PARRY: I will talk to Coldstream about his fucking guards. If he thought it was orange why did he let me in?

UNDY (*entering*):   Oh, I love this place! I do love this place! I love its columns and its architraves, I love its Greekness! I could have been Romulus or Remus coming up them steps . . .

PARRY: They weren't Greeks, Ralph, they was Romans.

UNDY: The guard says 'what's the password?' Velvet, says I. No, he says, not velvet. It is fucking velvet, says I, if it's not velvet, what is it? Orange, he says —

PARRY: We have just been through this, Ralph.

UNDY: Oh, you have, have you?

PARRY: Where's Frank?

HAMBRO: Frank is in the vault.

PARRY: In the vault?

HAMBRO: He wants to — feel the ingots.

PARRY: Feel the ingots?

HAMBRO: Yes.

PARRY: **Feel the ingots?**

HAMBRO: That's what I said. I do think someone's got to talk to Frank.

UNDY: This is a palace you got here, Billy. The King will never have a better.

HAMBRO: No. He can't afford it, can he?

PARRY: Not on what we give him.

STREET/MONCRIEFF (*entering*):   Are we late?

HAMBRO: Marginally.

STREET: I cannot stay late. I am in a slight hurry.

HAMBRO: We don't have much to discuss that concerns the Navy.

UNDY: What slight hurry is this, Stan? We have not met for three weeks, have we?

STREET: A masque in Putney.

UNDY (*disbelief*): A masque in Putney?

STREET: My wife is expecting me.

UNDY: His wife is expecting him. Well, if his wife is expecting him, what's it matter we have not met in three weeks?

STREET: Don't be silly, Ralph.

UNDY: I'm surprised he could make it at all, what with his wife expecting him.

HAMBRO: Ralph . . .

UNDY: A most commanding lady is Joanna . . .

PARRY: Are we ready for the oath?

UNDY: We govern, and are governed in our turn, it seems, all our conference must hang on Stanley's wife. Does she know she governs the country, Stanley, may I ask?

HAMBRO: Ralph.

UNDY: I thought we had got rid of absolute monarchy, but no, there is Stanley's wife more terrible than Louis le whatsname or the Tsar, kicking her heels in Putney, Christ help us —

PARRY: **The oath, Ralph!**

UNDY: Ludicrous.

HAMBRO: Please.

UNDY: It is. (*They stand round the table, join hands over the bottle.*)

MONCRIEFF: Mobberley's not here.

PARRY: Fuck.

HAMBRO: F — R — A — N — K!

STREET: Leave him out of the oath.

UNDY: Can't.

HAMBRO: This once.

UNDY: Can't.

PARRY: As Stan's in a rush. Agreed?

UNDY: Bloody hell.

ALL: Agreed.

HAMBRO: Ralph?

UNDY: Stan's wife commandeth.

HAMBRO: Go on, then, Bob.

PARRY (*reciting the oath*): To those whom God grants power grant honour, equity and conscience too —

ALL: Semper fidelis, Semper honorabilis, Semper, Semper —

UNDY: Oh, Christ, what has Frank —

ALL: Semper, Semper —

MOBBERLEY (*dragging some gold bars on a small trolley*): **Got a bit of England, sir!**
PARRY: Oh, put it back, Frank —
MOBBERLEY (*picking up a bar*):   In my grubby paw got boys and girls —
HAMBRO: Just give us the keys —
MOBBERLEY: **Got woods and fields and shops and rivers —**
HAMBRO: Put them on the table, there's a good —
MOBBERLEY: **An' fish an' fences, gardens, cradles, virgins, cots!**
HAMBRO: Frank, I am the Governor of this place!
MONCRIEFF: Leave him.
MOBBERLEY: Leave me, Billy. I am hanging on to **my bit.** (*He sits at the empty chair.*) Did I miss anything?
UNDY: You missed the oath.
MOBBERLEY (*putting the gold bar on his lap*):   Fuck the oath. (*He turns to his neighbour.*) I am keeping my gold indoors.
PARRY: You can't
MOBBERLEY: 'ho says so?
PARRY: You can't because we lend it to people.
MOBBERLEY: I don't wanna lend it.
STREET: You've got to. It's the system.
MOBBERLEY: Who's system? Not my system!
UNDY: I thought Frank was au fait with economics.
HAMBRO: No . . .
UNDY: Frank, I thought we had a civil war to get this straight. I spent four years on horseback chasing over garden fences to sort this out. Four years! And now you want to take your gold home and rip up the floorboards. **I have a wound five inches long in my groin says England's got to have a bank!** (*Pause.* MOBBERLEY *looks confused.*)
MOBBERLEY: I keep getting bits of paper.
HAMBRO: They are not bits of paper, they are credit notes . . .
MOBBERLEY: It's still paper, ain't it?
HAMBRO: **It's got my signature on!**
UNDY: All right, Billy.
STREET: I'm in a slight hurry, if you remember, so may I suggest —
MONCRIEFF (*paternally*):   Hang aboot, hang aboot, will ye? Take your mind back to before the war. You may remember, before the war, the King told us to pay him money. Ordered us to, ye cud na argue with it. But we did na want to pay him

money, so we had the war, all right? Now, we have a new King, an' he still wants money. He has to ha' the money from somewhere, it stands ta reason. But noo, instead o' givin' it to him, we lend it to him instead. Are ye clear on that, Frank? An' ye canna lend money if it's under the bed. (*He smiles.*) Now, goo an' put it back in the vaults, and when ye wanna see it, ye can see it, can't he, Billy, he can coom and look at his stuff. That's noo a lot to ask, is it?

HAMBRO: I suppose not.

MONCRIEFF: Of course he can. Okay? (*Pause*)

MOBBERLEY: Sorry, I am being dense.

MONCRIEFF: Noo, noo, not at all. It's a complicated subject. Off ye goo. (MOBBERLEY *gets up, tows his trolley away.*)

STREET: Now, can we get down to business? (HAMBRO *rises to his feet.*)

HAMBRO: I want to stop the terror.

PARRY: Why?

HAMBRO: Well, why not?

UNDY: Yes, why not, Bob? I think we've had enough of randy cavaliers knocking the eyeballs out of puritans. It's all right for a fortnight, but I had a Dutchman lose an ear last week and he was here to place a contract.

PARRY: They must have their fling.

UNDY: I think they've had it. Christ, all the republicans are still in hiding.

PARRY: No. Let 'em rampage a while yet, or they will turn their attention elsewhere. Let 'em beat the communists, and the pamphlet writers and the free love and the Christ-on-earth mob, let 'em carve the king's initials on their arses.

UNDY: I would be perfectly happy for that, but they are getting indiscriminate.

HAMBRO: They are getting out of hand, Bob.

PARRY: They are meant to be out of hand, they are cavaliers, aren't they? They have been rotting in foreign brothels for ten years, they are bound to be out of hand.

UNDY: They are blinding my customers.

PARRY: All right, and what do you intend to do with them?

HAMBRO: Enlist them in a regiment. Give them a uniform with lots of tassel and gold facing. Call them The King's Own and send them on an expedition from which they won't come back.

PARRY: They are too old for expeditions. They are antiquated thugs who lost their estates for monarchy and if we don't let 'em rollock they will sit about on doorsteps and start to think —

UNDY: What with, Bob?

PARRY: And they will think —

UNDY: What with, exactly?

PARRY: With what is left of their brains —

UNDY: Never had any —

PARRY: Whatever happened to their little estates, and they will look around and they will see who has 'em —

UNDY: Never —

PARRY: And it will be us —

UNDY: Oh, bollocks, Bob —

PARRY: And we will be in deep shit I tell you.

HAMBRO: Bob, you are governing England now. I do think, when a man is governing England, he oughtn't to shudder so much.

UNDY: 'ear, 'ear!

HAMBRO: No one will undo the settlement. Let them rot in taverns and piss their grievances down the sink.

UNDY: 'ear, 'ear!

STREET: Shall we vote?

UNDY: Why not? Stan's in a hurry, mustn't forget.

HAMBRO: Those in favour of calling them off? (*A majority of hands are raised.*) It's off.

CHARLES (*off*): **Orange, he quoth!**

UNDY (*jumping up*): Fuck, it's the mad shagman!

HAMBRO (*clearing the desk*): Look casual!

MOBBERLEY (*entering*): I put 'em back —

UNDY: Siddown!

HAMBRO: It's a drink — it's only a drink!

CHARLES (*entering*): **Not enter my bank!**

GAUKROGER (*entering abjectly*): Did not know you, sir!

CHARLES: Did not know me! And have I not the conk? The conk which goes before me crying **Monarch?** Orange or velvet, here's the conk! (*He thrusts his face at* GAUKROGER, *catches sight of the bankers.*) Oh, there's a do! There's a do in my bank!

HAMBRO (*bowing*): Sir, a glass?

NODD (*entering*): 'ullo, Billy, workin' late?

CHARLES: An' Undy, an' Mobb'ley, what's this?

GWYNN (*entering*): Men only.

CHARLES: Come to show Nelly me bank, an' there's a beano!

HAMBRO: A seat, madam?

GWYNN: No, give us the keys.

CHARLES (*peering*): An' Parry! Well, fuck me, what's this?

PARRY: Well, we meet . . .

CHARLES: Oh, yer meet, do yer? An' who's that?

NODD: Dunno, 'ho is it? (STREET *bows*.)

CHARLES: Oh, Stanley, you too?

NODD: 'ho is 'e? Somethin' legal ain't 'e?

CHARLES: Something legal, he says. He is Chief Justice, yer ass. Well, I'm buggered at this . . . (*He sits in a chair.*)

GWYNN: Where's the gold, Charlie?

CHARLES: Give her the keys.

HAMBRO (*taking them off the table*):   There are three doors to the vault, each one with an eight-lever lock —

CHARLES: Don't blind her with science, she is after rubbing her bosoms over the bricks.

GWYNN (*taking the keys*):   Can I 'ave one?

HAMBRO: Can you have one?

GWYNN: A gold brick. (*Pause. She looks at* CHARLES.)

NODD: Go on, give 'er one. (*Pause*)

HAMBRO: I should like nothing more, only —

NODD: No, no, stuff all that. Give 'er one.

HAMBRO: It isn't that simple.

CHARLES: Why ain't it?

HAMBRO: Each brick represents —

CHARLES: Represents what?

HAMBRO: The accumulation of other men's wealth.

NODD: Well, that's why she wants it. She ain't a nana. Give 'er one, then. (HAMBRO *looks resolutely at the floor.*)

GWYNN: Oh, Charlie, 'e don't want to! (*He looks at him.*) Ain't you mean, when you got such a lot?

NODD: Take it. G'arn take it. (*Pause.* CHARLES *gets up.*)

CHARLES: I may not. Do you see, Noddy? I may not.

NODD (*to* GAUKROGER):   Oi, you! You git down there an' bring us a brick! (GAUKROGER *looks at* HAMBRO.) Look smart, then! (*He doesn't move.*)

CHARLES: No, I may not . . . (*He moves away.*)

NODD: Oh, you crew of fuckers —

CHARLES: Nodd —

NODD: What's yer racket, eh? Down 'ere in the dead a' night, what is it?

CHARLES: Nodd —

NODD: It's a conspiracy, ain't it? When two or three are gathered together, charge 'em, it's treason an' you know it —

CHARLES: Nodd, you will make enemies of powerful men —

NODD: Fucked if I care —

CHARLES: I can't save you. Even my dad — my dad who was absolute and had God sitting in his eyeballs — could not save his pals, his bumloves and his vicars — they look at you so darkly, Nodd, take a warning from their looks! (*He goes up to them mockingly.*) Oh, do not hurt my Noddy, he is a slumboy, all cock and prattle, do not murder him, you will make all Southwark weep . . .

UNDY: His Majesty has had a long evening . . .

CHARLES: He thinks I'm tired —

UNDY: Perhaps a carriage —

CHARLES: No, Ralph, you are too kind, you are too generous, he offers me a carriage, such a nice, nice man . . . I do like Ralph . . . (*He turns to go, stops.*) What are you doing here? (*They are silent.*) Well, I can't bring charges, the chief lawyer's here himself!

NODD: Turn the mob out!

CHARLES: The mob — the mob — his touching adulation of the mob —

NODD: My mates —

CHARLES: Oh, Christ, spare us your mates —

NODD: Give over —

CHARLES: He thinks to terrorize you with his mates, the legion of the half cut, don't it touch you, Ralph, with its naivety?

NODD: All right, fuck yourself —

CHARLES: Mobs, no, **show 'em the look that stops their hearts!** (*He leans on the table, intimately.*) You will like this, I know you will, and you Billy, you will love this — (*He turns to* NODD, *who is feeling in a bag.*) **Hurry up, we're waiting!** Give it to Nell, she can handle flesh, Nell, show the gentlemen the way you kiss, there is no kissing like her, you would think all the kissin' I done there was nothing left to be discovered, but there is, there is! (GWYNN *takes the head of* BRADSHAW *from* NODD *and holding it in both hands, kisses the mouth.*) Watch her lip now! Can yer see, Ralph? Do come nearer, and you Mobberley, she has a kiss as long as the coast, oh, she makes yer faint, she does! (*He goes close to* HAMBRO.) Was he ever done like that, I ask yer, Billy, was he, do yer think?

HAMBRO: I don't know who kissed him.

CHARLES: Oh, Billy don't remember who lipped him, Robert, you would know! (PARRY *shakes his head.*) Nobody? And you were peas once in the pod of the Republic! Oh, look at his one eye, the single eyeball does look sad to be rejected, his one eye that says **long cold nights of serious thought.** Scaring, ain't it, Mobb'ley. **The man who thinks us to death!** Show Ralph!

UNDY (*as* GWYNN *moves near him*):   'ullo, Dick, 'ow are yer?

CHARLES: Oh, now, wit! Ralph's mordant wit! Look him in the eye, Ralph, the eye please, fix it . . .

UNDY (*looking*):   Been having late nights again, old son . . .

CHARLES: **No, look at him!**

UNDY: I am looking at him.

CHARLES: I hear he never slept.

UNDY: Well, you can see that.

CHARLES: But worked all nights.

UNDY: So they tell me.

CHARLES: Planning new commonwealths.

UNDY: Very likely . . .

CHARLES: Ever more common. Ever less wealthy.

UNDY: He 'ad some funny ideas . . .

CHARLES: Writing constitutions in the starry night, while moths struck the window . . .

UNDY: Quite . . .

CHARLES: While the rain lashed, plotted the extinction of private property . . .

UNDY: Wouldn't put it past 'im . . .

CHARLES: **Plotted the extinction of you, Ralph!** (*He leans closer, quoting from the 'Harmonia Britannia'.*) 'And there were some called rich, who gathered to themselves the labour and the inventiveness of others, and kept them brutally in place, but these were like a nightmare or bad memory, for in Harmonia there was neither gold nor money, but such things were laughed at as a superstition and a dead weight in the pocket . . . ' There, I know my Bradshaw, banned book but I got him in my library . . . (*He tilts the head up and down.*) Word perfect, ain't I? Yes, he says . . . (*He tosses the head to* NODD.) Stick him back in the bag, he makes their bowels go loose, or Ralph all witty, which is the same thing, same stink, ain't it? Nell, wish the gents goodnight . . .

GWYNN: Ta ta —

HAMBRO (*arising, bowing*):   Sire, good night —

CHARLES: Down poodles, down spaniels!

NODD: Woof, woof!

GWYNN: Ol' buggers, aincha?

CHARLES (*to* GAUKROGER):   Orange or velvet?

GAUKROGER: Whatever you say, Sire —

CHARLES: Oh, you are too accommodating! And me only a

monarch too! (*They go out.* HAMBRO *etc., remain standing, silently. Pause.*)

UNDY: Billy . . .

HAMBRO: I know . . .

UNDY: No, let me say this —

HAMBRO: I know what you're going to say —

UNDY: I still wanna say it —

HAMBRO: If you must —

UNDY: I must. **Why in Christ's name did we bring that back?**

PARRY: Have a drink, Ralph —

UNDY: Fuck the drink —

PARRY (*offering* MONCRIEFF):   Andrew?

UNDY: **Why!**

HAMBRO: I think you know why.

UNDY: **Out — fucking — rageous!**

STREET: Sit down, Ralph . . .

UNDY: **Impert — inence!**

HAMBRO: Ralph, he knows. And that is all that matters.

UNDY: I got my pride!

HAMBRO: **He knows.** (*Pause*) The rest is shrill and squealing. Never mind the squeal. I don't.

ACT TWO

Scene One

Beside the Thames in Essex. DEVONSHIRE *in a cloak, looks out. At a distance, a* FOOTMAN.

DEVONSHIRE: I do feel clean here. I do feel clean. The wind off the estuary. The cockle-women shouting I can't hear. And the low cloud racing, and the grey flat water, the thin surf on the mudbank, really it is better than a marine landscape by Mr. Van Oots and in any case I don't think I like sex. (*Pause. She breathes.*) Oh, this is pure, this is absolute life, I never felt so whole and so completely independent, this is the third letter in a week begging me back and in verse too! All very flattering but really it is pure dick, a woman should never forget a poem is actually dick, should she? I don't believe before Mr. Van Oots anyone went near a beach, you can't smell the seaweed in a painting, can you?

FOOTMAN: **Oi, get back!**

BEGGARS (*throwing themselves before her*): Alms, miss!

DEVONSHIRE: Or the beggars, for that matter . . .

FOOTMAN (*wading in among them*): **Fuck off!**

DEVONSHIRE: You are in pain, I know you are, you don't have to tell me, and I tell you that I am too! Does that sound callous? (*They look at her. She goes towards them.*) To look at me you'd think she knows no pain, now, wouldn't you? I'm sure you say that, privately. Admit you say that.

BEGGARS: No —

DEVONSHIRE: Oh, you do, you do! Her lovely this, her lovely that, compared to us in our rags and shanties, you do, of course you do, you think I have no agonies. But there are pains and pains, aren't there? (*They look blank.*) No? (*They look blank.*) Pains of the mind?

BRADSHAW: Yes.

DEVONSHIRE: Somebody knows! And they are, if anything, worse than the pains of hunger or whatever you are on about, because there is no cure. No, no cure! I have a pain like that. Believe me. Now, hurry off before Sam gets awful — (*She dips in a purse and throws small change about.*) . . . and think of me sometimes, and see the pain is not all on your side, mm?

FOOTMAN: All right, scarper!

BRADSHAW (*not moving*): Tell you about your pain.

FOOTMAN: Fuck off, I said —

BRADSHAW: Go on, let me —

FOOTMAN (*to her face*): **Oi!**

DEVONSHIRE (*turning away*): Don't kick her. I don't own the beach.

FOOTMAN: Above the tidemark —

DEVONSHIRE: Oh, sod that — (*Pause.* FOOTMAN *stands away.*)

BRADSHAW: All my knowledge. Give it to you. All my life.

DEVONSHIRE: Why?

BRADSHAW: Because you're shallow.

DEVONSHIRE: Oh, I am, am I?

BRADSHAW: And a bit cruel with it.

DEVONSHIRE: Do watch it dear, Sam will kick you in the head.

BRADSHAW: Yes. (*Pause*)

DEVONSHIRE: This is my beach and so is everything else that you can see. I am twenty-four and have miscarried seven times. That is wicked, isn't it, of God? Have you miscarried?

BRADSHAW: Yes.

DEVONSHIRE: It is particularly cruel because I care for men. Last week I thought the floor of my body was being bitten out, by rats, by dogs, I thought my whole floor going, have you had that?

BRADSHAW: Yes.

DEVONSHIRE: I cannot keep a child in, absolutely cannot, yet I conceive from a look, what is the matter with God, my womb is only fit for a nun, or is He trying to tell me to be a nun, is that His way, do you think? I will die from one of these drops. I would keep away from dick if I could, but you cannot be as good as I am, looking as I do, and keep away from them, can you? I am trying to appreciate views instead, but he writes so beauti-fully, my rump, my rump, he goes on about, keeps him awake at nights, my whispering hair and so on, I go back tonight, I know all poems are dick but I go back, I will die of him, it is silly but he makes me feel alive. What's your advice? I believe in asking strangers for advice, you cannot trust your friends. I believe in essence all your friends wish you dead. Say yes or no.

BRADSHAW: Yes.

DEVONSHIRE (*turning on her*): You only want to get me killed! (*Pause*) Really, what kind of advice is that? Forty years old, are you, and you say one syllable. Get off my beach. Sam . . . (*She goes to leave.*)

BRADSHAW: **How dare you turn your back, I have given you the education of a lifetime!**

DEVONSHIRE: All you said was yes.

BRADSHAW: Yes was all you asked for.

DEVONSHIRE: I'm not to be taken literally.,

BRADSHAW: I will tell you what yes means, shall I? (*Pause*) Shall I?

DEVONSHIRE: Go on.

BRADSHAW: Yes means no resistance. Yes means going with the current. Yes means lying down when it rains and standing up when it's sunny. Yes urge. Yes womb. Yes power. I lived with a man whose no was in the middle of his heart, whose no kept him thin as a bone and stole the juices from him. No is pain and yes is pleasure, no is man and yes is nature. Yes is old age and no is early death. Yes is laughter, no is torture. I hate no. No is misery and lonely nights. Do you follow or shall I say it again? (*Pause. Then* DEVONSHIRE *unclasps her cloak and lays it over* BRADSHAW's *shoulders.*)

DEVONSHIRE: Take all the cockles off the beach. (*She turns to go.*)

BRADSHAW: Let me be your servant.

DEVONSHIRE: I don't need a servant.

BRADSHAW (*crawling to her feet*): I will give you service of my life's blood though you are the worst bitch in the kingdom and pay me never. Employ me. I'll turn the kitchen spit with my teeth.

DEVONSHIRE: And you think me shallow?

BRADSHAW: Perfection. (*Pause. She looks at* FOOTMAN, *who shakes his head. She smiles.*)

DEVONSHIRE: I live in Blackfriars. (*She goes out, followed by* FOOTMAN, *who is barely offstage when he turns and runs back.*)

FOOTMAN: Yor're no skivvy! I seen you! All you old republicans, six months ago you wouldn't call no geezer master, now look at yer! **I'm the true skivvy! You will kill the trade you bleeders!** Coming! (*He runs off again.* BRADSHAW *is on her knees when* SCROPE *enters.*)

SCROPE: I do not, of the obscene career I've witnessed, care to specify which gave me the most horror, watching old women cheated from behind a bush, or in this instance tucked behind a dune, seeing you fondling the foot of the most callous whore to flounce in daft courts. **Take off that purple badge of shame, please** . . . I do believe I saw Mr. Bradshaw thin and gaunt with pain creep over the water . . . his kind eyes in the candlelight while we planned constitutions and just wars . . .

BRADSHAW: Have a cockle . . .

SCROPE: I believe no woman came nearer to touching saint-liness than you and you — do not eat with your mouth open, I do hate that doglike manner!

BRADSHAW (*opening the cloak*): Come under with me, there's a cruel wind off the water . . .

SCROPE: I was thinking today just where his greatness lay, and it lay in this, that nothing was ever set firmly in his mind, but he would challenge every thought and beat it round his head like a bear set on by dogs, stagger it from corner into corner, was it good, was it proper, the bloody bear pit of his mind! (*He sits beside* BRADSHAW. *She covers him.*) And me . . . it is my misfortune to have served him, who blew out my little candle with his great light . . . when I might have written . . . might have . . . **Lost my chance now!** (*He begins to sob.*)

BRADSHAW: Oh, don't cry for Christ's sake —

SCROPE: I have to! I'm not ashamed of tears!

BRADSHAW: You only cry because you want to impress me.

SCROPE: Rubbish.

BRADSHAW: You do. To show how great your soul is. From now on I am banning crying. You've been snivelling on and off since Norwich.

SCROPE: I've not . . . !

BRADSHAW: A red eye in the wind, some wail coming out the hay at night. Tears are a rebuke, to man or nature. Protests, aren't they? I don't protest, and I'll be happy. See if I ever cry again. (*Suddenly* BALL *bursts out of cover, waving a sword.*)

BALL: You never paid your drink in Roxworth! Took the ale and scarpered! Oh, trail of scrounging and cruel little knocks, I **am entitled to punish in the name of the Stuart. Get over there you!**

SCROPE: Oh God . . . !

BALL: **Over or I cut yer!** (SCROPE *rolls into a ball, away from*
BRADSHAW.) I have hunted you from your bed madam, from
the smell of your sheets I have, show me your face, your thin,
dry lips, show me, you may not leave your domicile if you were
of the rule of antichrist the Commonwealth, you broke the
regulation, did you think I'd let my fancy go? **I am come into my
rights!** (*He swings to* SCROPE.) Stay there you ball of scrawn
and bollock **I am the governor now!** (*He turns back to*
BRADSHAW.) Listen, I have been drinking and not paying
either, but I may do 'cos I suffered, no publican gives me a
cacky look I bust his lip for him, I have been drinking and I love
you, stand up, it offends me to see a woman crouching, is he to
do with you? What is he? Be my darling, I have a thing about
you, you could be as rough as fifty hellbags, I still got a thing for
you, I don't know what my passion's coming to, to be honest
you are nothing to stare after, why am I fixed like this?

BRADSHAW: It happens.

BALL: Fuck, it does, and I shall love you on this shore, or stab
you, I am that bewildered! Let me worship, God, Your eyes are
tired and yet full of secrets, I wrote you a poem, no, I tell a lie, I
wrote thirty, thirty sonnets in one night, there is cavalier art for
you, I was up to dawn and squinting by a candle in the guest-
room of some inn, 'sir, your boots on the boards keep us awake'
cries the publican, 'balls to your kip,' says I, 'I am creating, I am
sonnet mad for Bradshaw!' Read this one, or shall I? (*He takes a
paper from his pocket.*) This is the best, this is the cream, in the
Italian manner, I should bawl it in palazzos but this stinking
beach will do it, shall you read it or shall I?

BRADSHAW: You.

BALL: I am a poor reader —

BRADSHAW: Oh, don't say that —

BALL: All right — (*He swings back to* SCROPE.) **Don't shift or
I'll split your liver!** (*He turns back.*) It goes, I start — Christ,
this beach stinks — I call it — 'A Love Unexpected' — it is
twelve lines in the Tuscan manner — **I don't think I can do it
justice** — notwithstanding that, I — I — it — (*He lets his hand
droop.*) I will fuck you or I shall go mad. You have given me
hell these last ten nights.

BRADSHAW: The poem.

BALL: No, no —

BRADSHAW: Perhaps I —

BALL: No, no, the poem, stuff it — (*He thrusts it back in his
pocket.*) There is a hut over there, go into it —

BRADSHAW: You are going to force me —
BALL: Yes. Quick now.
BRADSHAW: I prefer you read the poem —
BALL: **Look, I am an agent of Charles Stuart, all I do is legal, naught is wrong, see?** (*Pause*) I worship, I bring my poor love to the altar, over there out the wind now . . .
BRADSHAW: God help me to do this . . .
BALL: He will, Christ knows you are perfect to me . . . (*She seems to prepare herself, then goes out. BALL looks round quickly, then follows her. SCROPE staring, quotes from the 'Harmonia Britannia'.*)
SCROPE: 'And there will be love betwixt man and woman of a sort not known yet, founded on freedom of will and desire, so that she shall not be hampered by false modesty nor him by his cult manliness . . . ' (*He shudders with a paroxysm of impotent anger.*) Oh, all you who come after, make your revolution right! (*He takes the book from his pocket and flings it into the mud, weeps. Pause. BALL returns.*)
BALL: It is a funny thing this, and I have never found it otherwise, that I come off so miserable I could weep or join a priesthood. I am off to fish in some pond, have an awful need for some tranquility . . . (*He goes a little way, stops, holds out the poem.*) Will you give her this? I think love would be to come off and be happy . . .

SCROPE *takes the poem. BALL walks off. After a pause, BRADSHAW returns, by a great effort of will she resumes exactly the posture she occupied before his arrival. Pause.*

BRADSHAW: You know, do you, for seven years Bradshaw did not come near me?
SCROPE: How should I know?
BRADSHAW: Well, I tell you. Could not come near me for the power of his thought, his nightmare. So I was untouched.
SCROPE: Oh.
BRADSHAW: So this one licked me. (SCROPE *turns away.*) **Licked me and opened me again.** (*Pause*) And I —
SCROPE: Go, shall we?
BRADSHAW: Felt sorry that he left me so depressed . . . (*Long pause.*)
SCROPE (*bitterly*):   You seem — you take this — very — Oh, I don't know, cowlike, stand up to nothing now, but bend down and so on, no tears or protest, wisdom of compliance and so on,

but — well, I — (*He faces her.*) Suppose I — what if I —

BRADSHAW (*seeing the direction*): Scrope, I don't wish it —

SCROPE: Wish it? What's this wish it? What are wishes, what are tears?

BRADSHAW: I don't —

SCROPE: You don't ? And how do you know I have not also found you beautiful? What of my compulsion? I have slept beside you on trestles and on bales in barns and never once out of respect for him —

BRADSHAW: Him?

SCROPE: Him who was my master, yes, out of respect not once lifted my hand to you, yet any coloured, drunken royalist can take you and —

BRADSHAW: Oh, God . . .

SCROPE: And you regret he did not feel a pleasure! What of me, I have the same thing, don't I —

BRADSHAW: I saw you as a friend, I —

SCROPE: No friend, never! I am a man, too! (*Pause*)

BRADSHAW: I could not keep him off. You I can easily push over . . .

SCROPE: **Well, where's the justice in that!**

BRADSHAW (*standing up to go*): Don't know the word . . .

SCROPE (*grabbing her roughly*): Do it with me, now —

BRADSHAW: Look —

SCROPE: **Must! Must!**

BRADSHAW: You'll only hate me for it —

SCROPE: No —

BRADSHAW: What about your honour —

SCROPE: Never mind it —

BRADSHAW: You know what you'll be like, don't you, it'll be recrimination and —

SCROPE: **Never mind it, I said, never mind!** (*Pause. She turns to him. He buries his face in her breasts.*) Oh, my love, oh!

Scene Two

A garden in London. MILTON *is staring blindly at a rose.* CLEGG *is watching him, with* SCROPE.

CLEGG: I hide Mr. Milton in my garden, though the penalty for concealing him is death, and me, who is court poet, double death of some description. I do this for literature, though I hate his views, though his politics offend me and his poetry upset my gut, I do it in case one day he writes a good thing in adversity. I am a very decent man, especially since I am so minor I will be forgotten quicker than my eyes melt into muck and no one prints my plays. I could happily denounce him out of envy, but I don't, Mr. Milton always knew how to cultivate his enemies, didn't you, John, in case the Commonwealth collapsed? He doesn't answer, but then he is chock-a-block with cunning. This is Mr. Scrope, who is educated, persecuted, and all the rest. He won't answer yet. (*Pause. They wander.*) I am a King's man, and a property man, and a Bishops' man, and everything John hates man, yet I hide him in my roses, I do believe I am the best that England makes, and have tolerance, which is more than John does. I am the author of a tragedy, 'Mayhem in Attica', in which the moral strength of the nation is shown to be inseparably linked to its respect for property. I have shown this to John, who says the Commonwealth was not opposed to property, on the contrary, John has a little bit himself. It is a fine play, but I warrant will be unknown to posterity, unlike John's stuff. I shall be buried in some obscure grave and no one will traipse to visit me, I don't know why I save him from execution, I must be mad, but you see I have my envy under firm control, it was envy brought the Civil War on, though John calls it justice, no, it was envy and it could not last . . .

SCROPE: I'm afraid I am not acquainted with your work, Mr. Clegg . . .

CLEGG: What a surprise! He has not heard of me! You hear that, John?

SCROPE: I have heard of you —

CLEGG: He **has** heard of me! Well, more surprising still, I am heard of! Forget the name, don't waste a useful space inside your memory for such a mediocre talent, there is Mr. Milton there —

SCROPE: Of course I know Mr. Milton —

CLEGG: Oh, you do, do you? Well, fancy, heard of Mr. Milton, John, your luck is in! How well do you know my plays?

SCROPE: I am not a play-going man —

CLEGG: Well, no surprise, there has been a slight dearth of theatre the last twenty years! You shall see 'Mayhem in Attica', I have been promised a production, I cannot say when, but the promise is there, for what a promise is worth, not a lot in the theatre, I assure you, but it exists. (*He grins at* SCROPE.) No, I tease you, don't waste your time on a man whose statue there is no subscription for, dogs will shit on my grave and lovers grapple on it, and none will say 'Here lies Clegg who spared Milton and had a mediocre talent.' No, stay at home and read John. Do you care for roses?

SCROPE: Yes.

CLEGG: I hope I shall not be sent any more of you atheistic wretches to shelter, I am a King's man after all and fought your lot at Worcester, cut a man's arm off and nearly fainted, where were you?

SCROPE: I was at no battles.

CLEGG: No more was John, but then you do well with a pamphlet, do you?

SCROPE: I was Secretary to the Council . . .

CLEGG: Oh, and took down all their evil in a book! I have a garden full of enemies! Am I not the best of men? I dread to think the boot were on the other foot, you would put my eyes out. Want a cordial, John? Look, I wait on him and yet I hate his views. (*He goes out to fetch drinks.* SCROPE *nervously advances to* MILTON, *stops, hesitates.*)

SCROPE: I wonder, sir, if you feel able to elucidate us . . . as to the failure of our struggle . . . (*He ignores this.*) The errors in our calculation and —

MILTON: Shit and God. (*Pause*)

SCROPE: Yes?

MILTON: Man.

SCROPE: Yes?

MILTON: **Shit and God.** (BRADSHAW *enters.*)

BRADSHAW: I had forgot the peeing you do with a child —

SCROPE: Shh!

BRADSHAW: What?

SCROPE: This is Milton.

BRADSHAW: Don't he know a woman pisses?

SCROPE: **No, he doesn't. Please shut up.**

BRADSHAW: He must do, didn't he go to bed with one?

SCROPE: **I beg you don't embarrass me.** (*Pause. She goes to* MILTON, *who has not moved.*)

BRADSHAW: I had a husband sat by you, and hatched a thing or two together, 'De Rerum Magisterium' or something, you would know Latin, on our lawn one summer, side by side in deckchairs with cloud scudding over Suffolk, in the sunshine writing revolution, now I kip in barns or gutters, there's a turn-up for you, your name is a good excuse for knifing and my old man's hanging on Blackfriars, oh, don't look so tragic, you are all right, they don't kill poets —

SCROPE: Our primary task must be — in my estimation — the examination of our errors —

BRADSHAW: Bradshaw left his bed in dead of night — did you do this — grappling for a pencil — mutter, mutter — kicks the pisspot over — wakes the house —

SCROPE: All is not wasted if error can be the educator of the future —

BRADSHAW: Night after night this — I said for all the warmth you bring, you might sleep in your study — and dropped his linen everywhere — are you like that — found items of his underwear on stairs — shitty drawers he could not bring himself to part with —

SCROPE: This is not true —

BRADSHAW: And scratching! You never saw a barmy cat more vicious with itself, could bleed sometimes from some raw eczema itch — here — behind the ear — look — mad fingers — **are you watching!**

SCROPE: **This is John Milton, you bitch.** (*Pause. She looks at* MILTON.)

BRADSHAW: Put your fingers on me. Read my face. I'm not the woman I was, am I? Tell me I'm not! (*He does not move.*) Thank you. (*Pause. She looks at him.*) I do think it's impossible to respect a genius when he's out of luck. I do. I quailed before you once, couldn't bring myself to speak — not that Bradshaw wanted me to , did he — just cart the sandwiches this way and that — but really, you made me tremble, and now you move me so little I could — (*With a sudden inspiration, she slaps his face.*)

MILTON: **Aaaggghhh!**

CLEGG (*returning with a tray*): Oh, don't do that . . .

MILTON: **Aaaggghhh!**

SCROPE (*to* BRADSHAW): **I hate you for that!**

BRADSHAW (*in delight*): No, look —

SCROPE: **Hate you for that!**

BRADSHAW: See what I did!

SCROPE: **Ugly! Ugly!**

MILTON: **Aaaggghhh!**

CLEGG: I always said, you need not fight the rebels, just lock

them in a chamber and they will die of arguing within a
week —

SCROPE: **Ugly! Ugly!**

CLEGG: Have a cordial . . .

BRADSHAW (*going to* MILTON):   Oh, don't cry. I didn't hurt
you —

SCROPE: **Hurt she says!**

BRADSHAW (*turning to him*):   I didn't! (*And to* MILTON.)
Listen, if you knew how it mattered I could do that! You don't,
do you? You have no idea! I feel so grateful I could slap you
again! (*To* SCROPE.) **Don't worry I shan't!** (*To* MILTON.) Try
to understand me. I have broken myself into pieces to do
this . . .

MILTON: I do not like women.

BRADSHAW: No, of course . . . (*Pause. She looks at*
CLEGG.) Find Scrope some little task. He will copy out your
Latin, and feel his honour is all safe. And when the shout dies
down, get him in some college —

SCROPE: **Do not dare to intercede for me!** (*Pause. She turns to
him.*)

BRADSHAW: Good bye. (*She holds out a hand.*)

SCROPE: I will not shake your hand.

BRADSHAW (*fondly*):   Oh, my little lover —

SCROPE: **Do not say that, please!** (*Pause. She goes out.*)

MILTON: She slapped my face because her heart is broken. I
find that comprehensible. When the war is won, wage war on
the victors. Every civil war must be the parent of another.
Those given laurels praise then execute. And their executioners, when the time comes, execute them too. Any amount
of war a man will take, will acquiesce in his own destruction
even, provided that he knows the change takes place. That is
the God in him. But if after the first war, you only heap praise
on the victors, they will make themselves your masters, even
ape the first oppressor and invite him back. Any amount of
power a man will take, provided we permit it. That is the shit in
him. Next time, should we start there must be no finish, or we
shall slap one another's faces in the gardens of our enemies . . .

Scene Three

A gate in Blackfriars. BRADSHAW *is looking up at something black and shapeless on a spike. Long pause. She conquers herself.*

BRADSHAW: I was deceived. Bradshaw was an African. I never stripped in daylight, nor him either. How was I to know he was an African? **No wonder we had revolution, the Moors had got into our beds.** I can't think why there's flesh on it, the birds here are so finicky. **What's the matter, isn't the meat good enough for you?** (*A soldier appears.*) **That is perfectly good man, you fussy buggers!**
SHADE: Now, then.
BRADSHAW: Why is he black?
SHADE: Sunshine, ain't it?
BRADSHAW: It's a bit well done for me, but never mind. I can find a use for it, get it down, ducks.
SHADE: You wouldn't be the fuss to ask . . .
BRADSHAW: Well, no, there is a wicked shortage of cagmag, isn't there? People will use anything to make a stew. And they call this a restoration! A restoration of what, starvation? **Who said that!** (*She pretends to look behind her.*) Come on, give us it, he was my husband.
SHADE: And I'm Father Christmas.
BRADSHAW: What do you expect, the cock to rise? Look, I have the other quarters in the bag — (*She opens a large bag.*)
SHADE: Oh, fuckin' 'ell . . .
BRADSHAW: Nip up and get it, there's a love. They were so good to me at Moorgate, they even wrapped it up, like butchers —
SHADE (*moving her on*):   Come on, darling, get along —
BRADSHAW: Don't hustle me —
SHADE: Move, then —
BRADSHAW: Who owns the pavement —
SHADE: I do —
BRADSHAW: Get it for me — listen — **Who are you shoving — will somebody witness this!**
SHADE: You barmy bitch —
BRADSHAW: **Somebody witness this!** — (*She is pushed to the ground. The* SOLDIER *walks off.* BRADSHAW *remains on her knees.* DEVONSHIRE *appears, with the* FOOTMAN. *She looks at her.*)

DEVONSHIRE: I was shagged. You were shagged. I am pregnant. You are pregnant. I do not know the father, and I warrant, no more do you. It is a shambles being a woman. I would chuck it all up if I met a doctor who could do the trick. (*She starts to go.*)

BRADSHAW: Use me.

DEVONSHIRE: How, dear? I have no need of a skivvy.

BRADSHAW: I have a lifetime's cunning.

DEVONSHIRE: You were not cunning enough to keep someone's cock out of your purse.

BRADSHAW: Give me one month as your housekeeper, and I will save you my wages by cutting the rest.

DEVONSHIRE: You could not pay them less than me. They'd scarper.

BRADSHAW: People will always go beyond the point they say they stick at. I will bring you change on payday, watch.

DEVONSHIRE: You are certainly persistent.

BRADSHAW: I will manage servants as only one who's grovelled knows how to. A duchess really has no idea how to use a servant. Even her blows are full of charity. Trust me. (*Pause. DEVONSHIRE scrutinizes her.*)

DEVONSHIRE: If you give birth I will not have it on the premises. I hate the sound, you see.

BRADSHAW: If I'm lucky it 'll die.

DEVONSHIRE: And take you with it, darling.

BRADSHAW: Chuck me on the dungheap if it do.

DEVONSHIRE: You have what I most appreciate in servants, a complete lack of self esteem. Follow us, and when we reach home, kick someone out an attic. (*She turns to go.*) What's in the bag?

BRADSHAW: Only a few bits.

DEVONSHIRE: You're not fond of possessions?

BRADSHAW: No.

DEVONSHIRE: I like my servants very Christian, who see the world as futile tinsel. Otherwise they're nicking. Sam, take her bag. (*DEVONSHIRE walks off.*)

FOOTMAN: You cut my wage like fuck, darling. I am a sodding Christmas tree, dangling with grandads and crippled kids.

BRADSHAW: Make it up from your subordinates.

FOOTMAN: Like fuck I —

BRADSHAW: Sam, be realistic.

FOOTMAN: **I ain't Sam to you**.

BRADSHAW: Or find another situation. I am the bitch now,

and you're only pussy. Find a mouse to torture. (*She goes out, watched by* SHADE *and the* FOOTMAN. BALL *enters, with a bottle.*)

BALL: Quick, pink bum, or I'll crack your arse . . . (FOOTMAN *takes up the bag and goes.*) Oh, this is a country for shit lickers now. There is more lace than dinner. **Whose dog are you!**

SHADE: Stuff it, Andy.

BALL: Stuff yerself, I'm pissed on misery.

SHADE: Nothin' new.

BALL: Nothin' new, nothin' new! Oh, you skinny little shivering hound, lock yer teeth for Christ's sake, I crave a decent conversation, even the conversation has deteriorated since I came back —

SHADE: Oh, yeah —

BALL: **It has, you spunk, it has!** And half the soldiers are in spectacles, some manhood has vanished —

SHADE: Oh, yeah —

BALL: **Foreskin it has!**

SHADE (*turning to go*): Go under the bridge and have a kip with all the other pissed ol' cavaliers, I got a job to do —

BALL: **They have withdrawn our certificates!**

SHADE: I know, mate.

BALL: **I am no longer a King's man, what of that!** No, it is a weird thing but I loved this fucking nation, and what is it —

SHADE: Good question —

BALL: **Come 'ere I said what is it!**

SHADE (*stops*): What?

BALL: The nation, you tit hair, what is it? Is it hills? Is it rivers? Is it scenery? You answer me.

SHADE: Buggered if I —

BALL: You answer me! Because it can't be people, can it? It can't be you. Because I wouldn't raise a fart for you. They have gone off, they have, I mean just look at **you** —

SHADE: Yer pissed, mate —

BALL: I am pissed, but I can look at you, and really you are a shambles of an English man, I say that — no offence intended — but to my mind you are not a man at all, you are something — (*He waves his hand vaguely.*) altogether — (SHADE *goes to leave.*) **I lost some lovely comrades in the war you cunt!** (SHADE *stops again.*) The nation, you see, is going down. Got to save the King, see? **Cut the gangrene out**.

SHADE (*nodding at him*): Okay, mate . . .

BALL (*suddenly tossing his bottle at the spike*):   Oh, you bleeders, where's my race?

*The bottle strikes the spike and dislodges the trunk. It has barely
touched the ground before BRADSHAW appears, issuing a fine
scream. She scoops up the remains and runs off with them. SHADE
makes a futile gesture of resistance.*

SHADE: Hey — Hey —
BALL: Hey he says! **Oh, you great English bastard.** Hey, he
says! (*He jeers.*)

Scene Four

A banquet. Guests, music, a wedding cake.

DEVONSHIRE: I do not want a husband.
CHARLES: No, but baby wants a dad.
DEVONSHIRE: You are the dad.
CHARLES: Oh, you'd believe any old rumour! I must say I can
imagine nothing nicer than you and Hambro locked together in
the bed. It takes the edge off my misery to inflict him with a
bitch like you . . .
DEVONSHIRE: I hate you, Charles.
CHARLES: No, it's only passion back to front . . .
NODD (*passing*):   Cheer up, darlin', Charlie 'll still slip yer one,
won't yer, Charlie, if yer good. Chin up!
DEVONSHIRE: If there is one thing I hate above all others it is
cheerful cockneys. Go into a corner and get pissed.
HAMPSHIRE: Gloria, you were never more beautiful.
DEVONSHIRE: Oh, don't be a silly old liar. (*She turns to*
CHARLES.) Charlie, call it off.
CHARLES: Who says I ain't a mighty mover of destinies, fling-
ing coldbummed bankers down with Lady Roaring Hips? These
old republicans will fuck shears for an earldom.
DEVONSHIRE: Call it off.
CHARLES: I could lie beneath the mattress just to hear old
Hambro grieve. Will he shove sovereigns up your slit? Tell all,
won't you, and call the infant Ajax, you must admire its tena-

city, no prod or quinine's shaken it, nor baths in boiling cowshit, I believe.

DEVONSHIRE: I hate its guts.

CHARLES: No!

DEVONSHIRE: I tell you I do.

CHARLES: Wait till it's grinning at your tits.

DEVONSHIRE: I will pinch its little pink bum.

CHARLES (*drifting away*): Oh blimey, Gloria, what pleases you?

BRADSHAW: Don't be angry with me. You look beautiful.

DEVONSHIRE: I don't want Hambro touching me. Has he promised? Has he sworn?

BRADSHAW: I have his assurance.

DEVONSHIRE: Good.

BRADSHAW: You are so perfect I could kiss you myself.

DEVONSHIRE: Do, then. (BRADSHAW *kisses her.*) Do you like me very much?

BRADSHAW: Yes.

DEVONSHIRE: I sometimes think I am unloved.

BRADSHAW: How could you?

DEVONSHIRE: And my life stinks.

BRADSHAW: Never.

DEVONSHIRE: I have no bloody friend but you. It is my day and I never felt more like hanging myself.

BRADSHAW: Wedding nerves. I wanted to hang myself.

DEVONSHIRE: Really? Promise me!

BRADSHAW: Oh, yes, hanging wasn't half of it! And you are so lucky, he promises he will not pester you. This is a wedding you can really enjoy!

CLEGG (*passing*): Her radiance doth dim the stars,
Come Hymen, banish Mars,
In splendid nuptial forget our wars,
Oh, lucky fate of Royal Whores!

DEVONSHIRE: Sam, one of these days, I shall have you daggered in an alley . . . (*She turns, moves off.*)

CLEGG (*to* BRADSHAW): Well, ain't you done well, miss, for an old red?

BRADSHAW: I get by, Mr. Clegg, thank you.

CLEGG: Visit me again, and we'll piss over courts and all this lark, I got some lovely satires.

BRADSHAW: No.

CLEGG: Go on, I love your belly.

BRADSHAW: Very well. I have to be consistent.

CLEGG: Good. (*As he moves off.*) By the way, they took your Mr. Scrope for calling God a liar. But Milton's safe. (*He advances towards* HAMBRO *who enters.*)
Bring gold, bring silver to her feet,
Dives of our day we humbly greet!

CHARLES (*greeting* HAMBRO *and his best man,* McCONOCHIE): Oh, Billy, ain't you smart and passionate! Let me kiss your hungry face! (*He embraces him.*) Be sweet to my daughter — **and don't sodomize her you floppy catkin** — I call her my daugthter, well, why not, **I'm giving her away, ain't I?** Yer earldom don't give access to all her crevices — (*He sees* McCONOCHIE.) Oh, and you brought your best-man! Clegg, got some verses for my favourite Scot?

McCONOCHIE (*bowing*):   Good day, sir.

CHARLES: Sam, lines for the great specialist!

CLEGG: Willingly — only — off the top of my head, I didn't come prepared —

NODD: Ain't that what yer paid for?

CLEGG (*with aplomb*):   Where should we be,
                    If from Dundee,
                    Had not appeared this prodigy?
                    (*Cheers and applause.*)
                    To banish drips from sickly cocks,
                    McConochie, we kiss thy socks!
                    (*Boos and applause.*)
Top of my head, I said, didn't I!

McCONOCHIE: Sir, I am deeply honoured by yer verse . . .

CHARLES: McConochie knows the pattern of our underneaths like a general knows a map of the terrain, don't you, know our **ins and outs?** No court in Europe's got the like of him. **Thank the prodigy, Ted!**

HAMPSHIRE: I do thank him —

CHARLES: No, thank him properly, down on yer knees —

McCONOCHIE: Noo, noo, there is noo need —

HAMPSHIRE (*kneeling*):   I thank him, I thank him —

CHARLES: **What is this rumour they want McConochie in Hanover!**

McCONOCHIE: Oh, it's no a temptation to me, I —

CHARLES: **I shall have you in chains first!** (*He turns away.*) Oh, Gloria hangs back, sweet virgin, hurry to your husband's side! It brings tears to your eyes, don't it, I do think there is no better union than beauty and success! (*He draws her by the hand.*) I've seen weddings where the couple was both beautiful, no, rubbish, this is the **raw old union of gain and expediency!**

HAMBRO: She moves with the grace of ten heifers . . .

CLEGG: They come like angels out the cloud,
Breathless meeting of the shy and proud,
In aristocracy unite the nation,
Flesh and gold's infatuation!

The couple offer a dry kiss. Applause.

PONTING: Speech! Speech!

CHARLES: Nodd! Fetch it! Fetch my present!

McCONOCHIE: I call upon the Right Honourable, Sir William Hambro!

CHARLES: Oh, Gloria, do smile you bitch!

PONTING: Her uncle swears she is a virgin!

SOUTHWARK: Billy, I can hear a baby crying!

CHARLES: Yer speech! Yer speech!

SOUTHWARK: Wah, wah, wah! Wah, wah!

HAMBRO (*staggering*):   I hate this — cock out — big balled — shagging lot —

PONTING: Christ, Hambro's pissed —

HAMBRO: I hope they all die of burst livers in some **snobby brawl!** Knocked down in some — vomit bucket — (*Cheers and abuse.*) Die like — bullocks rolling in the gore — eyes wild and — out of focus —

SOUTHWARK: Billy, watcha on about?

HAMBRO: **I'm speakin, aren't I?** Their old shag history going past their eyes — and dirty boots —

PONTING: Shuddup! (*Something is thrown.*)

HAMBRO: And dirty boots — going in — and in —

SOUTHWARK: Yer pissin' down yer leg, banker!

HAMBRO: **Dirty life and dirty death!** (*Roars of abuse.*) **I hate big arsed men who live like cattle!** (*Roars*)

CHARLES: Billy's language comes out like the old red agitators, no wonder he don't drink too much . . .

HAMBRO: **I like my life —**

HAMPSHIRE: Yer like to poke where yer mates have been —

HAMBRO: **No, you silly bugger, do you think I'm mocked?**

PONTING: I can hear a baby!

HAMBRO: **Oh, you great bullock, do you think I'm mocked by that? You aren't in your time and I am, see?** All that happens is as I want it, and everything suits me!

McCONOCHIE: I think we cud move on now —

HAMBRO: **Every day I pick up the paper I shall say 'Good', see?** The smoothness of my time. My life without rage, **see?** (*He collapses into his chair as* NODD *brings in a large, wrapped object.*)

CLEGG: This gift to you from he who reigns,
Reminder of old times and gains,
The spirit of lost dreams retrieves,
The muse of History giggles in her sleeve!

DEVONSHIRE: This is something horrible.

CHARLES: Nobody say that Billy made it easy, he did not! While others passed him, spraying brilliance, Billy crawled, fly on the pane, silent progress of his sticky feet, the rockets fell back past him, spent, but did not shake him. The Fly in History. Nobody laugh at flies.

DEVONSHIRE: What is this?

CHARLES: Open it.

DEVONSHIRE: I don't want to —

CHARLES: Open it!

HAMBRO *takes the string from* DEVONSHIRE, *and pulls it. The wrapping falls from the figure of* SCROPE, *his lips cut off, around his neck a massive copy of 'Harmonia Britannia'*

DEVONSHIRE: Is that supposed to be funny?

CHARLES: Funny? I did not say it was funny. I said it was a present. Does a present have to be funny? It is a **sad present.** I have invented the **sad present.** Thank me, Billy, for inviting an old colleague whose name was somehow left off the list of guests. (*He turns to* SCROPE.) If you can't come as a guest, you shall come as a present. He was caught saying God did not exist. **He does exists, he's over there!** (*He looks at* HAMBRO.) Billy, do welcome him, he is the most famous note-taker in history. There will be girls with books of shorthand on their knees and ignorant, oh, ignorant, of what a great forebear they had in him! **This was England's greatest secretary,** wrote down in his copperplate **off with my old dad's head.** Remember, Billy, you was there . . . ?

DEVONSHIRE: Get him out.

CHARLES (*to* SCROPE):   Speak, can you? Tell us what you know of the filthy act of History? (*He cups his hand to hear.* SCROPE *hesitates.*) Mmm? Can't hear yer, mm?

SCROPE: a — a — er — ee —

CHARLES: Mmm?

SCROPE: Arr — the —

CHARLES: Come again?

SCROPE: **Long liff the commonwealth ohh equals!**

CHARLES: Oh, no, that's old stuff, ain't it —

SCROPE: **Down wiff the sin ohh money and monarchy!**

CHARLES: Oh, dear, I never asked him to say this!

SCROPE: **Long liff the atheist re — hub — lic!**

CHARLES: Stop spoiling Billy's banquet with all this old stuff, really, it was a youthful abberation, wasn't it, **this old red muck!**

SCROPE (*in tears and frustration*):   **The sin off kings — disease of riches —**

BRADSHAW: Shut up.

SCROPE (*seeing her*):   **Aaaggghhheddaway!**

BRADSHAW: Just shut up.

SCROPE (*recoiling from her*):   **Aaaggghhhheddaway!**

BRADSHAW: What do you think you've got there, dignity? Really, I have seen some idiots, crashing about the doorposts of time and history, shouting out their old abuse, but you, what have you discovered, your **manhood** or something? You absurd thing, you should be nailed to a board. **Shut up,** (*She looks around.*) Excuse me. No. I'm perfectly all right. Well, I am, aren't I? Look, I have clean drawers on, courtesy of madam, starched underthings. And lips. Not rose bud. Not what they were, of course, but lips. (*She curtsies, turns away.*)

CHARLES: Kiss the bride, then, Billy —

BRADSHAW: Lips . . .

CLEGG: Of such unions as this,
          Shall spring the race none can resist,
          Throughout the globe, all under heaven,
          Raise the cry, the Earl of Devon!

ALL (*toasting*):   The Earl of Devon!

HAMBRO: It's my thing in her belly. (*Pause. He looks around.*) It's my thing in her belly.

Pause. Then CHARLES *leads a cheer.* HAMBRO *smiles. Suddenly one of the servants flings off his wig and is revealed as* BALL. *He rushes forward and stabs* HAMBRO *in the back.* HAMBRO *falls across the table.*

BALL: **I save the King! I save the King! Cavaliers and Stuarts, Ho!** (*Uproar.* BALL *climbs on the table.*) **I stand in blood of rubbish! Church and King! Parliament is abolished, we have struck for England and the monarchy. Keep still there, play the** anthem, send out messengers to every village, ring the bells! (*Nobody moves.*) Ring the bells, then! (*There is no response.*) Charles Stuart, be a King! (CHARLES *doesn't move.*) England calls you! Be a King! (*Silence*) Come on, then. (*Pause*) Come on, I have liberated yer. (*Pause*) Oh, come on, be a fucking monarchist. (*There is no response.* BALL *lets out a terrible wail.*)

CHARLES: Drink my health and get off the table. (BALL *sways, closing his eyes, he drops the dagger. Men close round him and haul him off the table.*)

DEVONSHIRE: Oh, God! Susan! I miscarry, oh!

A second uproar. BALL *is hauled out.* CHARLES *sweeps from the room, followed by the assembly, who remove* HAMBRO's *body.*

DEVONSHIRE (*as she is borne away*): Susan! (BRADSHAW *does not move. She finds herself alone in the room but for* McCONOCHIE. *He stares at her.*)

McCONOCHIE: A'm dooin' verry well here, as ye can see . . . (*Pause*) Ye ken A noo relish the idea o' discovery . . . (*Pause*) It's noo more than a — (*Suddenly* BRADSHAW *flings herself into his arms, crushing him in an embrace.*) A'd be grateful therefore, if ye — (*She sobs.*) Wuld ye be so kind as — (*She kisses him.*) A have noo desire to be — (*Suddenly he dissolves into tears.*) Noo — noo — noo —

BRADSHAW: Shh . . .

McCONOCHIE: A canna — canna —

BRADSHAW: Shh . . .

McCONOCHIE: A want a muther, A want a muther!

BRADSHAW: You mustn't, no —

McCONOCHIE: A do! A do!

BRADSHAW: You must not weaken, you must not weaken — (*She weakens herself, kissing him.*)

McCONOCHIE: A hate this place . . .

CHARLES *enters, unaware of them.* BRADSHAW *puts her hand over* McCONOCHIE's *mouth, pushes him off.* CHARLES *holds up* BRADSHAW's *head in his hands.*

CHARLES: Oh, Billy, we are standing in your blood . . . (*He kneels by it.*) Drink, Dick, at the puddle of yer enemies . . . (*He holds the head to the blood. He begins to weep, then to laugh.*)

This ain't remorse, only when I'm depressed it looks like
it . . . (BRADSHAW *makes a movement.* CHARLES *turns.*)
Who's that!
BRADSHAW: Me . . .
CHARLES: The cavalier, he thought he stabbed for me . . . he
loved something I'm only pretending . . . (*He goes towards her.*
BRADSHAW *winces at the sight of the head, recoils a moment.*)
Don't be like Gloria . . . if you listen to me I'll give you a bit of
Surrey . . . I am terribly cold, hold my fingers in your lap
. . . (*She takes his hand. They sit on the floor.*) Have you a child
there? I have no children I dare acknowledge, the Queen's
womb's like a walnut, I felt it with my tip once, have you heard I
got a melancholy character?
BRADSHAW: Yes . . .
CHARLES: So I never know if I am talking sense or it's the
membranes shifting, there must be some truth, mustn't there, or
is it all biology? I don't think anybody cares whether monarchs
live or die now —
BRADSHAW (*recovering*):   Oh, don't say that —
CHARLES: No, no, don't be shallow, don't makes soft replies,
the cavalier, he knew after my dad there would be no English
monarch would do anything but tickle crowds for bankers, I
looked in that man's eyes and I was all humiliation, may I touch
your belly? It's round as a football. I think a woman in late life
and pregnant is a precious sight, look, the light is going , say no
if you want to, I am sick of forcing women . . . (*She strokes his
head.*) Pity me, will you? I make you very gently, I am no
rocking billy, overlook my shallowness if I say that I love you,
but I do now, you kind woman . . .

CHARLES *falls asleep on her. With infinite caution,* BRADSHAW
*extricates herself, covers the sleeping figure with a cloak. She is
about to pick up the head when she is aware of* McCONOCHIE
*looking at her. He seems to shudder, then turns away in disgust,
and slowly walks off.* BRADSHAW *takes up the head, covers it
and is about to leave when the sound of jangling keys in heard. The*
FOOTMAN, *now a janitor, appears.*

FOOTMAN: Lockin' up. (*Looking away,* BRADSHAW
attempts to pass.) Oi. (*She stops.*) For six months I 'ave 'ad no
work, you cow. (*She looks at him. Suddenly, he strikes her
violently.* BRADSHAW *forces her hand to her mouth to prevent
a cry. He forces her to the ground and beats her. She utters no*

sound. He finishes, jangling the key.) Lockin' up.
(BRADSHAW *staggers out.*)

Scene Five

The garden in Suffolk. CROPPER *is standing in an apron.*
BRADSHAW *enters carrying a sleeping baby in her arms. She
leads, by a rope, the broken figure of* BALL, *who himself is
carrying the bag of remains. They halt.*

BRADSHAW: What have they done to my house?
CROPPER: Burned it. (*Pause. She looks at* BALL.) Who is
that?
BRADSHAW: My husband. (*She shrugs.*) He wasn't always
like that, but they put him on a rack. Well, they had to find out,
didn't they, if he was a conspiracy? He was a conspiracy, but a
conspiracy of one. In some ways I prefer him now. He was
awfully — boisterous — before. I came here because —
because there is nowhere to go in the end, but where you came
from, is there?
CROPPER (*going to* BALL):   Welcome. Would you care for a
drink?
BRADSHAW: They had his tongue out, by special order of the
King. It was very good of him, the magistrates were out to get
him chopped. I mean, he killed a banker. All the bankers were
. . . frothing . . . you can imagine . . .
CROPPER: Forgive me if I —
BRADSHAW: Yes —
CROPPER: If I — rather hate you for a minute —
BRADSHAW: Yes —
CROPPER: To go away and then —
BRADSHAW: Come back —
CROPPER: As if —
BRADSHAW: Absolutely, yes — do get him a drink, having
no tongue his mouth gets all — (CROPPER *goes out.*
BRADSHAW *goes to fetch the bag off* BALL, *who makes a
clumsy grab for her.*) Yes . . . yes . . . (*She laughs, he grunts.*
CROPPER *reappears with a glass. She watches, uneasy.*) Oh,
don't be frightened, it's me he loves. (*She gives him the water.*

BRADSHAW *drops the bag down.*) I brought Bradshaw back.
(CROPPER *turns in horror. Pause.*) —

CROPPER: You —

BRADSHAW: In the bag. The dad. (*Pause*) Well, look at it.
(CROPPER *shakes her head.*) Oh, listen, I have been put to
some little inconvenience retrieving that — (*She shakes it again.*)
Look at it, then! (*Pause.* CROPPER *concedes, looks in the bag.
Closes it again.*)

CROPPER: It is not him.

BRADSHAW: Who is it then?

CROPPER: It is not —

BRADSHAW: It's not? It is! Don't tell me I don't know my
own —

CROPPER: It's bones !

BRADSHAW: Yes, of course it's bones, what did you expect?
It's bones, obviously. Naturally, it's bones —

CROPPER: And he —

BRADSHAW: What's wrong with bones? (*Pause*)

CROPPER: I learned Latin.

BRADSHAW: Latin. What's that?

CROPPER: I read his book. By night. Run my dirty finger
through the words. Mice in the skirting. Husband groaning in
his kip. The sentence coming to me like a birth in the pale
morning. I am translating it. 'Harmonia Britannia'. I am printing
it. (*Pause*)

BRADSHAW: Oh, look, it's raining . . .

CROPPER: Quickly, come to the house. (*Thunder.*
BRADSHAW *doesn't move.*) Give me the child, quick . . . !

BRADSHAW *does not move.* CROPPER *takes the baby from
her, hurries away. After a few moment* BRADSHAW *goes to*
BALL, *puts her arm round him. She pulls a scarf over his head,
then they go, clasped together, towards the house.*

THE CASTLE
A Triumph

What is Politics, but the absence
of Desire . . . ?

CHARACTERS

STUCLEY	A Knight
BATTER	A Servant
KRAK	An Engineer
SKINNER	A Witch
ANN	A Changed Woman
NAILER	A Priest
CANT	A Villager
HUSH	A Villager
SPONGE	A Villager
HOLIDAY	A Builder
BRAIN	A Builder's Mate
POOL	A Circuit Judge
SOLDIERS	
PRISONERS	
WOMEN	

ACT ONE

Scene One

A Hill. A MAN, *wrapped against the rain, stares into a valley. A* SECOND MAN *enters. He stares at the first.*

BATTER: Thinking, this is a puddle, this is. This is a wet and bone-wrecking corner of Almighty negligence. Thinking, oh, these shifting sheets of dropping damp. Christ, I did wrong to, or Mohammed, is it? Oh, my sun, my date trees, you poor bugger, out of hot bricked yards and cool mosaics, **You have to be a great hairy English bastard to wear this! Oi!** (*He tears open his clothing, exposing his chest to the weather.*) England, your great frozen paw, Oi! (*The other has not moved.*) You are looking on my meadow. On my meadow which — (*He stares in disbelief.*) **No cunt has mown!** (*He turns to* ANOTHER *off.*) Have you seen this!

STUCLEY *enters, follows the direction of his finger.*

STUCLEY: Oh, the faithless bastards . . .
BATTER: Fallow, every fucking thing!
STUCLEY: Oh, the disloyal bastards . . .
BATTER: Not one in cultivation!
STUCLEY: My first glimpse and —
BATTER: And the wood not coppiced!
STUCLEY: My first glimpse and —
BATTER: And the pond not cleared, and no bugger with the cattle!
STUCLEY: **All bastard rotten!** (*He turns to* BATTER.) Ask them what they — my territory — what they —
BATTER (*running off*):   Hey!
STUCLEY: They have stripped me of every kind thought by this. Lying in their mess and squirming in the hot straw I

imagine, while we suffered, **I apologize I feel so ashamed!** (*He shakes his head in despair.*) All the good things I told you of this place and we clap eyes on the dead opposite. I'm glad it's raining, good! Piss rain you bastard sky, all I ever said is contradicted, good! All the glowing eyes round camp fires is pure fuck now, I'm lord of pigshit and made a proper fool of . . .

BATTER (*running, shouting*):   **It's us! Stucley and retainers after seven years!**

STUCLEY: You stick yourself in every sordid place, and run your ribs against the stakes, chucking blood down by the panful, and what do they do? They roost! They roost and shit the good estate in your absence, Christ, we will break their hearts for this! What are you staring at?

KRAK: I am looking at this hill, which is an arc of pure limestone . . .

STUCLEY: So it is, it is, yes, oh, I am so full of good, why does everything betray me? **Because it is the way of the world! Good!** All tenderness is doomed to ridicule, poetry is lies and mercy only fit for giggling over! **Is my wife dead?** Must be, must be because I love her so, she's dead, it stands to reason, **where is she buried?** What was it, fever? Fever, merciful fever? No, she was banged to death by bandits, **can you find someone or not?**

BATTER: Some filth is coming, I don't know who, some staggering filth, but I wouldn't know my mother after this time, if Christ had gilded her. (*A WOMAN enters.*) Do you know us or not?

CANT: You're Batter.

BATTER: She knows me! And my face ploughed up with scars!

CANT: Done much murder?

STUCLEY: **Done much murder? Done much murder? I'm your Lord you white rag, you!**

CANT: How beautiful you are, you great male things, I would kiss you if you'd let me, or in the bush there something better —

STUCLEY: **What?**

CANT: Oh, come on, we've had old men here, who only move by memory, not great stallion bits like yours, all —

STUCLEY: **What is this!**

CANT: My man's not come back so you do his business for him — here — (*She goes to lift her skirts. STUCLEY knocks her aside with a staggering blow.*)

STUCLEY: I won't be fouled by you, mad bitch, what's happened here, what! I slash your artery for you! (*He draws a knife.*) Down you, in the muck and nettle! (*She screams.*) **My territory!**(*He straddles her.*)

BATTER: **Hey!** (STUCLEY *wounds her, she screams.*)

STUCLEY: My shame, you — **look what you've made me do!** I've — I've — (*He tosses the knife away, wipes his hand.*) To come home and hear vile stuff of that sort is — when I am so clean for my lover is — no homecoming, is it?

KRAK: So much emotion is, I think, perfectly comprehensible, given the exertion of travelling, and all your exaggerated hopes. Some anti-climax is only to be expected.

STUCLEY: Yes. (*He shrugs.*) Yes.

KRAK: The only requirement is the restoration of a little order, the rudiments of organization established, and so on. The garden is a little overgrown, and minds gone wild through lack of discipline. Chaos is only apparent in my experience, like gravel shaken in water abhors the turbulence, and soon asserts itself in perfect order. As for the absence of hospitality, that does not offend me either, but I should like a desk at some stage. (*Pause.* BATTER *stares at him.*)

BATTER: Well, I'll be fucked. (*Pause*) No, I will be. He raddles my brains, he does. He pits his long, dark fingers in my ears and stirs them up. **Give me my brains back, you!** (*He laughs, prods* CANT *with his boot.*) Get up. Buzz down the valley and tell the oh-so-honest English Stucley's back with one mad retainer and a wog who can drawn perfect circles with shut eyes. Run! (*He chases her off.*)

STUCLEY: Wait! (*He looks to* KRAK.) I run to my wife's bedroom. Catch her unprepared and all confusion. Oh, my lord, etcetera, half her plaits undone! Oh, my lord and all — (*He chases off.*) Wait! (*Pause.* KRAK *is about to follow, when* A WOMAN *appears.*)

ANN: My belly's a fist. Went clench on seeing you, went rock. And womb a tumour. All my soft, rigid. What are you doing on my hill?

KRAK (*turning*): Looking. In so far as the mist permits.

ANN: It always rains like this for strangers. Drapes itself in a fine drench, not liking to be spied on. A woman, this country, not arid like your place. Not brazen. Were you captured and brought home to carry trays? (*He looks at her.*) My husband has turned skinny and beautiful. Was a fat puppy when he left. Why was he not slaughtered like the others? Stood around him, did they, taking arrows meant for him? The sole survivor of some mincing scrap? **No one requires you back, tell him**. (KRAK *bows*.)

KRAK: You are the lady of this place, perhaps I might introduce —

ANN: No. Manners are vile and servants worse. Get off my hill. (*He starts to go*.) **This was an ordinary afternoon and now you're here!** (*He goes. A* SECOND WOMAN *enters*.)

SKINNER: Stab him!

ANN: What —

SKINNER: Now! Stab him!

ANN: What —

SKINNER: I will!

ANN: Wait!

SKINNER: Wait, why wait!

ANN: You can't — we haven't — **we haven't discussed this** —

SKINNER: Fuck, he's running!

ANN: Catch him, then —

SKINNER: Can't, can't now, hey! Come and be stabbed! (*Pause*) He's gone into a thicket. (*Pause*)

ANN: I hope that wasn't — I do hope that wasn't — **the moment after which** — the fulcrum of disaster — I hope not.

SKINNER: Miss one moment, twice as hard next time. Miss the next time, ten times as hard the next.

ANN: All right —

SKINNER: Block the trickle before it's a stream, block the stream before it's a river —

ANN: **All right, I said.** Kill him later. What is he, anyway, a quaint slave to cook weird Turkish afters. The damp will do him if we don't.

SKINNER: You called him beautiful. Your husband. Beautiful, you said.

ANN: He was. The bone has made an appearance. (*Pause*) Well, he is. **He is**.

SKINNER: You won't —

ANN: I called him beautiful, I saw his face and it —

SKINNER: Go all cream and butter for his paddle, tell me —

ANN: Simple description of his face —

SKINNER: **I won't allow it.** (*Pause*)

ANN: You go so ugly, in a second, at the bid of thought, so ugly.

SKINNER: I love you, That's what makes me ugly.

ANN: And your eyes shrink to points, and your mouth collapses . . . (*They embrace.* CANT *enters*.)

CANT: Bugger cut me with a dagger, look! (*She exposes a breast.*)

ANN: Where are they?

CANT: In the big 'ouse, going barmy. Stucley's chucked the loom out, picked it up and dropped it in the shit 'eap. Batter's slicin' old men 'ho used to carry 'im round on their backs. Lovely. 'e works the point under their skin an' twists it. They wanna know 'ho made all the babies.

ANN: Nobody told them?

CANT: Too fuckin' true, nobody told 'em. So Stucley goes to the church for consolation and finds it locked an' pigeons shittin' up the belfry. 'e goes screamin' mad and puts 'is foot through all the winders. Only the wog stays still, kneels in the parlour cooking something 'e calls coffee. Look, my tit's bleedin'!

ANN: Tell him I'm here. On the hill, tell him.

CANT: Why ain't she 'ere, 'e says, plaited and fragrant? Plaited an' fragrant! Bugger!

ANN: Tell him. He'll come.

CANT: I'll see what mood 'e's in. An' fuck you if 'e's wavin' daggers, I won't say nothin'. (*She goes to leave, stops.*) Are they stayin'? (*Pause*) I'm only askin'. If they're stayin'? (*Pause, she goes out.*)

SKINNER: First there was the bailiff, and we broke the bailiff. And then there was God, and we broke God. And lastly there was cock, and we broke that, too. Freed the ground, freed religion, freed the body. And went up this hill, standing together naked like the old female pack, growing to eat and not to market, friends to cattle who we milked but never slaughtered, joining the strips and dancing in the commons, the three days' labour that we gave to priests gave instead to the hungry, turned the tithe barn into a hospital and **found cunt beautiful** that we had hidden and suffered shame for, its lovely shapelessness, its colour all miraculous, what they had made dirty or worshipped out of ignorance, do we now —

ANN: No —

SKINNER: Just deliver it —

ANN: No —

SKINNER: Our bodies and our labour up to their groping fingers?

ANN: No. (*Pause*)

SKINNER: I helped your births. And your conceptions. Sat by the bedroom, at the door, while you took the man's thing in you, shuddering with disgust and trying hard to see it only as the mating of dumb cattle —

ANN: It was —

SKINNER: Yes, and I managed. I did manage. And washed you, and parted your hair. I never knew such intimacy, did you? Tell me, all this unity! —

ANN: Never —

SKINNER: And my husband's bones are kicked around the hills of Asia. Husband. The suffocating thing in darkness. Oh, good for wars in foreign places, let them stab away for Christ or Mohammed! And I prayed to everything not one of them would crawl back to this valley, but I was not a good enough witch, was I?

ANN: No . . .

SKINNER: They crossed the world, missed floods and avalanches —

ANN: Loose planks on bridges —

SKINNER: Snake bites —

ANN: Falling trees and plague villages —

SKINNER: Angry parents of raped daughters —

ANN: Barmy tribesmen —

SKINNER: And rancid whores whose cunts dripped instant death, how did they? Europe is a million miles long, isn't it, how did they pick their way back here, **an ant could pass through a bonfire easier!** (ANN *laughs*. SKINNER *looks at her*.) How? (*Pause*)

ANN: Why are you looking at me like that?

SKINNER: How, then?

ANN: I suppose because —

SKINNER: You drew him. (*Pause*)

ANN: What?

SKINNER: Drew him. With your underneath. (*Pause*)

ANN: I do think — if we —

SKINNER: **Down there called to him across the spaces!**

ANN: Look —

SKINNER: **I hate God and nature, they made us violable as bitches!** (ANN *clasps her, as she sobs with anger*. STUCLEY *enters, holding a white garment. Pause*.)

STUCLEY: Put this on, please. (*They look at him*.) I found it in the bottom of a trunk. Do wear it, please. Change in the bushes, as you like this place so much.(*He looks at* SKINNER.) And you, Skinner's widow, clear off.

SKINNER: Don't be the wife to him, don't —

STUCLEY: Get out.

ANN (*to* SKINNER):   Go on. Trust me. Go on. (SKINNER *withdraws*. STUCLEY *still holds out the garment*.)

STUCLEY: Trust you? Why? (*He looks at her*.) You look so — (*Pause*) Trust you? Why? (*Pause*) Imagine what I — if you would condescend to — what I — the riot of my feelings when I look at — (*Pause*) Trust you to do what exactly? (*Pause*) In seven years I have aged twenty. And you, if anything, have grown younger, so we who were never boy and girl exactly have now met in some middling maturity, I have seen your face on tent roofs, don't laugh at me, will you? (*Pause*)

ANN: No.

STUCLEY: That is a ploughman's hag and you — what is it, exactly? (*Pause*) I found the church bunged up with cow and bird dung, the place we married in, really, what — (*Pause*) So I prayed in the nettles. (*Pause*) Very devout picture of young English warrior returning to his domain etcetera get your needle out and make a tapestry why don't you? Or don't you do that any more? (*Pause*) Christ knows what goes on here, you must explain to me over the hot milk at bedtime, everything changes and dreams are bollocks but you can't help dreaming, even knowing a dream is — (*Pause*) It is quite amusing coming back to this I was saying to the Arab every hundred yards I have this little paradise and he went mmm and mmm he knew the sardonic bastard, they are not romantic like us are they, Muslims, and they're right! Please put this on because I —

ANN: No.(*Pause*)

STUCLEY: This wedding thing, you were sixteen years my senior and a widow and I trembled, didn't I, and you said, do not feel you must do anything, but may I kiss you I have always loved your mouth **why won't you put it on**. (*Pause*) So there we were thinking — it is not a desert, actually, it is full of fields and orchards the Holy Land — and some said tell my old lady I was killed and married Arab women or Jewesses, some of them. Fewer were killed than you might think, much fewer, after all we left with fifty and it was tempting, obviously, but I thought she — wrongly it appears — she — (*Pause*) Have children in two continents, most of them. Not me, though. Not in one, alas. (*Pause*) I thought the time had come to — it was meant to be two years, not seven, but you know — or perhaps you don't — how wars go — coming back was worse than anything — what we did in Hungary I would not horrify you with — they got more barmy by the hour. Not me, though. I thought she'll take my bleeding feet in her warm place, she'll lay me down in clean sheets and work warm oils into my skin and food, we'll spend whole days at — but everything is contrary, must be, mustn't it, I who jumped in every pond of murder kept this one thing pure in my head, pictured you half-naked on an English night, your skin which was translucent from one angle and deep-furrowed from another, your odour even which I caught once in the middle of a scrap, do you believe that, even smells are stored, I'm sorry I chucked your loom out of the window, amazing strength comes out of temper, it's half a ton that thing if it's — trust me, what does that mean?

ANN: You've not changed. Thinner, but the same. For all the marching and the stabbing. Whereas quietly, here I have.

STUCLEY (*tossing the garment aside*):   Fuck the garment! Get to bed with me and we'll stir up long forgotten feelings, go down deep to floors of fornication we've not —

ANN: It isn't possible —

STUCLEY: **It is, you lie down and you part yourself**. (*Pause*) They say coarse things, by habit almost. Not me, though, I tried to keep my language wholesome and — not difficult if you have faith —

ANN: You shouldn't have —

STUCLEY: I shouldn't have? What? What shouldn't I?

ANN: Have struggled to be pure.

STUCLEY: No struggle! If you have faith!

ANN: Have kept the perfect husband for me —

STUCLEY: **Why not, because you were not equal?** (*Pause*)

ANN: No. (*Pause. He is suspended between hysteria and dis-belief.*)

STUCLEY: I think when God says — **crush this bastard** — I wish there was a priest here, but there isn't so I offer you my version, you hark to my theology — He really is the most **thoroughgoing of all deities**, no wonder we all bow down to Him, His grasp of pain and pressure is so exquisite and all compre-hending, what human torturer, what miserable nail-wrenching amateur in pain could pit his malevolence against the celestial wit and come out on top, no man I assure you could conceive of so many alleys by which to turn a brain. As if I had not swallowed every vileness conceivable and still stand on two feet, He chooses to hamstring me not by your death — that I had always reckoned possible, that I expected hourly to be splashed in my face, but no, He has me from her own mouth hear my lady has acquiesced in the riot of her cunt! And I have just fought the Holy War on His behalf! Oh, Lord and Master of Cruelty, who has no shred of mercy for thy servants, I worship Thee! (*He kneels, lowering his head to the ground.*) There is no arguing with genius like this, I threw the dagger away, it's in the bushes somewhere or I might have slit you open, but He takes care of everything, He does, oh, praise Thee, praise Thee, now tell me she has children by the very interlopers who greeted me as I climbed my very own steps.

ANN: Yes.

STUCLEY: Yes! Yes! I know the source of our religion! It is that He in His savagery is both excessive and remorseless and to our shrieks both deaf and blind! I could be a bishop. I missed my chance, slicing black men on the banks of the Jordan, silly, that's for sloggers and boys obsessed with weapons, no, the bishops have got their tongues in God's arse and lick up the absolute, that's for me, **pass a bit of purple somebody!** How many bastards, then?

ANN: One and three died.

STUCLEY: And you past forty! Such fertility, the Lord denying even His own ordinances to make me squirm, she will be pupping in her dotage if it hurts me, and I spent enough juice in you to father forty regiments and not one bred, further evidence, if evidence you needed of His mighty genius, bow, bow, Thou who dost not miss a trick! (*He bumps his head on the ground.*) Bow, bow . . . (*He stops, laughing.*) Could be furious. Not me, though. (*He get up.*) I met somebody who put a lock on it. His lady's thing. Had locked it! Really, the barbarism! And got a lance through him at Acre and fell into the sea, and sank, down to the floor of the blue waters, man and single key. Well, you couldn't have two keys, could you! (*He laughs.*) You have to laugh, I do, I have great recourse to laughter, of the demonic variety, I could kill you and no one would bat an eyelid. (*Pause*)

ANN: Don't stay.

STUCLEY: Don't stay?

ANN: No. Be welcome, and pass through.

STUCLEY: One night and then —

ANN: Yes.

STUCLEY: What — in the stable, kip down and —

ANN: Not in the stable.

STUCLEY: Not in the stable? You mean I might —

ANN: Don't, please, become sarcastic, it —

STUCLEY: Inside the house, perhaps, we might just —

ANN: Useless sarcasm, it —

STUCLEY: Under the stairs, and creep away at first light —

ANN: Undermines your honour —

STUCLEY: **What honour you dishevelled and impertinent slag.**
(*Pause*) You see, you make me lose my temper, you make me
abusive, why not stay, it is my home.

ANN: Not now.

STUCLEY: Not now, why not?

ANN: There have been changes.

STUCLEY: I begin to see, but where do you propose we —

ANN: Go on.

STUCLEY: To where?

ANN: The horizon.

STUCLEY: I own the horizon.

ANN: Cross it, then. (*Pause*) I'm cruel, but I do it to be simple.
To cut off hopes cleanly. No tearing wounds, I'm sorry if your
dreams are spoiled but —

STUCLEY: It is perfectly kind of you —

ANN: Not kind —

STUCLEY: Yes, perfectly kind and typically considerate of
you, I do appreciate the instinct but —

ANN: Not kind, I say —

STUCLEY: **Yes!** Down on your knees, now —

ANN: What —

STUCLEY: On your knees, now —

ANN: Are you going to be —

STUCLEY: Down, now —

ANN: Childish and —

STUCLEY: Yes, **I was your child, wasn't I?** (*Pause. He suddenly
weeps. She watches him, then goes to him. He embraces her, then
thrusts her away.*) **Penitence for adultery!** (*He sees a figure off,
calls.*) **Hoi!** Tell me what's gone on, they've abolished the
apology! (*An* OLD MAN *enters.*) They do their sin with such
clear eyes! Are you a thief, or been up in my bedroom? The
more innocent you look, the more sunk in treachery, it stands to
reason! Do you know me?

HUSH: Yes —

STUCLEY: Oh, good, I'm known, **get down then!** It is going to
take — this restoration of authority — a lot of time and bruis-
ing, I can see!

ANN: Don't make him bend.

STUCLEY: Why not, old bugger!

ANN: We're done with bending here.

STUCLEY (*forcing him to the ground*): Done with it? It's nature!

HUSH: Forgive me, forgive me!

STUCLEY: Forgive, what for?

HUSH: Whatever offends you —

STUCLEY: Good! Oh, good! The first wise words since I set foot in my domain! He is not grey for nothing, he has scuttled through his eighty years with sorry on his lips, spewed sorry out for each and every occasion, good! I appreciate you, cunning licker of brute crevices, insinuator of beds and confidences. Kiss my hands and tell me what you did against me. The more extravagant, the more credence I attach to it, promise you.

HUSH: I did not praise you in your absence.

STUCLEY: Oh, that's nothing, you mean you abused me, surely?

HUSH: Abused you, yes.

STUCLEY: Excellent, go on.

ANN: This is disgusting.

STUCLEY: Disgusting? No, he longs for his confession!

HUSH: I did not tend your meadows or your stock —

STUCLEY: You mean you stole them off me?

HUSH: Stole them, yes. I did not pray for your safe return —

STUCLEY: Oh, shit this for a confession, this is the Valley of Wickedness, say you prayed for my slow-dying torture —

HUSH: Yes!

STUCLEY: Daily prayed the devil I would rot —

HUSH: Yes!

STUCLEY: Turned my house into a brothel, my bedroom, whooped in it —

HUSH: Yes —

STUCLEY: Go on, I am confessing for you, you do it!

HUSH: Adultery and fornication —

STUCLEY: On who? On her?

HUSH: On everyone!

ANN: I won't witness this —

STUCLEY (*grabbing her wrist*): Must witness it! (*To* HUSH. Stuck children on her, did you?

HUSH: Yes?

STUCLEY: No, in your words!

HUSH: I lay on her and others naked and did put my seed in them and —

STUCLEY: Oh, rubbish, it's beyond belief. I hate bad lies, lies that fall apart, there's no entertainment in them. Get on your

cracking pins, you tottering old bugger . . . (ANN *helps* HUSH
to his feet.)

HUSH: Thank you.

STUCLEY: Thank me, why?

HUSH: Because the worst thing in age is the respect. The smile
of condescension, and the hush with which the most banal
opinion is received. The old know nothing. Fling them down.
They made the world and they need punishing.

STUCLEY: Good, I've no regrets if half your bones are out of
joint.

HUSH: Me neither.

STUCLEY: I cherish nothing, cherishing's out, and what was
soft in me has liquified into a poison puddle. Not to be fooled.
That's my dream now, **thank you, universe!** (*Pause*) Educated
me. Educated me . . . (*He goes out.*)

ANN: Tell him nothing.

HUSH: I won't.

ANN: Not even thank you or good morning.

HUSH: No.

ANN: He'll kill you if he knows you fathered children on me.
Some vile Turkish torture. Do you want that?

HUSH: No.

ANN: Good. Half the children in this valley are off you.

HUSH: As many as that?

ANN: Yes, so keep your mouth shut.

HUSH: Promise you. (*He starts to go out.*)

ANN: Why do you love your life so much? (*He stops.*) So much
that even dignity gets spewed, and truth kicked into blubber,
and will itself as pliable as a string of gut? You have no appetite
but life itself, I mean breathing and continuing. (*He shrugs.*)
There can't be a man alive with more children and less interest
in the world they grow up in.

HUSH: I never sought my family . . .

ANN: No. You were led to the female and then turned back in
the field again . . . (*He turns to go.*) **If you achieve immortality I
shall be furious.**

Scene Two

Another day. BATTER *carries a desk on his back. He is followed
by an* OLD MAN *carrying paraphernalia.*

BATTER: Down here, you quivering old bum, you walnut bollock, and careful with the precious instruments! (*He lowers the
tools.*) This is the impedimenta of science, which in collusion
with his genius will wring transformation out the dozing landscape. And he is mine, in all his rareness, mine, as if I'd birthed
him, yes, **don't look at me like that,** I am his second mother!
Through me, brute flesh and knuckle, he has existence, who
might be just another husk of wogland, sons of Arabia blowing
in the sand, I saved him, I, who was running head to foot with
Arab gore, kicked back the door and saw him, and he stared
into my eye, my eyes which were — **the only blue** — the rest
being hot gore, and into my only blues his only browns stared
pleadingly . . . imagine it . . .

SPONGE: I can . . .

BATTER: You can . . . you can imagine nothing . . . This was
the middle of Jerusalem where every bastard male or female I
trod by was split and opened up to inquisitive old daylight. I
spared no one. Well, we had been outside in rain and snow for
seven months, there is snow in deserts . . .

SPONGE: I can imagine . . .

BATTER: No one who was not there can imagine anything.
Never say 'I can imagine' again. It's a lie, nobody can. And he
stared into the little lights of what must have been — my kindness — and I stopped, the dagger in my hand tipped this
way . . . and that . . . slippery in my fist. I pondered. **After
eighteen staircases of murder** . . . and of course, because I
pondered, the genius was safe. Funny. Funny that I pondered
when this was the very bugger who designed the fort; the pen
was in his fingers for some lethal innovation. **How many more
dead would that have cost?**

SPONGE: I can't imagine . . .

BATTER: Not that I care about death, not even my own. In
little avenues and parks they fret on death who have so rigor-
ously hid from life — (KRAK *comes in.*) Have you done
murder, genius? (*He goes to him, holds his hands.*) Not with
those hands, no, but that is **shit hypocrisy** — (KRAK *withdraws
from him.*) It is, because the line from a to b — you see, I have
education, too — the linear trapezoid para — fucking —
llelogram is **five hundred corpses long!** No offence to mathematics, no offence. (*Cries off.* STUCLEY *enters dragging a* MAN
by the neck.)

STUCLEY: Found him! Found him! My incumbent priest who
did the wedlock whilst squirming at his celibacy! True or false?

NAILER (*his neck wrenched*):   True!

STUCLEY: The knob beneath the vestment twirling at my vows! It's all here, everything we left is like old ruins underneath the grass! Are we making too much noise? I know you have to concentrate. (KRAK *is leaning on the desk, staring across the valley.*) This man married me, and when I was away, condoned my bitch's filth! I do believe, I do believe this, that human beings left without severity would roll back the ages and be hopping, croaking frogs, clustering thick on the female with the coming of the Spring, and sunk in mud for winter . . . !

KRAK: The castle is not a house. (*They look at him.*) The castle is not a house.

NAILER: No lord's land, we said, and no common land, we said, but every man who lives shall go as he pleases, and we threw the fences down and made a bad word of fence, we called fence blasphemy, the only word we deemed so, all the rest we freed, the words for women's and men's parts we liberated —

BATTER (*to* KRAK):   Come again?

NAILER: And freeing the words we also freed the —

BATTER: Not you. (NAILER *stops. Pause.*)

STUCLEY: What is the castle, then? (KRAK *does not respond.* STUCLEY *turns to* BATTER.) Lock this in God's house and make him wash it spotless and set up God's furniture again.

NAILER (*pulled out*):   God has no furniture.

STUCLEY: No, but the church has! (NAILER *and* BATTER *go out.*) I tell you, the world's here as we left it, just sunk a bit, like the Roman pavement, you scuff it up, you spit, and there's the sun shining out the mosaic, an old god never properly obscured, Mithras waiting for his hour. So with vicars who have gone barmy, there is the old tithe gatherer beneath some weed of fancy patter I bet you . . . (*Pause*) Go on . . . (KRAK *holds out a large paper.*) Has he made a drawing for me? (*He smiles.*) He has . . . (*He looks at* KRAK, *beaming.*) The Great Amazer! (*He takes it, looks at it.*) Which way up is it? (*He turns it round and round.*) I genuflect before the hieroglyphs but what —

KRAK: No place is not watched by another place. (STUCLEY *nods.*) The heights are actually depths.

STUCLEY: Yup.

KRAK: The weak points are actually strong points.

STUCLEY: Yup.

KRAK: The entrances are exits.

STUCLEY: Yes!

KRAK: The doors lead into pits.

STUCLEY: Go on!
KRAK: It resembles a defence but is really an attack.
STUCLEY: Yes —
KRAK: It cannot be destroyed —
STUCLEY: Mmm —
KRAK: Therefore it is a threat —
STUCLEY: Mmm —
KRAK: It will make enemies where there are none —
STUCLEY: You're losing me —
KRAK: It makes war necessary — (STUCLEY *looks at him*.) It is the best thing I have ever done.

STUCLEY's *long stare is interrupted by a racket of construction as a massive framework for a spandrel descends slowly to the floor. On the construction,* BUILDERS *and the master,* HOLIDAY. STUCLEY *goes out.*

HOLIDAY: Oh, Christ, oh, bleeding hell, somebody!
WORKMAN (*calling to someone above*):   Steady, Brian!
HOLIDAY: I never should, I never should, should I? Expose myself to — are we safe? Are we down yet?
WORKMAN: Cast off, Brian!
HOLIDAY (*whose eyes are shut*):   I am in the wrong trade, can I open my eyes, are we —
WORKMAN: Down, Harry!
HOLIDAY: Down, are we? (*He opens his eyes.*) Oh, lovely earth, immobile, stationary thing! (*He kisses it.*) Do you sympathize with my condition? I exaggerate of course, I exaggerate to win the pity of my workmen. It is a good thing to advertize your weakness, it obliges them to demonstrate their manliness. Are you afraid of heights? When I am up I am horrified in case I slip between the boards, and when I'm down afraid some hammer will be dropped and plop through my cranium. I have an eggshell skull and yet I am a builder, that is one of life's perversities. In thirty years I have built two castles and an abbey and this tilt to my head is permanent, I have one eye always on the sky which may at any moment hold my extinction in some falling implement, what is wrong with the women round here, I am actually fond of women, when I did the abbey had some decent conversation with the nuns but this — (*Enter* SKINNER, *draped in flowers.*)
SKINNER: **Old hill says no**.
HOLIDAY: Does it, never 'eard it —

SKINNER: **Rock weeps and stone protests** —

HOLIDAY (*calling off*): Brian, I will 'ave that templet for the blind arch when you're ready —

SKINNER (*turning to* KRAK): Weren't you loved? Some bit of you not nourished? Why are all your things hard things, compasses, nibs and protractors, the little armoury of your drawing board, have you looked at a flower, go on, take one, the superior geometry of the — (*He ignores her.*) **Why don't you look at a flower!**

HOLIDAY (*shouting up*): No, I won't come up there, I 'ave just been up there —

SKINNER (*turning back to* HOLIDAY): The flower — five petals — each petal identical — **Look at the flower, will you, it's got truth in it** — all right, don't look at it, why should I save you, why should I educate you —

HOLIDAY (*still addressing his foreman*): All right, do it your way —

SKINNER: Educate you, oh yes, educate him, look at him —

HOLIDAY: I said —

SKINNER: My breath, my knowledge, really, do you believe I'd — what — on this —

HOLIDAY: I said do it —

SKINNER: Waste my precious — on you — all my struggle through the dark, through clinging — really, on you — does he actually —

HOLIDAY: **I'm sorry, Brian, 'ow can I fucking concentrate!**

SKINNER: **Save you, you are not fit!** (*Pause. He looks at her.*) No, no, no time for it. Educate you and they pile up bricks, love to educate you but — oh, love to, but — look, the footings in already, go back where you came from, quick, this will not be finished, your coat is on the hook, run without stopping even though it hurts your hanging guts, run, I tell you, I know, I am the witch, quick. (*Pause. He stares at her.*) Quick . . . (BATTER *comes in, looks at her. She turns her head to him contemptuously, then flings up her skirts and shows her arse. She walks off.*)

BATTER: Supposed to be a woman. A woman, calls itself.

HOLIDAY: Never saw a nun do that —

BATTER: No, well, you wouldn't —

HOLIDAY: Not in all the —

BATTER: A nun wouldn't, would she? Not a normal nun —

HOLIDAY: Barmy —

BATTER: Barmy, yes —

HOLIDAY: They 'ad their moods, they 'ad their comings-over
as all women do, but — are these towers really going to be
ninety foot above the curtain? I don't complain, every slab is
food and drink to me, but ninety foot? Who are you — it's a
quiet country what I see of it — no, the woman's touched,
surely?

BATTER (*contemplatively*):   Skinner's arse . . .

HOLIDAY: What?

BATTER: He told me how he lay upon that arse, and she kept
stiff as rock, neither moaning nor moving, but rock. So when
the bishop asked for soldiers he was first forward, to get shot of
her with Christ's permission. And found a girl under the olives,
who moved with him and praised him. Well, he assumed so,
they had not a word in common. And he kept on, the difference
in women, the difference in women! But she outlasts him. There
is no justice, is there? (*He turns to* KRAK.) Is there? No
justice?

BRIAN (*entering*):   Michael wants you about the quoins.

HOLIDAY: I will see Michael —

BRIAN: The courses for the quoins, 'e says —

HOLIDAY: Thank you Brian —

BRIAN: Don't tally with the specifications —

HOLIDAY: I will attend to Michael! I will explain to Michael
'ow many courses there are to the quoins —

BRIAN: Okay.

HOLIDAY: I will simplify the already simple drawing which his
eyes are crossing over, but don't 'urry me! When you 'urry, you
forget, and when you forget, that is the moment the dropped
chisel is hastening to its rendezvous with the distracted 'ead. I
will join Michael, but at my own bidding, thank you. (BRIAN
goes out.) This is all new to me. This passion for the circle.
Leaving aside the embrasures and the lintels, there are no
corners. Are none of the walls straight? Perpendicular, yes, but
straight? (KRAK *ignores him.*) Out of curiosity, what was
wrong with square towers? (*Pause*) Just change, is it? Just
novelty? (*Pause. He desists.*) All right, I'm coming! (*He goes
out.* BATTER *watches* KRAK.)

KRAK: Dialogue is not a right, is it? When idiots waylay
geniuses, where is the obligation? (*Pause*) And words, like
buckets, slop with meanings. (*Pause*) To talk, what is that but
the exchange of clumsy approximations, the false endeavour to
share knowledge, the false endeavour to disseminate truths
arrived at in seclusion? (*Pause*) When the majority are, percept-

ibly, incapable of the simplest intellectual discipline, what is the virtue of incessant speech? The whole of life serves to remind us we exist among inert banality. (*Pause*) I only state the obvious. The obvious being the starting point of architecture, as of any other science . . .

BATTER: Very good, but why so big? I don't think even Acre was this big, the citadel, was it? The walls of this you could accommodate the parish in, all to be paid for out of what, I wonder? You have your methods, I expect, but these bitches never cropped for surpluses, and kept the sheep for pets as far as I can see, the wool was hanging off the hedges, paid for out of what, I wonder? (*Pause*) And when they throw open the shutters, where's the sky, they'll say, give us back our fucking sky, they will, won't they? All they'll clap eyes on is masonry and arrow slits, it will blot the old blue out and throw long shadows over them, always at the corner of their eye, kissing or clawing, even in the bedroom looking in, and drunken arses falling out of beer houses will search in vain for corners to piss in not overlooked. Why? (*Pause*) Or don't you spend words on me, perhaps I'm only, what — inert banality? What's that, you bilingual fucker, you have more words in a foreign tongue than I have in English, but then I have the dagger, who speaks volumes when it comes to it, **Inert Banality** I christen it! (*He kisses the blade. Thunder and black.*)

Scene Three

In semi-darkness, the figure of BRIAN *running from the building works. He is followed by* CANT, *pursued by* SKINNER. SKINNER *catches her.*

CANT: **I done nothin'!**

SKINNER: You unravel us! What we knit together you unstitch!

CANT: **I done no wrong, let go you!**

SKINNER: I don't hurt you, do I? Don't struggle and I — you are asking to be — (*She brings* CANT *to the ground.*) There, I do that because you — (*She sees her own clothes are muddied.*) look at me — we slither in their mess — this was all bluebell

once — patience, though, I am listening to you, I am all ears
why you were in the foundations with a brickie —
CANT: Wasn't!
SKINNER: Oh, this is too painful for excuses!
CANT: Well, I wasn't — what you were thinking — wasn't
anyway —
SKINNER: No —
CANT: **Definitely not!**
SKINNER: But while we're on the subject . . . (*Pause*)
CANT: I haven't — you know I haven't — ever really over-
come my — not ever conquered my weakness for — .(*Pause*) It
was easy before the builders come, but there are dozens of these
geezers and they — I gaze at their trousers, honestly I do,
whilst thinking, enemy, enemy! I do gaze so, though hating
myself, obviously . . .
ANN (*entering*): What?
SKINNER: In the footing with a brickie —
CANT: **Only to keep the rain off!**
SKINNER: What? Off what?
ANN: With her it is just — it is a hunger — I don't see what —
SKINNER: Punish her, of course!
ANN: When she is like she is ? What —
SKINNER: Yes!
CANT: **I don't wanna be punished!**
SKINNER: You give her the truth, and she rejects the truth —
CANT: Skinner, I don't want to be —
SKINNER: And rejecting the truth she wrecks herself, and
wrecking herself she wrecks others, and wrecking others —
CANT: Skinner —
SKINNER (*turning on* CANT): They occupy your mind with
that! **We made ourselves when we ditched that!**
ANN: You are too angry —
SKINNER: Angry? Me? What? Mustn't be angry, no, be good,
Skinner, be tolerant, her feelings being somewhat coarse what
do you expect of peasant women, farmworkers ever on their
backs, legs open in the crops, **listen**, we all bring to the world,
inside our skulls, inside our bellies, Christ knows what lumber
from our makers **but**. You do not lie down to the burden, you
toss it off. The whine 'I am made like that' will not wash, will it?
Correct me if I'm wrong, will it? We have done such things here
and they come back and straddle us, where is the strength if we
go up against the walls skirts up and occupied like that? (*Pause*)
I do think, I do think, to understand is not to condone, is it?

(*Pause*) I do feel so alone, do you feel that? (*Pause*) It always
rains here, which we loved once. I love you and I wish we could
just love, but no, this is the test, all love is tested, or else it
cannot know its power . . .

CANT: I'm sorry.

SKINNER: The words, the words go drip, drip, drip . . .

CANT: Said I'm sorry, didn't I! (ANN *indicates she should go.*
CANT *slips away.*)

SKINNER: Where there are builders, there are whores, and
where there are whores, there are criminals, and after the
criminals come the police, the great heap heaving, and what was
peace and simple is dirt and struggle, and where there was a
field to stand up straight in there is loud and frantic city. Stucley
will make a city of this valley, what does he say to you?

ANN: Nothing.

SKINNER: No, nothing, and every day I expected to be stabbed
or stifled, didn't you? What is this waiting for? You have been
here ten minutes and not said you love me. I suspect you
terribly without a shred of evidence, I shall spoil us with it. Is it
because you were happy with him once? You see, I never was,
never with a man, and you so fecund and me horribly
childless —

ANN: Not horribly —

SKINNER: Not horribly, no —

ANN: I don't declare my feelings —

SKINNER: No, you don't —

ANN: Can't be forever declaring feelings, you declare yours,
over and over, but —

SKINNER: Yes —

ANN: It is your way —

SKINNER: Ridiculous way —

ANN: I am not forthcoming with these statements you require,
you have to trust —

SKINNER: Yes —

ANN: Signs, more. (*Pause*)

SKINNER: I do. I do trust signs. (*Pause*) We do not make a
thing of flesh, do we, the love of women is more — they could
eat flesh from off your body, we — no, actually I could eat
yours, I could! Tell me why you love me!

ANN: I don't see that I need, do I, need to —

SKINNER: Oh, come on, yes, you do need to, and I will tell
why I love you, the more they bore into the hill the more we
must talk love, the bond, fasten it tighter! You are very cold this

evening, I am not imagining it, you'll say I'm imagining it, but —

ANN: Yes. (*Pause*)

SKINNER: What, then. (ANN *does not reply.*) They talk of a love-life, don't they? Do you know the phrase 'love-life', as if somehow this thing ran under or beside, as if you stepped from one life to the other, banality to love, love to banality, no, love is in the cooking and the washing and the milking, no matter what, the colour of the love stains everything, I say so anyway, being admittedly of a most peculiar disposition **I would rather you were dead than took a step or shuffle back from me.** Dead, and I would do it. There I go, **what is it you look so distant** .

ANN: I think you are — obsessive. (*Pause*)

SKINNER: Obsessive, me? Obsessive? (*Pause. She fights down something.*) I nearly got angry, then and nearly went — no — I will not — and — wait, the anger sinks — (*Pause*) Like tipping water on the sand, the anger goes, the anger vanishes — into what? I've no idea, my entrails, I assume. I do piss anger in the night, my pot is angerfull. (*Pause*) I am obsessive, why aren't you? (*Pause*) Every stone they raise is aimed at us. And things we have not dreamed of yet will come from it. Poems, love and gardening will be — and where you turn your eyes will be — and even the little middle of your heart which you think is your safe and actual self will be — transformed by it. I don't know how but even the way you plait your hair will be determined by it, and what we crop and even the colour of the babies, I do think it's odd, so odd, that when you resist you are obsessive but when you succumb you are not **whose obsession is this thing** or did you mean my love, they are the same thing actually. (*Pause*) They have a corridor of dungeons and somewhere are the occupants, they do not know yet and she fucked in there, not knowing it, of course, not being a witch could not imagine far enough, it is the pain of witches to see to the very end of things . . .

ANN: Yes.

SKINNER: What?

ANN: To all you say and yet — I think I must talk with my husband. (*Pause*)

SKINNER: Talk —

ANN: Yes, he is not as you —

SKINNER: Your what?

ANN: He also has got feeling and —

SKINNER: Talk to your what —

ANN: I have a right to sense as well as you!(*Pause*) Even Nailer
has recanted. Kneeling is back and they have not put the keep
up yet.

SKINNER: There is no talking between you and a man. No
talking. Words, yes, the patter and the eyes on your belt —

ANN: How shall we win!

SKINNER: I do not know how we will win! It is not a failing not
to know the end at the beginning. Our power comes out of our
love. Love also is a weapon. (*Pause*)

ANN: Yes. (*Pause*)

SKINNER: The way you say yes . . . (*Pause*) We lay under the
stars, and in the comfort of the trees swaying, the felled trees,
swaying, swore everlasting love. I will not accept that everlasting love, even as you swear it, is a lie, a permissible lie,
because you do not know the unforeseen condition. It is still
everlasting, there could be forty thousand murderers or forty
thousand starving children, violence or pity threatening, it still
takes precedence. — (*She turns swiftly*) Who is there, exactly?
(*She addresses the shadows.*) Are you interested in love? Give
us your opinion. I am in the grip of this eccentric view that
sworn love is binding — (KRAK *steps out of the shadows.*)

KRAK: Why not? If sworn hatred is. (*They look at him. He goes
to leave.*)

ANN: I wonder if you smile? I have never seen you.

SKINNER: Don't talk to him. Accuse him.

ANN (*ignoring her*):   Or laugh, for that matter. But most
laughter's false. I trust smiles better.

SKINNER: No, that's talking —

ANN: Have you no children? I somehow think you have not
looked in children's eyes —

SKINNER: **Do you think he listens to that mawkishness?** (*Pause*)

KRAK: Children? Dead or alive?

Scene Four

*Sound of whispered incantations and responses. Sections of build-
ing are lowered.* NAILER *is seen kneeling on the ground.*
STUCLEY *enters, holding a Bible.* NAILER *stops his devotions.*

STUCLEY: Christ's cock.

NAILER: Yes . . . ?

STUCLEY: **Is nowhere mentioned!** (*He flings the Bible at him.* NAILER *ducks.*)

NAILER: No . . .

STUCLEY: Nor the cocks of his disciples.

NAILER: No . . .

STUCLEY: Peculiar.

NAILER: The gospels are scrupulous in their avoidance of anatomical and physiological description. We have, for example, no image of Christ's face, let alone his —

STUCLEY: He was a man, though, wasn't he? A man, or why else did he descend to move among us?

NAILER: He was a man, yes —

STUCLEY: He was a man and I have lost five years trying to recover his dominions, five years for someone with no cock!

NAILER: He had one —

STUCLEY: He did have —

NAILER: For he was circumcised —

STUCLEY: He was circumcised, I read that, the circumcision, yes —

NAILER: Thereafter little reference, I admit —

STUCLEY: None whatsoever —

NAILER: Quite —

NAILER: What happened to it, then? (*Pause.* NAILER *shrugs.*)

NAILER: Chastity?

STUCLEY: There is one chastity and only one. The exclusiveness of desire, not willed, but forced by passion, that's chastity. (*He walks a little.*) No, this is a problem for the Church, you know it is. The deity made manifest knows neither pain nor ecstasy, what use is He?

NAILER: Be careful, please . . .

STUCLEY: Careful, why?

NAILER: You may be overheard.

STUCLEY: By whom?

NAILER: You may be oveheard, that's all —

STUCLEY: **By whom!**

NAILER: By Him Who Hears All, obviously —

STUCLEY: Fuck the lunatic! (NAILER *winces. Pause.*) I lay in a tent outside Edessa, while you frolicked in the English damp, while you licked the dew off widows' arses, tossed on my cot bleeding from the gums, roaring at the bowel and throat, the

flux of Asia shagging me both ends, and longing to know Him,
to have some sense of Him, to put my finger into Christ and feel
His heat, and what pained me, what agonized me I assure you,
was not the absence of a face but His castration, this Christ who
never suffered for the woman, who never felt the feeling which
makes no sense. (*Pause*) He can lend no comfort who has not
been all the places that we have. (*Pause*) And then of course, I
knew He had, and we'd been tricked. (*Pause*)

NAILER: Tricked...?

STUCLEY: I am of the opinion Christ slagged Magdalene.
(*Pause*)

NAILER: There is no reference —

STUCLEY: No reference, no —

NAILER: Or any indication in the gospels that I —

STUCLEY: There wouldn't be, would there?

NAILER: But all the —

STUCLEY: **Neutered — Bishops — Ripped — It — Out.**
(NAILER *stares at him.*) You restore it.

NAILER: Me?

STUCLEY: Yes. Fetch a book.

NAILER: Now?

STUCLEY: Why not now? (*He shouts off.*) **Book!**

NAILER: It is not in character, as I understand Him, He should
have exploited His position with the woman to —

STUCLEY: Exploited? Why exploited? The thing's called love.

NAILER: She had known sex, had traded flesh, but through
Christ's pity, came to the spiritual —

STUCLEY: Yes! And by His cock communicated that! (HUSH
enters with a volume and ink.) Down there, kneel, quick!
(NAILER *takes the pen, kneels.*) Christ finds the Magdalene
— you write — He sees and pities her — and pitying her, finds
her beautiful — get this down quick — put the illuminations on
it afterwards or we'll be all night —

NAILER: I wasn't doing the —

STUCLEY: The mob's dispersed — He raises her — He holds
her hands, her hands which have fondled knobs and money,
these hands all fresh from fornication He takes in His . . .
(*Pause*)

NAILER: Yes?

STUCLEY: Where were we?

NAILER: Mani habitat —

STUCLEY: Mani habitat?

NAILER: Her hands in His —

STUCLEY: No, put this in English!

NAILER: English?

STUCLEY: Yes, this is the Gospel of the Christ Erect! (*He is inspired again.*) And by His gentleness, touches her heart, like any maiden rescued from the dragon gratitude stirs in her womb, she becomes to Him the possibility of shared oblivion, she sheds all sin, and He experiences the — **irrational manifestation of pity which is** — (*Pause. He looks at* NAILER, *scrawling.*) Tumescence . . . (*Pause*) Got that?

NAILER: Yes . . .

STUCLEY: Now, we are closer to a man we understand, for at this moment of desire, Christ knows the common lot. (*Pause*) And she is sterile.

NAILER: Sterile?

STUCLEY: Diseased beyond conception, yes. So that they find, in passion, also tragedy . . . (NAILER *catches up, looks at* STUCLEY.) What use is a Christ who has not suffered everything? (*He wanders a little.*) They say the Jews killed Christ, but that's nonsense, the Almighty did. Why, did you say?

NAILER: Yes . . .

STUCLEY: Because His son discovered comfort. 'Oh, Father, why hast thou forsaken me?' Because in the body of the Magdalene He found the single place in which the madness of his father's world might be subdued. Unforgivable transgression the Lunatic could not forgive . . . (*Pause.* STUCLEY *is moved by his own perceptions.*) You see, how once Christ is restored to cock, all contradictions are resolved . . .

NAILER: The Church of Christ the Lover . . .

STUCLEY: Yes, why not? (*Pause.* NAILER *is inspired.*)

NAILER: Therefore — therefore — the missing symbol of communion is — is —

STUCLEY: What?

NAILER: Milk! Body, blood and semen!

STUCLEY: Oh, luscious bishop of the new born church! (*He shouts.*) Bring him his hat! (*He turns to* NAILER.) Put this out, then, from your box, up the little stairs and leaning over them, put out the agonized virility of Christ! Fetch him his hat!

HUSH: What hat?

STUCLEY: I don't care what hat, bring a hat! (*To* NAILER) Begin, today I bring you hope, all you who have no hope — that's everybody — today I bring you satisfaction, all you who have no satisfaction — that's everybody again — Christ is rescued from His enemies! Make out there's been a thousand year conspiracy — what's that?

HUSH (*carrying a tool bag*):   Couldn't find a hat, but this — (*He holds it upside down, shrugs.*)

STUCLEY: Yes — Yes! Place it on him, crown him! (NAILER *looks uncomfortable.* HUSH *puts the bag on* NAILER's *head.*) Oh, yes, oh, look at that! The dignity, the patter, and the aged mush! All creases, not of wisdom, but repented filth, but who knows that? I'd think to look at him, oh, terrible hours in the celibate cell! **Don't tell me I can't ordain you,** that is taking your new enthusiasm to excess, I ordain you, I ordain you, first among episcopates of Christ the Lover, I ordain you, I ordain you, etcetera, look — (*He dismisses* HUSH *with a gesture.*) I must pay the builder and you have to help. (*Pause*)

NAILER: Help? I've no —

STUCLEY: He thinks I'm asking him to turn his pockets out! No, I mean invoke Christ the Lover round the estate. I mean increase the yield of the demesne and plant more acres. Plough the woods. I want a further hour off them, with Christ's encouragement, say Friday nights —

NAILER: They have already given up a day to the estate —

STUCLEY: You cannot have a castle and a forty hour week! (*Pause*) Now I'm shouting. I'm shouting at God's rep! Genuflections, genuflections, I mean we cannot be defended without sacrifice. Don't they want to be safe?

NAILER: They gather on Fridays, it is the night the women talk —

STUCLEY: There has to be a stop to that. The excessive talking. Talking here is a disease. Say it offends the scriptures and will blight their wombs —

NAILER: They know full well it doesn't —

STUCLEY: **Look, are you recanted or not?** (*Pause*)

NAILER: I only — beg to remind you — children they have had in bumper harvests here. (*Pause*)

STUCLEY: Yes. I am forever tripping over them.

NAILER: They also are a wealth.

STUCLEY: More's the pity I've no tin mine to stuff them in, but they can clear the heath — (ANN *enters. He turns on her.*) We have the keep up to your horror! For some reason I can't guess the mortar is not perished by your chanting, nor do the slates fall when you wave the sapling sticks. (*He goes towards her.*) As for windows, none, or fingernails in width. Stuff light. Stuff furnishings!

ANN: The cattle have been driven off the common.

STUCLEY: Yes. The common is too big.

ANN: Too big?

STUCLEY: To be misused like this. The common will be smaller and the rest given for sheep.

ANN: Sheep.

STUCLEY: You know, wool grows on them! (*He laughs, then turns.*) **You discuss things like a proper wife!** (*Pause*) Terrible impertinence. (HOLIDAY *enters.* STUCLEY *swings on him.*) Am I imagining, or is the rate of building falling off? I look out of my window and the same low, ragged outline —

HOLIDAY: Ragged?

STUCLEY: Outline in the sky, which does not double as I wish it would —

HOLIDAY: Double?

STUCLEY: Are you short-staffed or something? Of course not double but it's static —

HOLIDAY: It's not a marrow it's a castle —

STUCLEY: It's static, I swear it is —

HOLIDAY: I have one hundred labourers and they are shifting four courses every fortnight —

STUCLEY: Yes, you have all the answers, doesn't he, all the answers, and I have only got my eyes, why don't you look me in the eyes?

HOLIDAY: I do, but briefly —

STUCLEY: Briefly, like a liar —

HOLIDAY: No, I have a thing about —

STUCLEY: Me, too, even now your are —

HOLIDAY: Yes, I am scanning upwards for the —

STUCLEY: **Well, look.** (*Pause.* HOLIDAY *stares him in the eyes.*)

HOLIDAY: There are — scaffolding up — (*He points with a finger.*) And someone — butter-fingers might — **what?**

STUCLEY (*tearing off*): Where's my genius? My engineer!

ANN (to HOLIDAY): Give up . . .

HOLIDAY: Wha'?

ANN: Give up.

HOLIDAY: She is most persuasive, I must say, with 'er monosyllables. If you must know, I would rather be erecting hospitals myself.

ANN: Do, then.

HOLIDAY (*to* BATTER, *shuffling off*): Monosyllabic wisdom.

ANN: Do!

HOLIDAY (*turning*):   For what? Gratitude? Mix with straw and
   eat it? Lovely gratitude, yum, yum!
ANN: First you do it, then you see. But first, you do it.
HOLIDAY (*shaking his head*):   See first.
ANN: You can't see first. Everyone wants to see first. See after-
   wards. (HOLIDAY *goes out.*)
BATTER (*following*):   How the drowned man crossed the
   swamp . . . (*Pause. She looks at* NAILER, *who is kneeling in
   prayer.*)
ANN: What are you doing? (NAILER *mumbles.*) Have you
   seen yourself? (*Mumbles*) Find you a mirror . . . (*She delves in
   her pockets.*)
NAILER: All symbols can be ridiculed. On the one hand,
   authority is costume, but on the other —
ANN: Never mind the words, Reg, look at the —
NAILER: I don't need to —
ANN: Look — (*She holds up a small mirror.*)
NAILER: Thank you, I am perfectly aware what —
ANN: **Look!** (*He looks.*) What's that? (*Pause*)
NAILER: A mitre. (*Pause*)
ANN: A mitre? Reg, you have got a bag on your —
NAILER: I am sick of your wisdom! Women's wisdom! Sick of
   it!
ANN: Now, don't be —
NAILER: Argument, opinion, and debate! The whispering until
   the candle toppled in the wax —
ANN: Reg —
NAILER: Long nights of dialogue —
ANN: Reg, there is a tool bag on your head. (*Pause. He regards
   her with contempt.*)
NAILER: Oh, you literal creature . . . It was tool bag . . . it is
   no longer a tool bag, it is a badge . . . **If you knew how I
   yearned for God!**
ANN: Which god? (*Pause, then patiently.*)
NAILER: The God which puts a stop to argument. The God
   who says, 'Thus I ordain it!' The God who puts His finger on the
   sin.
ANN: Sin . . . ?
NAILER: **Why not sin?** (*Pause. He gets up.*) And no more Reg.
   (*He looks at her, goes out. A wind howls over the stage.*)

Scene Five

STUCLEY, KRAK, *leaning on a wind.*

STUCLEY: There never was a wind like this before! You got a
buffetting, but this . . . !
KRAK: It is the relationship between the air and the mass —
the wind is trapped between the towers and accelerates to three
times its velocity —
STUCLEY: He's changed the climate! What can't he do? (*He
takes him by the shoulders.*) You Turk. You Jew. You pedant.
Make it snow. (KRAK *looks at him.*)
KRAK: You ask a great deal of a simple engineer —
STUCLEY: No, stuff your reservations, make it snow. (*Pause*)
Because you can, you ice-cold shifter of old worlds, you can . . .
(*Pause. Flakes of snow flurry over the stage.* STUCLEY *laughs,
seizing the bewildered* KRAK *and lifting him bodily in the air.*)
STUCLEY: I could chuck you into space and you would circle
round my system like a star, twinkling at me from that secret
eye! (*He drops him.*) Play snowballs with me! I did love
boyhood more than anything! Play snowballs!
KRAK (*looking at the few flakes*):   There is scarcely —
STUCLEY: Chase me, then! (*He turns to run.* KRAK *waits.*)
Oh, it is beneath his dignity . . . (*Suddenly he flings himself on*
KRAK. *They struggle.* KRAK *asserts his superior physical
strength and forces* STUCLEY *to the ground. For a moment, he
threatens his life. Then he releases him.* STUCLEY *gets to his
feet, amazed.*)
STUCLEY: What? (*Pause*) What? (*Pause*) Could have ruptured
my throat! (*He rubs the place.*) I do hate men of intellect. The
curtain of the intellect, the mathematics, the poetics, concealing
what dog itch, I wonder. (*Pause*) That hurt, that did . . .
(*Pause*) Old man . . .
KRAK: More arches.
STUCLEY: Where?
KRAK: The outer work. Double the arches. Double the ditch.
(*He scrambles up, hurries out.*)
STUCLEY: Builder! (*He follows. Pause.* SKINNER *enters with*
CANT, *hands reaching for the snow.*)
CANT: 's not settling . . .
SKINNER: Fuck!
CANT: Stoppin' . . .
SKINNER: Fuck and fuck!

CANT: Got some bits . . .

SKINNER: **Lost my craft!**

CANT: Don't say that, you got some —

SKINNER: Laid a carpet three feet deep here once!

CANT: Remember it . . . (SKINNER *covers her face. Pause.*) P'raps the brew was —

SKINNER: You did the brew . . .

CANT: May be the toads weren't fresh enough —

SKINNER: Not the toads . . .

CANT: Or sprawning — that was it! A sprawning toad shall not —

SKINNER: Not the toads! Shut up about the toads. The power's gone . . .

CANT: Not gone, just —

SKINNER: Gone! (*Pause*)

CANT: I don't think you should — just because of — (SKINNER *kneels, her face covered.*) Skinner? (*Pause*) Because one —

SKINNER: Leave me alone, will you? I thank you for your kindness, but — (CANT *withdraws. A heavy snowfall. SKINNER does not move. In the silence the sound of a metallic movement. Armoured figures appear from different directions. They congregate, are motionless.*)

BALDWIN (*at last*): The oath!

ROLAND: The oath!

REGINALD: The oath!

ALL: We do vowe no peace shall be on earth, no ear of wheat standen, no sheep with bowel in, no hutte unburn, no chylde with blood in, until such tyme we have our aims all maken wholehearte and complete!

REGINALD: Baldwin!

BALDWIN: Here!

REGINALD: Reginald here!

BALDWIN: I see your armour, Reginald!

THEOBALD: Theobald here!

ROLAND: I see your badge! (*Pause*) The flaming cow ran with its entrails hanging out —

BALDWIN: I cut the dog in half —

THEOBALD: One blow —

BALDWIN: The dog in the two halves went —

THEOBALD: The head this way —

ROLAND: Its entrails caught around a post —

REGINALD: Double-headed axe went —

ROLAND: Its entrails caught around a post —
BALDWIN: Two-handed sword went —
ROLAND: Pulled out the seven stomachs of the flaming cow —
THEOBALD: Village bell went —
BALDWIN: Cut the dog in half —
REGINALD: The head this way —
THEOBALD: Ding —
BALDWIN: Cut the boy in half —
REGINALD: Or girl was it —
THEOBALD: Ding —
BALDWIN: Eighty millimetre gun went —
THEOBALD: Ding —
ROLAND: The seven stomachs of the bowelless cow —
REGINALD: Tracer from the half-track went —
ROLAND: The cow now with no entrails went —
BALDWIN: The mounting of the Bofors went —
REGINALD: Into the rick, into the thatch —
BALDWIN: Spent cases rattled on the deck —
THEOBALD: Or girl was it —
ROLAND: The cow now with no entrails went —
THEOBALD: Bereft of entrails —
ROLAND: Stomachless —
BALDWIN: The boy in two halves through the village went —
THEOBALD: Ding —
REGINALD: Or girl was it —
BALDWIN: The flaming messenger of our approach —
ROLAND: Barked its —
THEOBALD: Bellowed its —
REGINALD: Screamed its —
THEOBALD: Crack division —
BALDWIN: Crack division —
REGINALD: Spent cases rattled on the deck —
THEOBALD: I fear naught, Baldwin!
BALDWIN: Fear naught!
ROLAND: Encrimsoned and imbrued!
REGINALD: Down came the thatch and in the pig squeal and
    the woman squeal and the man squeal and the —
THEOBALD: Fear naught, Reginald!
ROLAND: Defend the right!
REGINALD: Down came the thatch!
THEOBALD: Baldwin!
BALDWIN: I see your armour! (*Silence.* HOLIDAY *enters.*)

HOLIDAY: Yep? (*He looks around.*) Somebody ask for me? (*Pause*)

SKINNER: The bricklayers are guilty, too.

HOLIDAY: Come again?

SKINNER: The bricklayers are guilty, too.

HOLIDAY (*turning away*): No, someone asked for me . . .

SKINNER (*as he goes*): You mustn't look up all the time.

HOLIDAY: 'ullo, advice from every quarter —

SKINNER: Because it will not come from there. (*He stops.*)

HOLIDAY: What won't? (*She does not reply. He is about to go, then, looking around him.*) I saw your arse . . . (*Pause*) Excuse me, but I saw your arse — you showed your arse and I — they say you don't like men — which is to do surely, with — who you 'ad to do with, surely . . . (*Pause*) Anyway, I saw your arse . . . (*He turns, despairingly, to go.*)

SKINNER: All right.

HOLIDAY (*stops*): What — you —

SKINNER: All right . . .

The walls rise to reveal the interior of a keep.

ACT TWO

Scene One

The hall, unfinished. KRAK, *in a shaft of light.*

KRAK: He wants another wall, in case the first three walls are
breached. The unknown enemy,the enemy who does not exist
yet but who cannot fail to materialize, will batter down the first
wall and leaving a carpet of twitching dead advance on the
second wall, and scaling it, will see in front of them the third
wall, buttressed, ditched and palisaded, this wall I have told him
will break their spirit but he aches for a fourth wall, a fourth
wall against which the enemy who does not exist yet but who
cannot fail to materialize will be crucified. As for the towers,
despite their inordinate height he orders me increase them by
another fifteen feet. A fifth wall I predict will be necessary, and

a sixth essential, to protect the fifth, necessitating the erection
of twelve flanking towers. The castle is by definition, not
definitive . . .

BRIAN (*rushing*):   **Ron's 'ead! Ron's 'ead!**

STUCLEY (*flying in*):   **The build — A! The build — A!**

BRIAN: Took yer eyes off, Ron!

STUCLEY: His eggshell! Someone tapped it with a spoon!

BRIAN: Took 'is eyes off and down comes a brick!

BATTER (*smartly*):   Was not, idiot. Found him lying in the
ditch, haunches naked and dew drops on his hairy arse.

STUCLEY: What!

BATTER: Trousers down and head bashed.

STUCLEY: What!

BATTER: Woman murder!

BRIAN: Trousers down and —

BATTER: Woman murder! (*They look at him.*) Well, what else,
he was not pissing under scaffolding.

BRIAN: Ron would never —

BATTER: Ron would never, 'e knows. To piss would be to take
your eyes off what's above, or soak your legs. No, this was
woman murder, most undignified he looked —

STUCLEY: **Who will translate my blueprints now!** (ANN *enters.*
STUCLEY *turns on her.*) Who did this, you! Oh, her mask of
kindness goes all scornful at the thought — what, me? (*He
swings on* BRIAN.) **You do the job!** (*And to* ANN.) And such a
crease of womanly dismay spreads down her jaw, and dignified
long nose tips slightly with her arrogance — what, me? **It stops
nothing, this.** (*To* BATTER.) Find the killer who tried to
hinder the inevitable! (*As* BATTER *leaves, with* BRIAN.)
Listen, I think morality is also bricks, the fifth wall is the wall of
morals, did you think I could leave that untouched? (*He turns to
go, stops.*) Gang meets at sunset by the camp! The password
is — (*He whispers in* KRAK's *ear.*) **Don't tell!** (*He goes to
leave.*) Gang meets at sunset and no girls! (*He hurries out.
Pause.*)

ANN: Gravity. Parabolas. Equations. The first man's dead.
Gravity. Parabolas. Equations. Are you glad? (KRAK *does not
move.*) Say yes. Because you are. That's why you're here. Grey
head. Badger gnawed about the ears and eyes down, bitten old
survivor of the slaughter, loosing off your wisdom when you
think yourself alone, I know, I do know, grandfather of slain
children, aping the adviser, aping the confidant, but actually,
but actually, I do know badger-head, you want us dead. And
not dead simply, but torn, parted, spiked on the oaks, limbs
between the acorns, a real rucking of the favoured landscape,
the peace when you came here made your heart knot with
anger, I know, the castle is the magnet of extermination, it is
not a house, is it, the castle is not a house . . . (*Pause*) I am so
drawn to you I feel sick. (*Pause*) The man who suffers. The man
who's lost. Success appalls me but pain I love. Your grey misery
excites me. Can you stand a woman who talks of her cunt? I am
all enlarged for you . . . (*He stares at her.*) Now you humiliate
me. By silence. I am not humiliated. (*Pause*)

KRAK: They cut off my mother's head. She was senile and
complaining. They dismembered my wife, whom I saw little of.
And my daughter, with a glancing blow, spilled all her brains, as
a clumsy man sends a drink flying off the table. And her I did
not give all the attention that I might. I try to be truthful. I hate
exaggeration. I hate the cultivated emotion. (*Pause*) And you
say, come under my skirt. Under my skirt, oblivion and com-

pensation, shoot your anger in my bowel, **cunt also is a dungeon!**
(*Pause*)

ANN: Enthralling shout . . . (*Pause, then he suddenly laughs.*)
And laugh, for that matter . . . (*Pause, then he turns to leave.*) I
mean, don't tell me it is virgins that you want, the unmarked
flesh, untrodden map of girlhood, the look of fear and unhinged
legs of — (*He returns, slaps her face into silence. Pause.*) You
have made my nose bleed . . .

Scene Two

The PROSECUTORS *descending. A court assembling.*

NAILER: Thank you for coming.
POOL: Thank you for asking me.
NAILER: The rigours of travel.
POOL: Not to be undertaken lightly.
NAILER: No, indeed. Indeed, no. His trousers were down.
POOL: So I gather.
NAILER: I do think —
POOL: The absolute limit.
NAILER: And misuse of love.
POOL: Make that your angle.
NAILER: I will do.
POOL: The trust which resides in the moment of —
NAILER: Etcetera —
POOL: Most cruelly abused. Make that your angle.
NAILER: Thank you, I will.
POOL: Fucking bitches when your goolies are out . . .
NAILER (*to the court*):   A man proffers union — albeit outside
the contract of marriage — a man proffers union — albeit
without the blessing of Almighty God — he offers it by tacit
understanding, by signs, by words negotiates this most delicate
and sacred of all —
SKINNER (*from the dock*):   **Ann!**
NAILER: Lays down, abandons, puts aside all those defences
which the male by nature transports in his demeanour, and in
the pity of his nakedness —
SKINNER: **Ann!**

NAILER: Anticipating the exchange of tenderness, arms outstretched for the generosity of the feminine embrace —

SKINNER: **Where are you, you bitch** — no, mustn't swear —

NAILER: A crime therefore, not against an individual — not
against a single man most cruelly deceived —

SKINNER: Descend to swearing — better not —

NAILER: But against that universal trust, that universally
upheld convention lying at the heart of all sexual relations
marital and illicit —

SKINNER: Temper and so on, no, no, no, Skinner, stop it, it's
the daylight got me going — beg pardon —

NAILER: And thereby threatening not only the security of that
most intimate love which God endowed man with —

SKINNER: Daylight — got me going — sorry —

NAILER: For peace and for relief but —

SKINNER: I am not ill-tempered as a matter of fact, I don't
know where that idea's come from that I — and anyway I know
you hate it, loudness and shouting, you do, such delicate
emotions and I — **they have done awful things to me down
there** — do my best to be — to be contained — that way you
have, you — **There is a room down there and they did terrible
things to me** — I mean my cunt which had been so — which we
had made so — **Thanks to you was dead** — so it wasn't the
abuse it might have been, the abuse they would have liked it to
be had it been a living thing, were it the sacred and beautiful
thing we had found it out to be and — am I going on, I do go
on — are you — so thank you I hated it and the more they hurt
it the better I — I was actually gratified, believe it or not, yes,
gratified —

NAILER: But the very act of procreation itself, which is col-
laborative, which is, for its success wholly dependent on —

SKINNER: They have this way you see, of relating the torture
to the offence — the things they say — you wouldn't — are
you in here, I can't see — put your hand up I can't — am I
being reasonable enough for you, not shouting am I, actually
I'm half dead — where are you sitting, I — (*She looks around.*)
I call it daylight but it's relative — **I want to see your hand**
— Can I have a stool or not? (*A* MAN *goes to fetch it.*) **Not one
with a spike in the middle!** They think of everything — they
do — imaginations — you should see the — **Invention down
there** — makes you gasp the length of their hatred — the
uncoiled length of hatred — mustn't complain though — was I
complaining — was I — beg pardon — I have this — tone

which — thanks to your expertise is mollified a little — (*The* MAN *returns with a stool.*) **What does that do, bite your arse?** (*She looks at it, on the ground.*) Looks harmless, looks a harmless little stool, boring bit of carpentry **don't believe it!** (*She goes towards it, extends her fingers gingerly.*) Spring trap! (*She leaps back.*) Spring trap! Legs fly up and grip your head, seen stools like that before, didn't think I'd fall for that, did you, not really, didn't think I'd — (*She sits on it, in utter exhaustion.*) You have ₒo kill them, don't you? Death they understand. Death is their god, not love. Because after he was dead they built nothing, for one day **They built nothing.** And because all things decay, in actual fact for one day the castle went backwards! I mean — by virtue of erosion and the usual rot — there was less castle on Monday than on Sunday! And what did that? **Death did!** I call it death, they call it murder, they call it battle, I call it slaughter etcetera, etcetera, the word is just a hole down which all things can drop — I mean, I put a stop to him. (*Pause*) And he was quite a nice man, as far as they — there is a limit to those even of the best intentions — he talked of mutual pleasure — really, the banality! It really hurt my ears — after what we had — to talk of — **mutual pleasure** — can you believe — the very words are . . . (*She dries.*)

STUCLEY: We are up against it. We are, we really are, up against it. (*He walks about.*) Having hewn away two hills to make us safe, having knifed the landscape to preserve us we find — horror of horrors — **the worst within.** (*Pause, he looks at all of them.*) I find that a blow, I do, I who have reeled under so many blows find that — a blow. Who can you trust? **Trust!** (*He shrieks, the word is a thing butted at them.*) I say in friendship, I say in comradeship, I say without malice **you are all traitors!** (*They deny it.*) Thank you, thank you, you deny it, thank you, the vehemence I love it, thank you, lovely vehemence orchestrated and spontaneous **thank you but.** (*Pause*) Things being what they are I have no choice, times being what they are I feel sure you understand in everybody's interest it is crucial I regard you all as being actively engaged in the planning of my murder — no, not really, not really, silly, but as a basis for —

NAILER: Yes.

STUCLEY: He knows! (*Pause*) I have changed my view of God. I no longer regard Him as an evil deity, that was excessive, evil, no. He's mad. It is only by recognizing God is mad that we can satisfactorily explain the random nature of — you say, you are the theologian.

NAILER: It appears to us He was not always mad —

STUCLEY: Not always, no —

NAILER: But became so, driven to insanity by the failure and the contradiction of His works —

STUCLEY: I understand Him!

NAILER: The absurdity of attempting to reconcile the simultaneous beauty and horror of the world is abolished by the recognition of His —

STUCLEY: **They are building a castle over the hill and it's bigger than this.**(*Pause*) Given God is now a lunatic, I think, sadly, we are near to the Apocalypse . . . (*He turns.*) Gatherings of more than three we cannot tolerate.

NAILER: The church —

STUCLEY: I exclude births, deaths and marriages! And periodical searching of all homes I know you will not wish to hinder, what have the innocent got to conceal, it stands to reason all who complain have secrets, juries are abolished they are not reliable, quaint relics of a more secure time, I sleep alone in sheets grey with tossing, I cannot keep a white sheet white, do you find this? Grey by the morning. Does anyone find this? The launderers are frantic.

BATTER: Yes.

STUCLEY: You do? What is it?

BATTER: I don't know . . . it could be . . . I don't know . . .

STUCLEY: Why grey, I wonder?

SKINNER (*stands suddenly*):   **What have you done to your hair?** (*Pause*) It's plaited in a funny way, what have you — **It's vile.** (*Pause*) Well, no, it's not, it's pretty, vile and pretty at the same time, **Did you take him in your mouth, I must know.** (*Pause*) If I know all I can struggle with it, I can wrestle it to death, but not the imagined thing, don't leave anything out, **Of course I am entitled to a description.** (*Pause*) This floor, laid over flowers we once lay on, this cruel floor will become the site of giggling picnics, clots of children wandering with music in their ears and not one will think, not one, **A Woman Writhed Here Once.** The problem is to divest yourself of temporality, is that what you do? (*She looks at* NAILER.) I gave up, and longed to die, and yet I did not die. That all life should be bound up in one randomly encountered individual defies the dumb will of the flesh clamouring for continuation, life would not have it! I hate you, do you know why, because you prove to me that nothing is, nothing at all is, **The Thing Without Which Nothing Else Is Possible.** (*Pause*) I am aching from my breasts to the bottom of my bowel, but that is just desire, poof! And deprivation, poof! Love and longing, poof to all of it! **Am I to be hanged or drowned?** If you haven't had love ripped out your belly, dragging half your organs with it, don't talk to me, you haven't lived! Only the suffering to pass the sentence, you, for example . . . (*She indicates* STUCLEY.)

STUCLEY: Tie her to the body of her victim. (*Pause*)

SKINNER: Tie her to —

STUCLEY: And turn her loose.

SKINNER (*in horror*):   Now hold on, what —

POOL: The mercy of Almighty God be —

SKINNER: What about my execution —

POOL: Be upon you now and always —

SKINNER: **My hanging . . . !**

A reverberating explosion. Running to and fro.

Scene Three

STUCLEY: You heard that!

BATTER: Of course I fucking heard it . . . (*Another boom.*)

STUCLEY: **Another one.**

BATTER: All right, another one . . .

STUCLEY: Why?

BATTER: Can't think.

STUCLEY: What is it!

BATTER: Can't think, I said —

STUCLEY: Comes from the East, you know!

KRAK: Yes.

STUCLEY: What! (*Pause*)

KRAK: A castle.

STUCLEY: What?

KRAK: There is a one. (*Pause*)

STUCLEY: There is one . . . (*A third boom.*)

KRAK: You knew, and I knew, there could not be only this one, but this one would breed others. And there is one. Called The Fortress.

STUCLEY: Bigger than this . . .

KRAK: Bigger. Three times the towers and polygonal. With ravelins beyond a double ditch, which I never thought of . . . (STUCLEY *stares for a moment in disbelief.*)

STUCLEY: Everything I fear, it comes to pass. Everything I imagine is vindicated. Awful talent I possess. **Don't I have an awful talent?**

BATTER: Yes . . .

STUCLEY: What's a ravelin?

KRAK: A ravelin is a two-faced salient beyond the outer-work —

STUCLEY: I want some —

KRAK: You want —

STUCLEY: Some ravelins, yes. Say a hundred.

KRAK: A hundred —

STUCLEY: Two hundred, then! (*A fourth boom.*) **And that noise, what is it!**

KRAK: The coming of the English desert . . . (*Pause*)

STUCLEY: Yes . . .

NAILER: Almighty! Almighty!

STUCLEY: Yes . . .

NAILER: Oh, Almighty, Oh, Almighty . . . !

STUCLEY: Extinction of the worthless, the obliteration of the melancholy crawl from the puddle to the puddle, from the puddle of the maternal belly to the puddle of the old man's involuntary bladder . . . Good . . . and they make such a fuss of murder . . . **Not me, though!** (*He sweeps out, with the others. ANN appears. She is pregnant. She looks at* **KRAK.**)

KRAK: There is one. With three times the towers and polygonal. With ravelins beyond a double ditch, which I never thought of, why polygonal, to deflect what, I wonder, some young expert who sits all night with his protractors, some thin German with no woman, it is the better castle —

ANN: Better —

NAILER: And the keep low, why? And banked with earth. He sleeps alone, the opposing engineer . . .

ANN: We find a rock.

KRAK: Stink of death to English woods. Hips on the fences. Flies a noisy garment on the entrail in the bracken.

ANN: I have your child in here.

KRAK: The trooper boots the bud open and sends my — (*Pause*) Said my, then . . . (*Pause. He smiles.*) Error.

ANN: It is you that needs to be born. I will be your midwife. Through the darkness, down the black canal —

KRAK: **What rock?**

ANN: Off the coast. A barren place with nothing to lure murder for.

KRAK: No such place.

ANN: No wealth. Nothing to draw the conqueror.

KRAK: All places will be conquered.

ANN: Useless pinnacle of gale-lashed —

KRAK: **No such thing.** (*Pause*) Hot pans of blazing sun, spiky rocks in frozen waters, sheep-gnawed granites in Arctic hurricanes, all pretexts for murder and screaming up the barren slopes —

ANN: **All Right, Wisdom! All Right, Logic!** (*Pause*) I have a child in here, stone deaf to argument, floats in water, all pessimism filtered, lucky infant spared compelling reasons why it should acquiesce in death. (*She turns to go.*)

KRAK: **Is there any man you have not copulated with?** (*She stops.*) I wonder . . . (CANT *runs across the stage, picks up a stone, chucks it at something off.*)

CANT: S'comin'! (*A second figure runs by.*)

BRIAN: S — T — E — N — C — H! (*And another.*)

MAN (*laughing*): Scarper! (*They turn, stare, as* SKINNER *staggers in. The decayed body of* HOLIDAY *is strapped to her front. She leans backwards from her burden, a grotesque parody of pregnancy.*)

SKINNER: Wind's a bastard, running ahead. And yet these walls make eddies, and running from me sometimes meet me slap! (*They stare at her.*) Not dead. Been feverish, of course. And much morning sickness all times of the day . . . (ANN *turns away her head.*) Lay in the bluebells, odd sight this, on my back, head turned to gasp great lungfuls of the scent and then could not get up, you'd know this, my gravity was somewhere else, legs like windmills, beetle on its back or pregnant female, you get used to it, nothing you can't get used to, **First Horror**. (*Pause*) Fashion of the rotted male, exclusive garment, everybody's wearing it **not to copy** and his organ butts against mine, would you believe, you can live without others, **Second Horror!** Why are you pregnant all the time, other women spent their fertility decades ago, but you — been at the herbs again? (ANN *weeps with despair.*) He is losing weight. If I lie still the crows take bits away, kind crows, my favourite bird they are so solitary or live in pairs not like rooks and I was fond of rooks once, no, the solitary bird is best, you have power over her, shut her up . . . (KRAK *does not move.*) He hates you. You do your hair like that, and yet he hates you. Does anyone remember what this place was once? They don't, they really don't, the children say the castle has been here a thousand years.

ANN: You should go. (*Pause*)

SKINNER: Go . . .

ANN: Yes. Not hang round here.

SKINNER: Go where? I live here.

ANN: No such thing as live here any more, go where you might find peace and rub the thing off you, where you won't be stoned. (*Pause*)

SKINNER: No.

ANN: Do you liked to be stoned?

SKINNER: Yes. (*Pause*) Yes to punishment. Yes to blows. (*Pause*)

ANN: What have I done to you? (SKINNER *laughs.*)

SKINNER: She thinks — she has the neck — she has the gall — to think she brought me to — she has to think herself responsible! (*She looks to* KRAK.) Careful! She's after your suicide! Hanging off the battlements for love! The corpse erect! Through her thin smile the knowledge even in death she got you up! (*Mimicking*) Did I do this? (*She turns to* ANN.) This is my place, more stones the better and pisspans, pour on! You and your reproductive satisfactions, your breasts and your lactation, dresses forever soddened at the tit, **It did get on my wick a bit,** envy of course, envy, envy, envy of course. I belong here. I am the castle also.

ANN: You do suck your hatreds. You do — suck — so. And he — also sucks his.

SKINNER (*as a group of hooded prisoners enters*): That way the dungeon!

ANN: Gulls at the sewer . . .

SKINNER: Bear left and wait, the torturer's at breakfast! (*They shuffle.*)

ANN: Snails on the eyes of the dead . . .

SKINNER: Tax evaders on the first rung, work-shy on the second!

ANN: Suck pessimism, suck fear . . . !

SKINNER: Don't hang about, the last lot came up again. Only some bits were missing! (ANN *hurries out. The gang shuffles further.* BATTER *appears, with a short stick.*) There are eighty-seven stairs and the last two flights they throw you off!

BATTER: All right, get along . . .
SKINNER: Hullo, Bob . . .
BATTER: Wotcha, darling . . .
SKINNER: Look well . . .
BATTER: Thank you . . . (*To the gang.*) 'ho said to stop?
SKINNER: Cold again . . .
BATTER: English summer . . .
SKINNER: Fuckin' 'ell . . .
BATTER (*as he passes*):   Take care . . .
SKINNER: Will do . . .

The prisoners and BATTER *depart.* SKINNER *takes an apple from her clothes and begins to eat it.* KRAK, *who has been watching in perfect stillness, suddenly kneels at her feet.*

SKINNER *stops, mouth open, apple aloft.*
SKINNER: What? (*Pause*) What? (*Pause*) What, you bugger, what?
KRAK: The Book of Cunt. (*Pause*)
SKINNER: What book is that?
KRAK: The Book of Cunt says all men can be saved. (*Pause*) Not true. (*Pause*) She pulled me down. I did not pull her. She pulled me. In the shadow of the turret, in the apex of the angle with the wall, in the slender crack of 39 degrees, she, using the ledge to fix her heels, levered her parts over me. Shoes fell, drawers fell, drowned argument in her spreading underneath . . . (*Pause*) European woman with her passion for old men, wants to drown their history in her bowel . . . ! (*Pause*)
SKINNER: Scares you . . .
KRAK: My arse. My arse, she says . . . (*Pause*)
SKINNER: Yes . . . ?
KRAK: Cunt you lend or rent, but arse you have to will . . . true ring of marrriage . . . brown button of puckered muscularity . . . the sacramental stillness born of hanging between pain and ecstasy . . . **In Shit I Find Peace Is It!** (*He scrambles to his feet.*) Don't tell them I came here —
SKINNER: Tell who . . . ?
KRAK: Where's cunt's geometry? The thing has got no angles! And no measure, neither width nor depth, how can you trust what has no measurements? Don't tell them I came here . . .
SKINNER: No . . .
KRAK: **Find Peace In Shit, Do I?** (*He looks around, goes out.* HUSH *enters with a dish. He places it at* SKINNER's *feet.*)
SKINNER: Wha's that?

HUSH: Lamb.
SKINNER: What?
HUSH: Stew.
SKINNER: What? (*He starts to slip away.*) It's an offence to feed me! (CANT *enters with a dish, lays it down.*) What —
CANT: Baked apple —
SKINNER: You —
CANT: Can't stay! (*She withdraws, running low.*)
SKINNER: Oh, God, Oh, Nature, **I am going to be worshipped.**

Scene Four

KRAK *is sitting at his desk.* STUCLEY *appears.*

STUCLEY: Saw you. (KRAK *looks up.*) Giving your brain away. (*Pause*) Saw you. (*Pause*) Whose brain do you think it is? (KRAK j*ust looks.*) Well, no. Cock's free but brains are property. (*He walks a little, stops.*) Deceit floats up, like fat on the tea cup. Like bones scuffed years after the murder, the knife, the stain, the knickers that refused to rot, **I followed you into the thicket, yes** . . . ! (*Pause*) Symposium of military architects. Twigs cracked but did they look, twigs shattered but did they look? Crouching with diagrams you might have slammed the doors of Asia and they would not have budged. **Supreme concentration of treasonable genius.** Are you listening or not?
KRAK: Drawn cunt. (*Pause*)
STUCLEY: What?
KRAK: In twenty-seven versions.
STUCLEY: The diagrams you traded with the Fortress, were they approximate or comprehensive, did they include the order of defence, the sally ports, which entrances were blind and which lead to the keep, **How safe are we after this?** (KRAK *holds up his drawing.*) The representation of that thing is not encouraged by the church. (*Pause. He is looking at it.*) It's wrong, surely, that — (*Pause*) I have never looked at one, but that —
KRAK: Gave him all my drawings. And got all his. They are experimenting with a substance that can bring down walls with-

out getting beneath them. Everything before this weapon will
be obsolete. This, for example, is entirely redundant as a con-
vincing method of defence —

STUCLEY: What —

KRAK: Its vertical profile, which I took further than any other
architect, renders it utterly vulnerable . . .

STUCLEY: What —

KRAK: It goes up, instead of down. Is high, not wide. Is circular
and not oblique. Is useless, in effect and an invitation to —

STUCLEY: **Only just finished it.** (*Pause*)

KRAK: Yes . . . (*He returns to his drawing.*)

STUCLEY: **Don't draw cunt. I'm talking!** (*Pause*) This is a
crisis, isn't it? Is it, or isn't it? You sit there — you have always
been so — had this — manner of stillness — most becoming
but also sinister — dignity but also malevolence — easy superiority of the captive intellect — **Is that my wife's bits** — I
wouldn't know them — what man would — I know, you
see — I am aware — I do know everything — I do — I think
you have done this all to spite me — correct me if I'm
wrong —

KRAK: Spite —

STUCLEY: Spite me, yes —

KRAK: Spite? I do not think the word — unless my English
fails me — is quite sufficient to contain the volume of the
sentiment . . . (*Pause*)

STUCLEY: You blind draughtsman . . . all the madness in the
immaculately ordered words . . . in the clean drawings . . . all
the temper in the perfect curve . . . (*He pretends to flinch.*)
Mind your faces! Duck his guts! Intellectual bursts! (*Pause*)
Tumescent as the dick which splits, splashing the ceiling red
with sheer barminess, **Robert!** (*Pause*) But I'm not spited. If you
do not feel spited no amount of spite can hurt you, Christ was
the same, **Robert!** (*Pause*) We burn people like this. Who give
away our secrets. Burn them in a chair. Fry them, and the fat
goes — human fat goes, spit . . . ! Does — spit! (ANN *enters*)
No. Robert I want. (*She looks at them.*) Violence not
abundance.

ANN: The ease of making children. The facility of numer-
ousness. Plague, yes, but after the plague, the endless copula-
tion of the immune. All these children, children everywhere and
I thought, this one matters, alone of them this one matters
because it came from love. But I thought wrongly. I thought
wrongly. (*Pause. She looks at* KRAK.) There is nowhere except

where you are. Correct. Thank you. If it happens somewhere, it will happen everywhere. There is nowhere except where you are. Thank you for truth. (*Pause. She kneels, pulls out a knife.*) Bring it down. All this. (*She threatens her belly. Pause*)

STUCLEY:　You won't. (*Pause*) You won't because you cannot. Your mind wants to, but you cannot, and you won't . . . (*Pause. He holds out his hand for the knife. She plunges it into herself. A scream. The wall flies out. In a panic,* SOLDIERS. *Things falling.*)

Scene Five

A haze of light.

SOLDIER ONE:　Raining women!

SOLDIER TWO:　Mind yer 'eads!

SOLDIER ONE:　Raining women!

NAILER:　The temper of the Almighty, who gave you abundance, imagine His temper! Standing before Him how will you say I did destroy that which it was not mine to dispense with —

SOLDIER TWO:　Mind yer 'eads! (*A fall.*)

NAILER:　The spirits of your unborn children will rise up in accusation saying —

SOLDIER TWO:　**And another!**

NAILER:　Oh, wickedness to so wantonly cast off the gift of life — (*A fall.*)

BATTER:　These bitches will put paid to the race . . .

SOLDIER ONE:　**To yer right!**

NAILER:　I cast thee out, saith the Lord, I cast thee from my sight —

SOLDIER ONE:　**To yer right!**

SOLDIER TWO:　**Another!**

NAILER:　**Stop it! Stop it or else . . . !** (*A fall.*) Oh, contempt, contempt of life!

BATTER (*looking up*):　That's it, that's it for today . . .

SOLDIER TWO:　No more for today . . . (*The* SOLDIERS *wander off.* CANT *appears.*)

BATTER (*to* CANT):　All right, get on with this . . .

NAILER (*rising to his feet*):　They must be locked away. All women who are pregnant. Chained at wrist and ankle, like cows in the stall. They bear our future in their innards and they kill it. **By what right!** All women big about the middle, lock up! (*He hurries out.* CANT *straightens the limbs of the fallen.*)

BATTER: Not theirs, birth. Not theirs, is it?

CANT: Dunno.

BATTER: Theirs only, I mean. What's your opinion?

CANT: No opinion.

BATTER: Go on, I won't tell.

CANT: No opinion! (*She carries on.*) Death is not yours, either.

BATTER: Wha'?

CANT: Not yours only, is it? Not an opinion.

BATTER: Come again . . .

CANT: We birth 'em, and you kill 'em. Can't be right we deliver for your slaughter. Cow mothers. Not an opinion. (KRAK *enters. He moves among the fallen.*)

KRAK: Warm women, cooling . . . (*He stops by another.*) Cooling women . . .

BATTER: Husbands want to kill 'em. Want to murder 'em, but they are murdered. Not finding anything to take revenge on, go barmy, mutilate the flesh they simpered over once . . . (*Pause*)

KRAK: She undressed me . . . (*They look at him.*) I lay there thinking . . . what is she . . . what does she . . . undressed me and . . . (*Pause*) What is the word?

BATTER: Fucked?

KRAK: Fucked! (*He laughs, as never before.*) Fucked! (*Pause*) Went over me . . . the flesh . . . with such . . . inch by inch with such . . . (*Pause*) What is the word?

CANT: Desire. (*He stares at her, then throwing himself at her feet, tears open his shirt, exposing his flesh to her.*)

KRAK: Show me.

CANT: Wha'?

KRAK: That!

CANT: Show —

KRAK: Desire! (*She hesitates.*)

BATTER: Go on . . . (*She puts her hand out, touches him unwillingly, mechanically.*)

KRAK: Not it . . .

CANT: Trying but I —

KRAK: Not it!

CANT: Can't just go —

KRAK: **Not it! Not it!** (*She runs out.* KRAK *shudders.* STUCLEY *enters, looks at him.*)

STUCLEY:Lost love . . . ! Nothing, nothing like lost love . . . (*He rests a hand on* KRAK's *bent head.*) And she was of such sympathy, such womanly wisdom I could not bring myself, for all the damage she had done me, bring myself to take revenge, any man would, you say, yes, any man would! Not me, though . . . ! (*He draws* KRAK's *head to his side.*) And you, dear brother in lost love, **I understand.** The very substance of the body wilts, like dummies who have lost their straw, we flop! Oh, I know, I know his filetting, **I too was filetted.** And all the valley sobs with grief, shh! (*He cups his ear.*) The howl of men bereaved . . . odd sound among the trees, oh, extraordinary brotherhood! (*Pause*) The new walls will be so low they cannot jump off. Not fatally. They will roll down the slopes only and — (*He stops, looking from one to another. They stare at him.*)

BATTER (*at last*): Come for a walk . . .

STUCLEY: A walk?

BATTER: Through the meadows. Through the trees.

STUCLEY: Rather not.

BATTER: Rather not . . . (*He looks about him.*) Just like Jerusalem, when we got in, the women were thick on the steps and clotting up the doors, you trod the rolling carpet of their flesh, oh, intoxication,! Rather not, he says!

STUCLEY (*resisting*): **What's this walk exactly!**

BATTER: And you were up there, first always, up the ladders —

STUCLEY: Was I? Dangerous . . .

BATTER: Dangerous, yes, England and —

STUCLEY: Saint George! **You're pushing me where I don't want to go.** (BATTER *sweeps him up in his arms.*)

BATTER: And light! So light, do you find that? (*The* SOLDIERS *make no move.*) Light as a child . . . (*He walks through them, and out.* KRAK *scrambles to his feet.*)

KRAK (*to the soldiers*): His last walk. His last walk. (*They ignore him.*) Listen, his last walk . . . ! (*He offers himself.*) Cut the skull through, will you! The one with the axe? Slice it round the top and sssssss the great stench of dead language sssssss the great stench of dead elegance dead manners sssssss articulation and explanation dead all dead **You don't hold women properly in bed.**

An effect of rain and time.

Scene Six

SKINNER, *festooned with the skeleton, outside the walls.*
BATTER *enters, with* NAILER. *Pause.*

BATTER: The Church of Christ the Lover. Fuck it.
SKINNER: What?
BATTER: New church. Tell her.
NAILER: The Holy Congregation of the Wise Womb.
BATTER: All right? (*Pause. She looks at them.*)
NAILER: Christ, abhorring the phallus, foreswore his male-
ness, chose womanly ways. Scripture in abundance for all this.
BATTER: All right?
SKINNER: I don't like wombs.
BATTER: You don't like —
SKINNER: Hate wombs. (*Pause.* BATTER *looks to* NAILER.)
  BATTER: She hates —
NAILER: I have been up sixteen hours assembling a theological
foundation for all —
BATTER: All right —
NAILER: **Not all right.** (*Pause*) We acknowledge the uniquely
female relationship with the origin of life, the irrational but
superior consciousness located in —
SKINNER: Sod wombs —
NAILER: Do listen, please (*Pause. He proceeds.*) The special
sensitivity of woman to the heart-beat of the earth — Romans,
VIII, verses 9 to —
SKINNER: He does go on —
NAILER: 17, which hitherto has held no special place in
doctrine but which henceforward will be —
SKINNER: **Palaver Of Dissimulators!**
NAILER: The foundation of the edict **Let There Be Womanly
Times!** (*Pause*)
BATTER: Wha'd yer think? (*Pause*) Well, do you wanna
church or not? (*Pause*)
SKINNER: She was all womb. Tortured me with her fecundity,
her moisture, birthing, birthing, very public, down among the
harvest, crouches, yells, and slings it round her neck, where did
I leave my sickle, oh, blood on her knees and afterbirth for
supper, and me like the arid purse of rattling coins, to her whim
and feminine mood of the moon stuff danced my service, and
then stabs it, **stabs it, the vanity of it!** (*Pause*) No womb lover
me. Witches' blight if I could manage it. I won't help you govern

your State, bailiff made monarch by a stroke of the knife . . .
(*Pause*)

BATTER: No . . . (*Pause*) You govern it instead. (*She quivers.*)

SKINNER: Now wait — now wait a minute — **wait!** Are you — **don't tease me** . . . !

NAILER: He is in a positive lather of good faith —

SKINNER: Some limp joke or spiteful provocation —

NAILER: None, I —

SKINNER (*grabbing* NAILER *by the collar*): **What** . . . ! **What** . . .

NAILER: You — are — hurting — my — throat —

SKINNER (*releasing him*): Some bastard — some twisted — scratch my brain — I can't — fingers at the old seat of suspicion — what's your — **yes! yes!** (*Pause*) Wait a minute, wait, what's your — get me swelling, get me gloating, dangle it before her eyes — she blobs about the eyes, the eyes are vast and breath goes in and out, in-out, in-out, pant, pant, the bitch is hooked, the bitch is netted, running with the water of desire **give me power what for,** look at me, all twitching with the appetite for — (*Pause*) All right yes . . . (*Pause.* NAILER *tosses down the castle keys.* SKINNER *looks at them, then with a lightning movement, snatches them off the ground.* **Execute The Executioners!** (*She leaps.*) All my pain, all my violence, all my scars say — hear my scars, you — **Suffering To Be Paid Out, Debts Extracted, Settlement In Yells!** Oh, she is not dignified, she is not charitable, the act of kindness from the victim to the murderer, grey eyes serene in pain absorbed, agony knitted into cloths of wisdom **Who Says!** Reconciliation and oblivion, **No! Great Ugly Stick Of Temper, Rather** (*She turns on her heel.*) Nobody say it's all because I'm barren! I have had children, I have done my labour side by side, and felt myself halved by her spasms, my floor fell out with hers and yes, I haemorrhaged (*Pause. They stare at her. She goes to the wall, runs her hand over the stone.*) I can't be kind. How I have wanted to be kind. But lost all feeling for it . . . Why wasn't I killed? The best thing is to perish in the struggle . . . (*She turns to* BATTER *and* NAILER.) No. (*She tosses the keys down.*) I shall be too cruel . . .

KRAK: Got to.

SKINNER: Who says?

KRAK: Got to! (*Pause. She looks around.*)

SKINNER: Out the shadows, who thinks the only perfect circle
 is the cunt in birth . . . (KRAK *emerges from a cleft in the wall.*)
KRAK: Demolition needs a drawing, too . . . (*Pause*)
SKINNER: Demolition? What's that? (*A roar as jets streak low.
 Out of the silence,* SKINNER *strains in recollection.*) There was
 no government . . . does anyone remember . . . there was
 none . . . there was none . . . there was none . . . !

SCENES FROM AN EXECUTION

CHARACTERS

GALACTIA	A Painter
CARPETA	A Painter
URGENTINO	The Doge of Venice
SUFFICI	An Admiral
RIVERA	A Critic
OSTENSIBILE	A Cardinal
PRODO	A Veteran
THE SKETCHBOOK	
SUPPORTA	Daughter of Galactia
DEMENTIA	Daughter of Galactia
SORDO	A Painter
PASTACCIO	A Prosecutor
OFFICIAL	
MAN IN THE NEXT CELL	
GAOLER	
LASANGNA	A Painter
FIRST SAILOR	
SECOND SAILOR	
THIRD SAILOR	
WORKMEN	

Scene One

A studio in Venice. A naked man sketched.

THE SKETCHBOOK: The sketchbook of the Venetian painter Galactia lying on her parted knees speaks of her art, speaks of her misery, between studies of sailcloth in red chalk the persistent interruption of one man's anatomy . . . On every margin where she has studied naval history his limbs or look intrude, the obsession alongside the commission . . .

GALACTIA: Dead men float with their arses in the air. Hating the living, they turn their buttocks up. I have this on authority. Their faces meanwhile peer into the seabed where their bones will lie. After the battle the waves were clotted with men's bums, reproachful bums bobbing the breakers, shoals of matted buttocks, silent pathos in little bays at dawn. The thing we sit on has a character. Yours says to me **kindness without integrity.** I don't think you will ever leave your wife.

CARPETA: I shall leave my wife, I have every intention of leaving my —

GALACTIA: No, you never will. I believed you would until I started this drawing, and now I see, your bum is eloquent on the subject, it is a bum that does not care to move . . .

CARPETA: I resent that, Galactia —

GALACTIA: You resent it —

CARPETA: I resent it and I —

GALACTIA: Resentment is such a miserable emotion. In fact it's not an emotion at all, it's a little twitch of self-esteem. Why resent when you can hate? **Don't move!**

CARPETA: You are the most unsympathetic, selfish woman I have ever had the misfortune to become entangled with. You are arrogant and vain and you are not even very good looking, in fact the contrary is the case and yet —

GALACTIA: You are moving —

CARPETA: I couldn't care if I am moving, I have my —

GALACTIA: You are spoiling the drawing —

CARPETA: I have my pride as well as you, and I will not lie
here and be attacked like this, you have robbed me of all my
resources, I am exhausted by you and my work is going to
the —

GALACTIA: What work?

CARPETA: **I have done no work!**

GALACTIA: Carpeta, you know perfectly well you only stand
to benefit from the loss of concentration you have suffered
through loving me. You have painted Christ among the flocks
eight times now, you must allow the public some relief —

CARPETA: **You despise me!**

GALACTIA: Yes, I think I do. But kiss me, you have such a
wonderful mouth.

CARPETA: I won't kiss you.

GALACTIA: Please, I have a passion for your lips.

CARPETA: No, I will not. How can you love someone you
despise?

GALACTIA: I don't know, it's peculiar.

CARPETA: Where are my trousers?

GALACTIA: I adore you, Carpeta . . .

CARPETA: **I am a better painter than you.**

GALACTIA: Yes —

CARPETA: **Fact.**

GALACTIA: I said yes, didn't I?

CARPETA: And I have painted Christ among the flocks eight
times not because I cannot think of anything else to paint but
because I have a passion for perfection, I long to be the finest
Christ painter in Italy, I have a longing for it, and that is
something an opportunist like you could never understand —

GALACTIA: No —

CARPETA: You are ambitious and ruthless —

GALACTIA: Yes —

CARPETA: And you will never make a decent job of anything
because you are a sensualist, you are a woman and a sensualist
and you only get these staggering commissions from the State
because you —

GALACTIA: What?

CARPETA: You —

GALACTIA: What?

CARPETA: Thrust yourself!

GALACTIA: I what?

CARPETA: Oh, let's not insult each other.

GALACTIA: Thrust myself?

CARPETA: Descend to low abuse —

GALACTIA: **It's you who** —

CARPETA: I am tired and I refuse to argue with you —

GALACTIA: Get out of my studio, then, go on, get out —

CARPETA: Here we go, the old Galactia —

GALACTIA: You are such a hypocrite, such an exhausting, dispiriting hypocrite, just get out —

CARPETA: As soon as I've got my trousers —

GALACTIA: **No, just get out.**

PRODO (*entering*):   Signora Galactia?

CARPETA: I want my —

GALACTIA: No! Ask your wife for some trousers, she'll make you some trousers, down on her knees, eye to the crutch, sew, sew, sew, little white teeth nipping the thread —

CARPETA: We can't go on like this, can we? We can't go on like this —

GALACTIA: Snip, snip, snip, lick, lick, lick —

PRODO: Signora Galactia?

GALACTIA: **I hate you, you are running my life**. (*Pause, then the door slams.*) I am losing my mind. My mind is breaking up and drifting in all directions, like an ice field in some warm current, hear the crack, drifting blocks of consciousness that took me forty years to put together, I look ten years older and I already looked old for my age, I cannot let myself be splintered like this, can I? I cannot! Who are you? What do you want?

PRODO: I'm Prodo, the Man with the Crossbow Bolt In His Head.

GALACTIA: Oh, yes.

PRODO: Come at two o'clock, you said.

GALACTIA: Yes . . .

PRODO: It is two o'clock.

GALACTIA: Yes . . .

PRODO: I am prompt because I am in demand. Where there is no demand, there is no haste. I would appreciate it if we got on, I am required by a Scotch anatomist at half past three.

GALACTIA: Yes.

PRODO: The fee is seven dollars but no touching. I also have an open wound through which the movement of the bowel may be observed, and my hand is cleft to the wrist, if you're interested. I suggest two dollars for the bowel, and the hand you can look at with my compliments. It is a miracle I am alive, I am a walking manifestation of organic solidarity and the resilience of the Christian state. Shall I proceed?

GALACTIA:	Please.

PRODO:	I will take my hat off. Are you ready?

GALACTIA:	Ready. (*Pause*)

PRODO:	Voilà. The tip is buried in the centre of my brain and yet I suffer no loss of faculties. Pain, yes, and alcohol may occasion blackouts. The shaft may be observed to twitch perceptibly at times of mental exertion. If you would care to set me a simple arithmetical sum I may be able to exhibit this phenomenon.

GALACTIA:	Incredible . . .

PRODO:	Go on, ask me.

GALACTIA:	Twelve plus five.

PRODO:	No, simple, simple.

GALACTIA:	Seven times eleven.

PRODO:	Seven times eleven . . . is. . . .

GALACTIA:	It's moving . . . !

PRODO:	Is seventy-seven! There is no other recorded evidence of a man sustaining traumatic damage to the brain of this order and retaining consciousness. Would you care to examine the bowel?

GALACTIA:	Why not, while we're at it?

PRODO:	I do not normally reveal this to a woman.

GALACTIA:	Try not to think of me as a woman. Think of me as a painter.

PRODO:	I will think of you as a painter. Are you braced for the exposure? I will lower my belt.

GALACTIA:	Good God . . .

PRODO:	Please do not faint.

GALACTIA:	I am not going to faint . . .

PRODO:	The passage of undigested material along the alimentary canal by the process known as peristalsis can be clearly observed. The retention of the bowel within the pelvic cavity is sometimes problematic given the absence of a significant area of muscularity.

GALACTIA:	Spilling your guts . . .

PRODO:	As you wish. That is nine dollars, please.

GALACTIA:	Are you bitter, Prodo?

PRODO:	Bitter?

GALACTIA:	For being left a specimen?

PRODO:	God gave me life. God led me to the battle. God steered the bolt, and in his mercy turned my maiming to my benefit. That is nine dollars, please.

GALACTIA:	Unbuttoning yourself in rich men's rooms . . .

PRODO: Thank you.

GALACTIA: Grotesque celebrity. Shudder maker. Clinging like a louse to dirty curiosity . . .

PRODO: Do you require a receipt?

GALACTIA: What about the battle, Prodo?

PRODO: I do not talk about the battle. Thank you. One dollar change.

GALACTIA: Oh, come on, I love your wounds, but tell me how you got them.

PRODO: A treatise on my condition is to be published in the Surgical Gazette. I am also featured on a box of matches, one of which I leave you as a souvenir. I hope you have enjoyed the trivial interest of my misfortune —

GALACTIA: Paint your pain for you.

PRODO: Oh, bloody hell, it's raining —

GALACTIA: Your butchery.

PRODO: Is there a short cut to the Rialto?

GALACTIA: Paint your anger. Paint your grief.

PRODO: I'll see myself out, thank you —

GALACTIA: **Idiot**. (*Pause*)

PRODO: What?

GALACTIA: Holding your bowel in. With an arrow sticking out the middle of your head. **Idiot**. (*Pause*)

PRODO: If you'll excuse me, I —

GALACTIA: I am painting the battle, Prodo. Me. The battle which changed you from a man into a monkey. One thousand square feet of canvas. Great empty ground to fill. With noise. Your noise. The noise of men minced. Got to find a new red for all that blood. A red that smells. Don't go, Prodo, holding your bowel in —

PRODO: **What sort of woman are you?**

GALACTIA: A midwife for your labour. Help you bring the truth to birth. Up there, twice life-size, your half-murder, your half-death. Come on, don't be manly, there's no truth where men are being manly —

PRODO: Don't trust you, got a mad eye —

GALACTIA: Shuffling away there, stop, will you?

PRODO: Afraid of you.

GALACTIA: Afraid of me? Me? Why?

PRODO: Hurt me —

GALACTIA: Never —

PRODO: Ruin it —

GALACTIA: What? (*Pause*) What?

PRODO: **My peace with life.**

GALACTIA: Listen. Listen, look at me, look at me, what sort of a face do I have? Look at it, is it a good face? Is it generous?

PRODO: It's all right —

GALACTIA: No, it's more than all right, it's a good face, it's an honest face, broad and generous —

PRODO: Yes —

GALACTIA: Of course it is, I know it is and so do you, I know my face, I paint it, over and over again, I am not beautiful and I wouldn't be beautiful if I could be —

PRODO (*sarcastically*):   No, you wouldn't be —

GALACTIA: I tell you I would not, I do not trust beauty, it is an invention and a lie, trust my face, I am a woman who has lived a little, nothing much, I have not been split up the middle like you have, but I have picked up a thing or two and I tell you I have never been at peace with life, I would not be at peace with life, there is no such thing and those who claim they have it have drugged their consciences or numbed their pain with futile repetitions of old catechisms, catechisms like your patter, oh, look at you. **Who did it to you, Prodo, and what for?** I will paint your violence for all the passing crowds who mock your daft appearance . . . (PRODO *sobs*.) There, there . . . we must be brave . . .

PRODO: Nightmares . . .

GALACTIA: Yes . . . yes . . .

PRODO: Down the bottom of the sheets all arms and legs . . .

GALACTIA: Go on . . .

PRODO: Bones going . . . air full of cracking bones . . . oars going . . . bones going . . .

GALACTIA: Yes . . .

PRODO: Flesh falling down . . . flesh raining down . . . bits going . . . everywhere bits going . . . rain of bits and **this tumult in my bed . . .!**

GALACTIA: Oh, my poor ridiculous man, I shall paint the why of all your terrors, shall I?

PRODO: Give me back my little peace . . .

GALACTIA: Why was the battle fought, Prodo?

PRODO: My little ease, you —

GALACTIA: Why? (*Pause*)

PRODO: Freedom, of course.

GALACTIA: Freedom . . .

PRODO: Glory, of course.

GALACTIA: Glory . . .

PRODO: The Honour of the Great Republic and the Humiliation of the Pagan Turk!

GALACTIA: Oh, look, the arrow's twitching! Round and
round it goes . . .

PRODO: **Doesn't!**

GALACTIA: Twirling, feathered thing, oh, look!

PRODO: **Doesn't!**

GALACTIA: Wonderful man, grappling with dim truths!

PRODO: What are you trying to do to me, Signora! (*Pause*)

GALACTIA: Truth, that's all, just truth. See yourself out, will
you?

PRODO: You are an unkind woman, you . . .

GALACTIA: Thank you for coming.

PRODO: Digging out my —

GALACTIA: Sketchbook! Sketchbook! Where have I —

PRODO: Horror of my —

GALACTIA: Laid it down and —

PRODO: **Stupid life.**

GALACTIA: Good bye.

SKETCHBOOK: The upper left hand corner shows a parting in
the angry sky; the clouds have opened and sun bursts through
the aperture, flooding the canvas and highlighting all the subjects that lie under the slanting beams, a dramatic diagonal that
draws the eye, pulls the eye down jerky surfaces of battle and
through passing horizontals to —

Scene Two

A palace in Venice. The Doge examines a drawing.

URGENTINO: I can't see my brother. (*Pause*)

GALACTIA: You can't see your —

URGENTINO: Well, of course I can see him, don't be obtuse.
Obviously I can see him, I mean I cannot see *enough* of my
brother. I like my brother and I want to see more of him. He is
the Admiral and he is not big enough.

GALACTIA: He is — fourteen feet high. (*Pause*)

URGENTINO: Listen, I do hope we are going to become
friends.

GALACTIA: Me too.

URGENTINO: I like to be friends with everybody. It is a weakness of mine. But if we are to be friends I think we have to understand one another. I know you are an artist and I am a politician, and we both have all sorts of little mannerisms, turns of speech, beliefs and so on, which neither of us will be happy to renounce, but for the sake of easy communication may I suggest we stop the little dance of personal regard and concentrate on facts? Simple, incontrovertible facts? My brother is Admiral of the Fleet and he does not occupy a prominent enough position in this drawing. There! Do you like my jacket? It's damascene.

GALACTIA: It's very fine.

URGENTINO: It is fine. I take clothes very seriously.

GALACTIA: I admire that in a man.

URGENTINO: Do you! We are going to get on! I pride myself on my good taste, and my good taste extends to artists too. You know Carpeta almost got this job? The cardinals on the fine art committee were hot for him.

GALACTIA: Is that so?

URGENTINO: I fought them bitterly. I said he is spent. He is spent, isn't he? Utterly.

GALACTIA: He is only thirty-five.

URGENTINO: What does it matter if he's seventeen? He's spent. Listen, I know artists pretend to be kind to one another, but be honest, you all hate one another's —

GALACTIA: That isn't actually the case —

URGENTINO: No, no, of course not, but when it comes down to it you —

GALACTIA: No. Actually. No.

URGENTINO: You won't admit it. I like that. All right, you won't admit it! Signora, I have taken a chance with you, do you know why? Because you sweat. Your paintings sweat. Muscle. Knuckle. Shin. No one drapes in your pictures. They clash. Kissing even, is muscular. You see, I have eyes, I look, but also I smell, I smell your canvas and the smell is sweat. Do you find me offensive? I am a devotee.

GALACTIA: I rejoice in your appreciation.

URGENTINO: Good! But listen, this is a State commission, an investment, an investment by us, the Republic of Venice, in you, Galactia. Empire and artist. Greatness beckons, and greatness imposes disciplines. Do you like these grapes? They come from Crete. We left two thousand soldiers dead there, but we have the grapes. Little bit of sand. Little bit of history.

GALACTIA: What are you trying to say to me?

URGENTINO: I am saying you have not been asked to paint the back wall of the vicarage. I am saying that a canvas which is one hundred feet long is not a painting, it is a public event.

GALACTIA: I know that. It's why I'm here.

URGENTINO: Good! You are ambitious, and ambition is a fine thing, but it involves changes of perspective. My brother is quite big enough, but is he in the right place? That is what I meant when I said I could not see my brother. I have a sense of humour, you see!

GALACTIA: Yes, yes —

URGENTINO: You see!

GALACTIA: I also have a sense of humour —

URGENTINO: Signora, obviously you have a sense of humour, only an artist with a sense of humour would place the Admiral of the Fleet in such an obscure position! For all his size, he does not dominate the drawing. Now, that is very witty of you, but you see, I am witty, too, so let's be serious, shall we?

GALACTIA: Are you faulting me for composition?

URGENTINO: Signora Galactia! Would I do such a thing? You are the artist! I only remind you of certain priorities. A great artist must first of all be responsible, or all his brush strokes, and all his colouring, however brilliant, will not lift him out of the second rank.

GALACTIA: I am painting the Battle of Lepanto. I am painting it in such a way that anyone who looks at it will feel he is there, and wince in case an arrow should fly out of the canvas and catch him in the eye —

URGENTINO: Excellent!

GALACTIA: So that children will tremble at the noise and cling to their parents as the ships collide —

URGENTINO: Excellent!

GALACTIA: Such a noisy painting that people will stare at it holding their ears, and when they have dragged themselves away, look at their clothes to see if they have been spattered with blood or brain —

URGENTINO: Marvellous! You see, you are passionate, you are magnificent!

GALACTIA: Make them breathless, make them pale!

URGENTINO: Yes! Yes! But also make them **proud**.

GALACTIA: Proud?

URGENTINO: Great art will always celebrate! Celebrate! Celebrate! Do you love Venice, Signora Galactia?

GALACTIA: I am a Venetian.

URGENTINO: So you are, but —

GALACTIA: I have said, I am a Venetian.

URGENTINO: Then praise Venice. I think I need say no more than that. Bring me another drawing soon.

Scene Three

A disused barracks in the Arsenal.

SUPPORTA: It's cold in here!

GALACTIA: Paint in gloves.

SUPPORTA: Paint in gloves?

GALACTIA: If you concentrate hard enough you'll forget the temperature. Anyway, it won't always be winter.

DEMENTIA: It stinks.

GALACTIA: Of what?

DEMENTIA: Men. There is a proper male stink in here.

GALACTIA: Of course. It used to be a barracks.

DEMENTIA: Vile.

GALACTIA: It is absolutely the right smell for the subject. If you are painting soldiers, you should live among soldiers.

DEMENTIA: It is disgusting coming here. If you wear a coloured scarf they take you for a prostitute.

GALACTIA: Wear black.

DEMENTIA: Why should I wear black? I'm not a widow.

GALACTIA: Listen, I asked to come here. When I asked for a place big enough to paint in I was offered all sorts of things, even a museum. But who wants to paint in a museum? Live among what you are painting, among who you are painting. Look at their faces, the way they move. You will never be anything but drapery painters if you do not want to look. I have tried to make you look since you were children. The habit of looking. Come here, look through the window.

SUPPORTA: I don't want to climb up on —

GALACTIA: No, look! The way they walk, the soldiers. It is not a walk, is it? It is a hip thrust, a pelvic deformation. Hip and thigh, the stiff buttock and the contorted face. The soldier when he is not dying . . . (*Pause*) Enjoy looking and stop thinking everyone wants to fuck you.

DEMENTIA: They do not pester you, you are an old woman!

GALACTIA: All right, nothing's proper, nothing's right! But it's a free room and you can get a hundred feet of canvas in it!

DEMENTIA: Male groin. Male swagger.

GALACTIA: I don't know why it frightens you. I never brought you up like it.

DEMENTIA: Doesn't *frighten* me.

GALACTIA: I was kissing at seven and gave birth at twelve.

SUPPORTA: Here we go —

GALACTIA: I had twelve lovers by my fifteenth birthday —

DEMENTIA: Oh, God, mother —

GALACTIA: For all that I knew nothing until I met Carpeta, nothing! At forty-six I find — I knew nothing. And Carpeta is spineless. Pity.

WORKMAN (*calling off*): Signora!

SUPPORTA: The scaffolders have finished.

DEMENTIA: There really isn't enough light in here.

GALACTIA: It's the afternoon.

DEMENTIA: There's still not enough light —

GALACTIA: Painters make too much of light. I can work by a candle.

DEMENTIA: There's no light, it stinks and I —

GALACTIA: Dementia, if you do not wish to be involved in this run away and look after your children —

DEMENTIA: Now, don't be silly, I am only saying —

GALACTIA: Go on, run away and —

DEMENTIA: Why do you have to be so —

WORKMAN (*approaching*): Finished it, Signora —

GALACTIA: Children's piss and husband's dinner, clean underwear and dinner party stuff, go on!

DEMENTIA: Why is she —

GALACTIA: So many people wanting — what — what is it?

WORKMAN: Finished the scaffolding. (*Pause*)

GALACTIA: Let me see. (*Pause*) No, you didn't listen to me.

WORKMAN: Three tiers you said —

GALACTIA: I said three tiers —

WORKMAN: An' that's what you —

GALACTIA: What do you think I am? Do you think I am a monkey? How am I supposed to crawl along —

WORKMAN: 'ho said you were a monkey? I never said you were a —

GALACTIA: Got to stand up there for six or seven hours, do you —

WORKMAN: Remind you what you said, you —

SKETCHBOOK: The sketchbook of the fifth daughter of the painter Galactia, known as Supporta, also an artist and scenery painter, in red chalk, shows her mother sitting with her legs apart, mouth hanging open like a rag, remonstrating with workmen in a vast room empty but for stools and scaffolding . . .

Scene Four

GALACTIA's *studio.*

GALACTIA: Do you like my flesh, Carpeta? Tell me you do, although it's coarse and the pores are dark as pepper. Aren't I all colours? White eyelids, mottled on my shoulders, blue veined in my thigh and red veined on my cheeks? Are you fascinated by me? I have a sagging basket of flesh where my children have swung, and my navel protrudes like a rude tongue. But my tongue! You love that, don't you, restless tongue! Do I exhaust you? Oh, God, I exhaust him, he has a weary look . . . (*Pause*) I want to show the effect of cutlasses on flesh, the way they slice out pieces, like a melon, flinging the scrap into the air. It is not something I shall ever see, but I imagine it. It is not important to witness things. I believe in observation, but to observation you must lend imagination. The Doge says I am to submit to him another drawing in which the Admiral is given greater prominence. Well, I shall do. I shall show him not only prominent but **responsible**. And a face which is not exulting but **indifferent**. No, let go of me, you always start to touch me when I think, what are you afraid of, don't you like me to think? You see, you feel my breasts as if — **I insist on thinking** even though you have your finger — **What is it you object to?** (*Pause*) What? (*Pause*) Oh, come on, you —

CARPETA: I have been displaced.

GALACTIA: By what?

CARPETA: The battle.

GALACTIA: Rubbish.

CARPETA: I have been. I am not on your mind.

GALACTIA: Of course you are on my mind —

CARPETA: Not all the time!

GALACTIA: No, not all the time, how can I —

CARPETA: You see! Not all the time!

GALACTIA: Oh, God . . . Oh, God, Carpeta . . . (*He sobs.*)

CARPETA: You make me — utterly childish . . .

GALACTIA: Yes . . .

CARPETA: Clinging . . . rag . . .

GALACTIA: I wish I were not sensual. I wish I had not got from my mother, or my father was it, this need to grasp and be grasped, because it drives me into the arms of idiots who want to crush me. Wonderful, idiotic crushing in the night. Can't you just crush me in the night? <u>I am very happy to be crushed in bed but I am a painter and you can't have that off me</u>. Oh, don't sulk, please don't sulk, there really isn't time for all this mending and accommodating to your sensitivity, which in any case isn't really sensitivity, it's brutality, but never mind that —

CARPETA: It is not brutality, it is possession —

GALACTIA: All right, you say it's —

CARPETA: **It is not brutality.**

GALACTIA: No . . . all right . . .

CARPETA: I am humiliated by my feelings for you. Humiliated. (*Pause*)

GALACTIA: Carpeta, how do you paint pity? You've always painted pity, and I never have. Tell me how to do it.

CARPETA: I don't think you could paint pity, Galactia.

GALACTIA: Why?

CARPETA: I don't think you have pity, so you can't paint it.

GALACTIA: Ah. Now you're being spiteful.

CARPETA: No. You are violent, so you can paint violence. You are furious, so you can paint fury. And contempt, you can paint that. Oh, yes, you can paint contempt. But <u>you aren't great enough for pity</u>.

GALACTIA: Great enough?

CARPETA: It's hard luck on you, because if you could paint pity, the Church would stand up for you, and if you could paint glory, you would have the State. But <u>you will please nobody</u>.

GALACTIA: You know what I think? I think you are marvellous at honouring yourself. Marvellous. But pity's got nothing to do with greatness. It's surrender, the surrender of passion, or the passion of surrender. It is capitulating to what is. Rather than pity the dead man I would say — there — there is the man

who did it, blame him, identify. <u>Locate responsibility</u>. Or else
<u>the world is just a pool, a great pool of dirty tears through which</u>
<u>vile men in boots run splashing</u>. You paint pity very well, but
you endure everything, and in the end you find Christ's
wounds — enticing. You find suffering — erotic. Your cruci-
fixions — there is something wrong with them. They love them
in the Church, the bishops wet themselves with appreciation,
but really they are rather dirty pictures, Carpeta. And if you
were normal, you would love a younger woman.

Scene Five

The barracks.

SKETCHBOOK: Painting the Turk.

GALACTIA: I scoured Venice for a Turk. I could not find a
Turk, but I discovered an Albanian.

DEMENTIA: The Albanian is staring at me. Will you ask him
not to stare at me.

GALACTIA: He sells pineapples on San Marco. Look at his
eyes!

DEMENTIA: I do not wish to see his eyes.

GALACTIA: Perfect head. Rotund, male head . . .

DEMENTIA: He is rubbing himself and staring at me. **Do keep
still!**

GALACTIA: At first I thought, paint him dead. With arms
flung out and backwards, falling headlong from the Muslim
deck, and then I thought, what a waste of a head, because who
will look at a head which is upside down? **Do stop whatever it is
you are doing, you will make my daughter angry**. So instead I did
a suppliance. I did a figure begging for his life, and I put him at
the feet of the great Admiral, with his palms extended, and I
thought I would put into his expression the certain knowledge
he would be murdered on the deck. So with one figure I transformed the enemy from beast to victim, and made victory
unclean. And I suspect, even as I draw it, they will hate this . . .!

SUPPORTA: Can I say something?

GALACTIA: Mmm . . .

SUPPORTA: I am your daughter and I love you.

GALACTIA: Yes . . .

SUPPORTA: But I am also a painter, and old enough not to flatter you.

GALACTIA: Yes . . .

SUPPORTA: And I know, as you do, that you are the best painter in Venice.

GALACTIA (*stops sketching*):   Have you noticed this, I wonder, that when someone is about to pay you a crippling and devastating compliment, they always preface it by saying they are not going to flatter you. What do you want?

SUPPORTA: You always spoil things.

GALACTIA: Do I?

SUPPORTA: Have to prove something. Superior insight, incisive wit. Whatever. I want to talk to you.

GALACTIA: I'm sorry. Yes.

SUPPORTA: It doesn't matter how they patronize you, or attack you for your promiscuity, you are still the best painter in Venice, and if you were not promiscuous, but severe, prudish and had no appetites at all, they would use that against you, they will always have to find something because you are brilliant and a woman.

GALACTIA: What are you trying to say, Supporta? The preamble is very comforting but what exactly —

SUPPORTA: You have this vast commission in front of you, which will prove beyond all argument what you are, and I am frightened you will waste it. (*Pause*)

GALACTIA: Waste it.

SUPPORTA: Yes. You will offend, and when people are offended, they cannot see the brilliance, only the offence.

DEMENTIA: I feel I am being burned here. Burned by eyes. I am going out to mix some paint. Look at it, sticks to you, sticky little Albanian thing! (*She goes out.*)

GALACTIA: Go on.

SUPPORTA: Give the people what they want, and they will love you. They will exclaim over you. And after that, no woman painter here will have to struggle against prejudice, because you will have proved us. You see, I think you have a responsibility — not to the State, but to Venetian women. Paint your feelings, by all means, that is your power, but let the public in, share with them. The drawing of the Turk insults them.

GALACTIA: You want me to paint like a man.

SUPPORTA: No —

GALACTIA: Yes, you want me to paint a man's painting.

SUPPORTA: I do not. What man can paint like you in any
case? The vigour, the effort, the agony? No man.

GALACTIA: And no man honestly hates murder, either. You
ask me to be responsible, when what you really mean is, 'celebrate the battle!'

SUPPORTA: I am thinking of you.

GALACTIA: Oh?

SUPPORTA: I am thinking how mean life is, how it gives you
one bite only. Think how they'll attack you, they'll say this
woman scorns us, mocks our sacrifice. You scour your own
mind, you hunt down your own truth, but perhaps you're vain,
too, not to compromise. Maybe you're arrogant, have you
thought of that?

GALACTIA: Arrogant, me?

SUPPORTA: You joke, but —

GALACTIA: Supporta, listen to me. The act of painting is an
act of arrogance. It is arrogant to describe the world and then to
shove the thing into the world's face. It is arrogant to compete
with nature in painting a flower, or to challenge God by imp-
roving views. To paint is to boast, and if you don't like boasting
you ought not to paint. Now, let me concentrate. I will negotiate with power because I have to. I will lick the Doge's crevices
if need be, because he has power. I am not wholly an idiot and I
like to eat and drink as well as you. **Mustafa I may be talking but
I am watching you.** Look at him, he can't sit still if Dementia is
out of the room, fidgets like a ferret in the trousers —

SUPPORTA: You will not listen to advice, will you?

GALACTIA (*to the Albanian*):   It's all right, she's coming back!
Do look at him!

SUPPORTA: You are adamantly self-opinionated and —

GALACTIA: Here she comes, look at her waist, her lovely
waist —

DEMENTIA: Will you not encourage him!

GALACTIA: His eyes, look! Look at his eyes, isn't he amazing?

SUPPORTA: **Intolerable**. (*Pause*)

GALACTIA: The Turk thinks he will die. How does he know
he will die? Because the Admiral's expression is bereft of
mercy, is a mask of —

Scene Six

The Admiralty.

SKETCHBOOK: Painting the Admiral. (*A clock ticks in the room.*) The preliminary sketch. (*Pause*)

SUFFICI: Do you like my face?

GALACTIA: Well, that's a bold question.

SUFFICI: I like bold questions.

GALACTIA: Normally they ask it in a different way. They say 'Is my face difficult to draw?' (*Pause*) It is difficult to draw.

SUFFICI: I have always been painted — cravenly.

GALACTIA: How do you mean, cravenly?

SUFFICI: The real me not attempted.

GALACTIA: What is the Real You? (*Pause*) Come on, what's the Real You?

SKETCHBOOK: The Admiral of the Atlantic, the Admiral of the Two Seas, the General of the Home and Distant Waters, is shown leaning on a desk with one fist underneath the chin, staring with a melancholy gaze into the middle distance, in red ink, the victor of Lepanto in civilian dress, patrician forehead weary from high office, he is —

SUFFICI: A homosexual gardener.

GALACTIA: You're teasing me.

SUFFICI: Garacci guessed it, and painted my fingers on the muzzles of my dogs in such a way that all the armour in the world could not conceal my nature . . .

GALACTIA: Garacci is superficial.

SUFFICI: I felt, for all the steel in which I was encased, naked. He is wonderful with hands, don't you think?

GALACTIA: I cannot stomach Garacci.

SUFFICI: My hands said The Warrior Prefers the Living Flesh. In no uncertain manner. But who looks at hands?

GALACTIA: They will look where they are told to look, where the composition compels their attention. I do hands better than Garacci, you'll see. Everyone will see the hands, it will be a hand painting, the hands of the killed, the hands of the killers, hands red to the wrists, hands without owners. Can you think of anything more pitiful than a severed hand? Or eloquent? I think it is the ultimate in pity. My lover says I have no pity, but you don't have to have Christ hanging off a tree trunk to show pity, do you? Hands are the points of contact between man and man, man and woman, the instruments of friendship, symbols of love and trust. And in battles they drop from the sky, and men shake stumps in anger, don't they? Raw things prodding. I must say I am furious to find you like this, so gentle and so subtle, I am drawing badly. I am drawing rubbish —

SUFFICI: Don't I keep still enough?

GALACTIA: Yes, terribly still, terribly dignified. I did not see you in the victory parade, I do not go to victory parades, I have only seen Garacci's portrait, and I thought it slavish and flattering, but I come here with my book and pencils, and blow me down, you have to hand it to him, he's done you right, you have the most compassionate face I've ever seen. Silly me, I should know the world is full of contradiction, but it's thrown me. See first, and look after. I saw you, and then I looked, and the two don't tally. Never mind, it must be that I'm not looking deep enough. (*A page is ripped from the sketchbook.*) Start again.

SUFFICI: From this window you can see the Fleet.

GALACTIA: Yes.

SUFFICI: Riding at anchor. Do you care for ships?

GALACTIA: I have spent a fortnight drawing them.

SUFFICI: Do you like them?

GALACTIA: The trader, in a good wind, bringing things, yes.

SUFFICI: And the warships?

GALACTIA: No.

SUFFICI: Why did the committee choose you, Signora, to paint the Battle of Lepanto?

GALACTIA: Because I do what no one else can. I paint realistically. Either that or the papers got mixed up.

SUFFICI: I feel sure they made the wise choice.

GALACTIA: Oh, now, don't be generous, sitting so still there with your grey eyes resting on your empire . . . (*Pause*)

SUFFICI: I think you are rather angry with me . . .

GALACTIA: Grey eyes with no chink for doubt to enter, only the little veiling of the lazy lid, the droop of bedroom miseries . . . (*Pause*)

SUFFICI: Go on . . . (*Pause*) My drooping eyelid? (*Pause*) Go on, I am not offended . . .

GALACTIA (*refusing*): Sometimes you have to admit they get things right, the bureaucrats; for all their corrupt deliberations, they pick an artist who might just **tell the truth**. And then God help us, it's blood and mayhem down the cold museums.

SUFFICI: My eyelid.

GALACTIA: I don't know whether Venice is a good republic or a bad one, I am not political —

SUFFICI: Me neither, what about my —

GALACTIA: The moment you go in for politics, you cavil, you split up the truth —

SUFFICI: Please — (*Pause*)

GALACTIA: I go from my belly. Yes or no. And when I show meat sliced, it is meat sliced, it is not a pretext for elegance. Meat sliced. How do you slice meat? (*Pause*)

SUFFICI: I think you are, for an artist, rather coarse.

GALACTIA: Coarse for an artist? It's an artist's job to be coarse. Preserving coarseness, that's the problem.

SUFFICI: And simple. By which I do not mean unintelligent. I mean there are things you choose not to know.

GALACTIA: Such as that Admirals like to run naked among flowers? I do know that.

SUFFICI: I mean, the Necessary War, and the Unnecessary war.

GALACTIA (*sarcastic*): Ah, now you are stretching me . . .

SUFFICI: You see, you mock so! So replete with your own belief, you bustle and assail me, you lend no space to opposition, or risk yielding me some credibility. You see the eyelid droops, but you are afraid of it, afraid to be sucked down into the well of a different truth. You have seen me, but you are not looking. They told me you were a better painter.

GALACTIA: Your sensitivity. Your great, swaggering sensitivity. Do not look at the armour, look at the fingers. Do not look at the sword, look at the eyelids. Ignore the blood, think of the buttocks in the garden. (*Pause*) Sorry, no.

URGENTINO (*entering*): I interrupt! Philistine bore invades the sitting!

SUFFICI: We were not progressing . . .

URGENTINO: I was passing Ponte Dore on my way to the Treasury and who do I meet, I meet Gina Rivera, distinguished critic, poet and sensualist, and I say at once, damn economics, didn't I, damn economics, let us creep into the Admiralty and see how artists work!

RIVERA: Yes.

URGENTINO: Look, her sketchbook on the floor, all hot with smudges and corrections, Gina, look! Touch it! Can she touch it?

GALACTIA: Why not?

URGENTINO: A critic should watch a painter. How many critics witness the moment of production? None! They let fly at the finished canvas and know nothing of its history! By the way,

Signora, the latest sketches are superb, they are perfect, I wish you to proceed at once to the painting. My brother is big enough.

GALACTIA: Good.

URGENTINO: Gina, finger the book, finger it, the smell of it! I am a fetishist for art, forgive my infantile enthusiasm!

RIVERA: The composition for the battle is most original, Signora.

GALACTIA: Yes, I try to be original.

RIVERA: You cannot try to be original. Either you are or you are not, surely?

GALACTIA: No, originality is as much an effort as anything else. It is sweated for, unfortunately.

RIVERA: It's inspiration, surely? You cannot labour for brilliance —

URGENTINO: Suffici, listen! Two of the most remarkable women in Venice, divorced, promiscuous and combative!

RIVERA: I am not divorced. It's you that is divorced.

URGENTINO: It is absurd that the critic and the artist are not better related, absurd! You are utterly dependent on one another and yet you squirm with mutual suspicion!

RIVERA: The critic is afraid of the artist and envies her power. She is ashamed of what she secretly believes to be an inferior gift, that of exposition. So instead of serving the artist, she humiliates her.

URGENTINO: There, that is a bad critic. There are good ones, too.

RIVERA: Of course.

SUFFICI: Signora Galactia has had a trying morning, coping with my face.

URGENTINO: What is wrong with his face? He has a lovely face!

GALACTIA: Yes.

URGENTINO: What I should like for my brother is this — clemency in victory, modesty in triumph, virtue in —

SUFFICI: Do shut up.

URGENTINO: All right, I leave him to your imagination! But show him for what he is — a tactical genius.

RIVERA: How does she do that? Show him holding a compass?

URGENTINO: Yes.

RIVERA: In the middle of a battle?

URGENTINO: Why not?

RIVERA: Because she is a realist.

URGENTINO: All right, she is a realist! I don't understand these terms.

RIVERA: It means she paints what happened.

SUFFICI: There is no such thing as what happened, surely? Only views of what happened. Just as there is no such thing as a man. Only images of him. (*Pause*)

URGENTINO: Excellent! Signora, I shall forever be dropping in your studio. It is the nature of a good patron that he shows his curiosity.

GALACTIA: I do not welcome visitors as a rule.

URGENTINO: I am not a visitor, as a rule. But this is not a private commission. It is the gold and silver of the Venetian people on your paintbrush, is it not? We must be off, we have had our treat. (*Pause*). Listen, listen! The murmur of the fleet, the whack of the wind in the canvas, that is a beautiful sound, the sound Odysseus heard as he kipped on his deck with dirty sailors . . . I spent three years in the Navy, didn't I? Didn't I? Cesare?

SUFFICI: Yes . . .

URGENTINO: Yes, he says. Eloquent yes. I was the Great Naval Disaster. But Cesare is a Great Man, a great, Great Man. We had different mothers, unfortunately. Come on, Gina, let's get out from under the genius's feet.

RIVERA: How do you paint a Great Man, Signora?

GALACTIA: I'm not sure, Signora. I know the conventions, of course.

RIVERA: The conventions, yes, of course . . . (*They depart. Pause.*)

GALACTIA: Carry on, shall I? (*Pause*) No? (*Pause*) Oh, now don't say you're not going to speak . . . ! (*Pause*) All right, don't speak . . .

Scene Seven

Inside a church. A priest intones a funeral oration.

CARPETA: I don't think you should stand next to me.

GALACTIA: Not stand next to you?

CARPETA: In public.

GALACTIA: What?

CARPETA: Shh.

GALACTIA: I don't understand. If I sleep with you I don't see —

CARPETA: Shh.

GALACTIA: **Everybody knows we —**

CARPETA: Please, this is a colleague's funeral! (*Pause*)

GALACTIA: He wouldn't have objected. He was never in his wife's bed, either.

CARPETA: I should be very grateful if you'd —

GALACTIA: It's funny but a funeral is calculated to make me want to fuck —

CARPETA: Please —

GALACTIA: Not fuck, exactly — mate.

CARPETA: I shall move away from you.

GALACTIA: You know, heat to heat, the procreative, mindless dog and bitch thing down the —

CARPETA: I am standing over there —

GALACTIA: **Don't dare move**.

CARPETA: You are hurting my —

GALACTIA: I haven't finished yet —

CARPETA: My wrist, you —

GALACTIA: All right, go! (*Congregational responses.*)

CARPETA: Please, why are you following me?

GALACTIA: Do you know what I hate?

CARPETA: No, and I don't —

GALACTIA: I hate the way you act in public. It disgusts me. Is it because you are a religious painter?

CARPETA (*to a bystander*): Excuse me —

GALACTIA: Who do you think you are fooling? The way you stick your nose up in the air, and your eyes go all —

CARPETA: Excuse me, excuse me —

GALACTIA: I know you have to please your patrons, but really! Farini hated all this, and so do I.

CARPETA: His wife wanted it. She wanted a proper funeral.

GALACTIA: She would have done. She hated him.

CARPETA: Nonsense.

GALACTIA: She could not dispose of him in life so she —

CARPETA: Shh!

GALACTIA: Catch Farini with a crucifix — hey, Sordo —

MOURNER: Shh!

GALACTIA: Sordo, imagine the old man watching this! We do terrible dishonour to dead men. And he was an atheist!

MOURNER: Be quiet!

GALACTIA: Fact! He was investigated by the Inquisition —

MOURNER: Rubbish.

GALACTIA: In 15 —

MOURNER: Rubbish.

GALACTIA: Oh, do stop saying rubbish, he was a great painter
and he couldn't stick God, I should know, he taught me.

SORDO: That isn't true.

GALACTIA: No?

SORDO: It isn't true, Galactia, that he —

GALACTIA: All right, correction, he wasn't a great painter, he
was a moderate painter and he hated God. Is that better? I was
being generous because he's dead.

SORDO: Galactia, you are drunk.

GALACTIA: Oh, God . . . !

SORDO: You are drunk and everyone —

GALACTIA: Why is it you cannot speak the truth without
someone saying you must be drunk? That or barmy? They put
Farini in the madhouse for saying the Pope could not tie his own
shoelaces — (*Protests*) They did — **fact!** He recanted. (*More
groans and complaints.*) I must get some fresh air. All this death
worship is getting up my nostrils, where's my lover? Oh, look at
him, he has the face of — now I see it, Carpeta's Christ paintings are self-portraits! And half an hour ago he had his
mouth — (*Shouts of protest.*) All right, I'm going! (*The door
closes. Sounds of the street.*) A dead painter, claimed. The
dissenting voice, drowned in compliments. Never happier than
when lying in the gutter with a bricklayer, drunk out of mind.
Human, warm, and round. And yet a frightful liar. Couldn't put
a brush to paper without lying — the happy poor, the laughing
rags of tramps and scabby dogs pawing the dirt. Guilty old
fornicator . . .

CARPETA: I wish you wouldn't do that.

GALACTIA: What?

CARPETA: Exhibit yourself.

GALACTIA: Is that what I do?

CARPETA: Yes.

GALACTIA: I thought I was keeping death at bay.

CARPETA: No, why do you —

GALACTIA: They worship death because, listen —

CARPETA: **Why do you? Why?** (*Pause*)

GALACTIA: I don't know . . . I don't know . . . I am not

happy, Carpeta, which is why I laugh so much. (*Pause*) I must work now.

CARPETA: Come home with me, my wife —

GALACTIA: I left Dementia finishing the oarsman's cuff, I want to see she —

CARPETA: My wife's at the —

GALACTIA: Your wife . . . (*She laughs a little.*)

CARPETA: Come home with me —

GALACTIA: Get off. (*Pause*)

CARPETA: It is all right for you to finger me in public, murmuring things in churches, naughtiness and desecration, but when I —

GALACTIA: Yes —

CARPETA: When I ask for what I —

GALACTIA: Absolutely —

CARPETA: What I —

GALACTIA: Egotistical And Monstrous Woman. (*Pause*) Yes.

Scene Eight

The barracks. A door slams.

SKETCHBOOK: Painting the Dying. The dead and dying occupy one third of the entire canvas, which is no less than six hundred and sixty-six square feet, an area not strictly in accordance with the sketch submitted to the authorities. They lie sprawled, heaped and doubled against gunwales and draped over oars, with expressions of intolerable pain, and by a method of foreshortening, their limbs, attached and unattached, project uncomfortably towards the viewer . . .

GALACTIA: Who's there? Oh, come on, who's — Look, I only have to call and —

RIVERA: Working late, Signora?

GALACTIA: People choose the most extraordinary times to visit you.

RIVERA: Candles . . . the incense of the pigment . . . rather a religious atmosphere . . .

GALACTIA: Is it.

RIVERA: A woman alone in a barracks.

GALACTIA: Not really alone. There are several hundred marines within shouting distance.

RIVERA: You squat up there like — skirts pulled up like — perched on your scaffolding — a full and undone breast — these nights are hot, I couldn't hold a brush for sweating, do you sweat, Signora? And the oil which trickles down. You have got smudges of burnt umber on your cheek.

GALACTIA: It's not umber, it's sienna.

RIVERA: I have just come from church. Do you like churches? The whispering of women! 'Lord, make me pregnant!' 'Lord, stop me being pregnant!' Women pleading, women dragging their pain up to the altar, and I thought, I must see Galactia, and there you are, sleeves rolled up like a plasterer . . . superb. The Doge is terribly unhappy. I thought I'd tell you.

GALACTIA: Yes.

RIVERA: You know.

GALACTIA: Yes. He visits me, and he feels sick. He is frightened I will paint some awful truth. So he walks up and down, and looks. And feels sick. (*Pause*) No fun being a doge.

RIVERA: Are you interested in politics?

GALACTIA: No.

RIVERA: May I tell you a little about politics, or would it spoil your concentration?

GALACTIA: Yes.

RIVERA: I'd like to anyway. (*Pause*) The Doge is actually a highly responsible patron of the arts. Dilettante, of course, and slightly vulgar. But then, to someone of your sensibilities, all patrons are vulgar, I expect. He loves artists, and the harder he loves them, the more vulgar he becomes, it's all rather pitiful, really, but —

GALACTIA: Bang goes the concentration. (*Pause*)

RIVERA: Sorry. The point is this. The Doge is insecure. It would not take a great deal to have him removed from office.

GALACTIA: Doges come, and doges go . . .

RIVERA: It isn't as simple as that, unfortunately.

GALACTIA: Isn't it?

RIVERA: There is a climate very favourable to painting here. To poetry, to sculpture. It is a climate that permitted the appointment of a controversial painter like yourself to represent the greatest triumph of Venetian history —

GALACTIA: Represent what?

RIVERA: The greatest triumph of Venetian —

GALACTIA: I think you've come to the wrong studio. On my

contract it says — I can't find the contract at the moment but it says — I'm sure it says — 'The Battle of Lepanto.' Nothing about triumphs of — triumphs of what?

RIVERA: The doge has taken an extraordinary risk in commissioning you. If you humiliate him, you aid his enemies and invite his fall. And if he falls, there will be a new incumbent, and I assure you, as someone who is interested in politics, none of the other candidates cares one iota for —

GALACTIA: You're a critic, aren't you?

RIVERA: Yes, but I must have something to criticize. (*Pause*)

GALACTIA: Excuse me, this figure of a man dying of wounds sustained during the greatest triumph of Venetian —

RIVERA: **It isn't that simple**. (*Pause*) I make no attempt to influence you on points of style, I only —

GALACTIA: The muscle hanging off the bone is rather difficult to do with you —

RIVERA: **Dirty Mess Of Truths, Signora, Clinging To The Mouth**. (*Pause*) It is really beautiful in here, and the candles catch your eyes. I am not ashamed of what I tell you, bringing world of muck against your doors. Absolutely not ashamed. How beautiful my clothes are, and my whiteness, most impeccable woman, drifting through galleries. But it is very violent, criticism. A very bloody, knocking eyeballs thing. Knives out for slashing reputations, grasping the windpipe of expression. I try to look nice, though it's murder I do for my cause. Good night. (*She withdraws.*)

GALACTIA: Sitting through the dark, thirty feet aloft on creaking boards, with moths gone barmy round the candles, someone's got to speak for dead men, not pain and pity, but abhorrence, fundamental and unqualified, blood down the paintbrush, madness in the gums —

VOICES OF THE CANVAS: The Dying — The Dying —

GALACTIA: The Admiral is a hypocrite. Humility my arse.

VOICES OF THE CANVAS: The Dying — The Dying —

GALACTIA: Algebraic. Clinical. Shrivelled testes and a sour groin.

VOICES OF THE CANVAS: The Dying — The Dying —

GALACTIA: The soldier does not smell his own lie but repeats the catechism of the State, bawling pack of squaddies yelling male love —

VOICES OF THE CANVAS: **The Dying! The Dying!**

GALACTIA: The painter who paints for the government recruits the half-wit and stabs the baby in its mess —

THE VOICES OF THE CANVAS: **The dying! The dying!**

FIRST SAILOR: **Oi!** (*Silence. Three drunk sailors have come in.*) Woman up a ladder . . .

SECOND SAILOR: Anybody seen my bed?

GALACTIA: This is out bounds to naval personnel, will you —

FIRST SAILOR: Oi! (*Pause*) Woman up a ladder . . .

GALACTIA: You will kick the paint jars over —

SECOND SAILOR: Seen my bed!

GALACTIA: You have kicked them over, stupid!

SECOND SAILOR: Beg pardon, looking for my —

THIRD SAILOR: 'ho are you callin' stupid?

SECOND SAILOR: Not a bed . . .

GALACTIA: Who is your commanding officer?

SECOND SAILOR: Table, not a bed . . .

THIRD SAILOR: 'ho is she callin' stupid?

GALACTIA: You have come to the wrong door, this is not a barracks, it's a —

FIRST SAILOR: Oi!

GALACTIA: Studio and I —

FIRST SAILOR: Oi! (*Pause*)

SECOND SAILOR: Wha'? (*Pause*) Christ . . . !

SKETCHBOOK: The sketchbook shows three seamen variously disposed about a massive canvas, mouths open, hands hanging at their sides. One of them holds a bottle loosely in his hand, as if, out of sheer amazement, he has forgotten to be drunk . . . (*The bottle splinters.*)

THIRD SAILOR: **Mur-der!**

FIRST SAILOR: Daggers! Rifles! Arms!

SECOND SAILOR: **Att-ack! Att-ack!**

FIRST SAILOR: Christ and the Republic, Ho!

GALACTIA: **Do not stab the canvas!**

SECOND SAILOR: Fire! Fire!

FIRST SAILOR: Look out, be'ind yer!

THIRD SAILOR: **Help! Help!**

FIRST SAILOR: Guard yer backs! (*The sailors rampage.*)

SECOND SAILOR: Cut-lass!

GALACTIA: Mind that tray of — (*A pile of bottles is scattered.*)

FIRST SAILOR: Slash the bugger!

THIRD SAILOR: **Mur-der! Mur-der!**

GALACTIA: **Mind my palettes, you —** (*A collapsing table and items.*)

SECOND SAILOR: Blood!

FIRST SAILOR: **Got-cha!**

THIRD SAILOR: **Aaagghhh!**

GALACTIA: **Get out! Get out of here, you** —

FIRST SAILOR: Ow! She 'it me!

GALACTIA: **Out! Out!** (*With whoops, two of the sailors run out. Pause.*) And you.

SECOND SAILOR: I think — I think —

GALACTIA: Look at this mess . . . ! How am I to work when you — when people like you — look at it!

SECOND SAILOR: I think I —

GALACTIA: Do you have any idea of the cost of these things? Have you?

SECOND SAILOR: Think I —

GALACTIA: Twenty dollars for an ounce of that, you —

SECOND SAILOR: Go and —

GALACTIA: Lunatics, I'll —

SECOND SAILOR: Be sick . . . (*Pause*)

GALACTIA: Sit still.

SECOND SAILOR: Be sick, Mrs. . . . (*Pause*)

GALACTIA: Why do you drink so much? Is it because — everybody is half cut round here, is it because —

SECOND SAILOR: Not the drink . . . (*Pause*) The picture. (*Pause*) Is death like that? In battle, is it? (*Pause*)

GALACTIA: Yes. I have never seen it, but I think so.

SECOND SAILOR: I think so, too. (*Pause*)

GALACTIA: Sit there, and I'll draw you . . .

SKETCHBOOK: The Young Sailor Struck. (*Pause*) The Young Sailor Struck does not exist in any of the preliminary sketches for The Battle of Lepanto, and a close examination of the paint reveals him to be an addition to the composition painted at a later stage. He is shown huddled against an abandoned cannon, staring with an expression of disbelief at the violence raging about him. It is the only face in the entire canvas of over two hundred faces which is in repose, and painted in a liquid, translucent colour in an almost religious manner, acts as a barometer of human incomprehension, in contrast to the fixed and callous stare of the Admiral Suffici against whom he is placed in diametrical opposition. The two figures are separated by a shoal of dying figures sliding out the canvas to the left, while to the right, in the third point of a triangular configuration, in utter desolation against the mayhem, The Man With The Crossbow Bolt In His Head covers his ears, rocking to and

fro at his oar, fathoming the shock of what's befallen him and
inviting us to share his passionate desire to be somewhere
else . . .

Scene Nine

A passageway in the palace.

OFFICIAL: Signor Carpeta?

CARPETA: Yes.

OFFICIAL: Take a seat, please. Have you brought your folder?

CARPETA: Yes.

OFFICIAL: What a big folder!

CARPETA: Yes, I do a lot of art.

OFFICIAL: Wait here, please.

SORDO (*emerging*):   Carpeta! You here, too!

CARPETA: Naturally.

SORDO: Same old faces. Same old hacks!

CARPETA: I don't think you should call yourself a hack, or you
will start to believe it.

SORDO: I do believe it! I am a hack. And so are you.

CARPETA: I have no wish to be included in your —

SORDO: You may not wish it, old son, but —

CARPETA: I resent that, Sordo. No, more than that. It makes
me angry. If you do not wish to paint seriously, you should not
paint at all.

SORDO: Excellent. What have you brought along, Christ
Among The Flocks, is it? Oh, don't be angry, it's as much a
performance as my self-denigration and twice as difficult to
keep up. They are looking for movement.

CARPETA: Movement?

SORDO: Yes, it's a secular subject.

CARPETA: What?

SORDO: Ah, well, you wait and —

OFFICIAL: Signor Carpeta!

SORDO: We must get together, have a talk some time —

CARPETA: Yes —

SORDO: They call us a school of painters but we never meet, except at funerals. Funny school!
OFFICIAL: Signor Carpeta!

Scene Ten

A room in the palace. The door closes.

OSTENSIBILE: Thank you for your folder.
CARPETA: Oh, I —
OSTENSIBILE: It's too big.
CARPETA: I'm sorry.
URGENTINO: Really, we scarcely need educating in the nature of your talent, Signor Carpeta.
CARPETA: Thank you.
URGENTINO: Or perhaps you thought the Head of State has not the time to keep abreast of current movements in the field of painting? Christ Among the Flocks! There, you see!
CARPETA: I am delighted you —
URGENTINO: This is Cardinal Ostensibile. He knows Christ Among the Flocks.
OSTENSIBILE: I have one.
URGENTINO: He has one! You see, you are among admirers here!
CARPETA: I also have a number of secular drawings which you may —
URGENTINO: The Cardinale, as you know, is Secretary of State for Public Education, which is to say he is very worried about Signora Galactia and so am I. Sit down, will you? Let me tell you straight away that any time I spend on the subject of art is not wasted. Art is opinion, and opinion is the source of all authority. We have just spoken to Sordo. He is spent, don't you think? Quite spent?
CARPETA: He is only thirty-seven . . .
URGENTINO: What does it matter if he's seventeen? He's spent.
CARPETA: Perhaps.
OSTENSIBILE: They pretend to be kind to one another, but

they are each other's cruellest critics. How well do you know Galactia?

CARPETA: I know her.

OSTENSIBILE: I didn't ask that, I said how well. Very well? Or hardly well?

CARPETA: Pretty well.

URGENTINO: They say you go to bed with her. Pretty often.

CARPETA: Do they?

OSTENSIBILE: Of course they may be wrong. And in any case to go to bed with someone is not to know them, I suspect. Were they to be known to one another, to go to bed would for most people, be something of a problem, I dare say. And, conversely, you might sleep with someone every night and after ten years turn around and say, in honesty, you knew them only 'pretty well'. I speculate.

CARPETA: I have had a relationship with Signora Galactia of a — of a rather casual nature which — which is rather casual . . .

OSTENSIBILE: Yes . . . Yes . . . (*Pause*)

URGENTINO: You see, I have the most profound respect for Signora Galactia, as a painter, as a woman.

CARPETA: Me, too. I think she —

URGENTINO: Don't interrupt —

CARPETA: I'm sorry —

URGENTINO: A profound respect. She is not spent. Most certainly she is not spent; she moves, she travels, a sort of meteor cleaving her way through dark spaces, undisturbed by gravities, I mean the gravities of greater stars, she is under no influence but her own will, she has by her perseverance — and possibly, perversity — achieved a following, she has a school of sorts, and she is brilliant. And the Cardinale and I thought, decided between ourselves, we could not let Venice fail to celebrate her genius, because for an art establishment like us, a cynical clique of bureaucrats like us, who like to pride ourselves on taste, to let a great fish through the net of our sponsorship would be a lapse. I tease you, but we hate to miss anyone.

OSTENSIBILE: We hate to miss you.

URGENTINO: We hate to miss you, too. And so we adopted her. Talent is rare and precious, and of course, explosive too. What is the matter with her, is she mad? (*Pause*)

CARPETA: Mad? Is she mad? She — yes, she may be a little mad, she — keeps asking me to leave my wife. And — so on. It is a sort of madness.

URGENTINO: Is it? I should have thought that rather depended on your wife. Or perhaps she loves you.

CARPETA: Loves me, well, she —

URGENTINO: Loves you. More than you are worth. I have seen the painting called The Battle Of Lepanto in various stages and it is not getting any better, it is getting worse, not from the technical point of view but from the moral one. And I ask you very frankly, is she a moral woman?

CARPETA: Moral? No, I don't think you could — not moral, no. (*Pause*)

OSTENSIBILE: How quickly can you paint a canvas of three thousand square feet, Signor Carpeta? (*Pause*)

CARPETA: A month.

URGENTINO: Now, that's silly —

CARPETA: No, I'm saying —

URGENTINO: I have heard of ambition, but that's —

OSTENSIBILE: Let him finish.

CARPETA: I'm saying I *could*, I *could* paint a canvas of that size in a month, only it wouldn't be —

URGENTINO: It damned well wouldn't, would it?

CARPETA: Be very — very good —

URGENTINO: Quite. You are not a rash man, Signor Carpeta. I am glad to see.

CARPETA: For a decent composition and — with the right assistants, I think — seven weeks.

OSTENSIBILE: You see, Signora Galactia has not been altogether fair with us.

CARPETA: No, no, she hasn't been —

OSTENSIBILE: She has —

CARPETA: Gone her own way —

OSTENSIBILE: Gone her own way, yes! Which is all very well in certain circumstances, but in a public matter such as this —

CARPETA: You have to think of — (*Pause*)

OSTENSIBILE: What? (*Pause*) What do you have to think of?

CARPETA: What — the circumstances — require. (*Pause*)

URGENTINO: Well, that's it, then, isn't it? Can you start today?

CARPETA: Yes.

OSTENSIBILE: The way you do Christ — the nobility of Christ — transmit that feeling to the officers.

CARPETA: Yes . . .

OSTENSIBILE: The battle is not — unwholesome — it is,

rather, the highest moment of self-sacrifice. It is as divine — in essence — as the crucifixion —

CARPETA: Yes . . .

OSTENSIBILE: And the soldiers are — not victims of a sacrifice but — a fraternity on Christian crusade, do you follow?

URGENTINO: Yes. But you must paint it for yourself! It is your painting!

OSTENSIBILE: It is his painting, yes!

URGENTINO: Congratulations! You are — from this moment, promoted to the pantheon of Venetian masters, yes, you are!

CARPETA: Thank you, it will be my finest opportunity to —

URGENTINO: Sordid financial matters can be arranged by others at a later date!

CARPETA: Of course, I long to satisfy both my own requirements as a painter and —

URGENTINO: Good bye! Good bye!

CARPETA: Thank you for —

URGENTINO: Do leave your folder. Yes, leave it. (*Pause. A door is closed.*) Why is it, I wonder, the base instinct is so often the spur to fine achievement? I suspect Signor Carpeta will, in seven weeks, do his greatest for us, though it will be modest enough as greatness goes . . . Do you want any of his drawings? (*Turned cartridge paper.*) There, that's quite good . . . and look! I swear that's Galactia naked . . . !

OSTENSIBILE: What about Galactia?

URGENTINO: She loves him . . . the great woman . . . dotes on . . . the little man . . .

OSTENSIBILE: Please.

URGENTINO: What about her?

OSTENSIBILE: We cannot overlook the provocation. We cannot, can we, on delivery of this calculated and obscene affront to History, lie down, can we? Say many thanks and put it in the basement? It is all meat and chopped up genitalia, it is not a battle and she knows it. We cannot simply overlook.

URGENTINO: No.

OSTENSIBILE: And she wouldn't want us to.

URGENTINO: She would hate it.

OSTENSIBILE: We have to make an appropriate response. (*Pause*)

URGENTINO: Prison.

OSTENSIBILE: You think prison?

URGENTINO: I think prison is — a little prison, not too much — is what this desperate woman wants . . .

OSTENSIBILE: Yes.
URGENTINO: Confirmation. Of our baseness. Is what she wants.

Scene Eleven

The barracks.

GALACTIA: It's done. (*Pause*)
CARPETA: Yes. (*Pause*)
GALACTIA: **It's done**. And you will be the first to see it. Do
   you know I have never shown a finished canvas to a man before,
   a man first, except my father, and he taught me? Do you know
   you are the first?
CARPETA: Yes.
GALACTIA: I do it because I love you. I love you, Carpeta.
CARPETA: Yes. (*Aside*) I believe there is nothing so exquisite,
   so refined in its cruelty, as to be the object of a passion which
   you no longer reciprocate . . .
GALACTIA: Kiss me . . . !
CARPETA (*aside*):   It is humiliating, not of the one who loves
   you, but of you yourself. Splashed with adoration, it burns your
   skin . . .
GALACTIA: Kiss me . . .
CARPETA (*aside*):   And your lips moan. Sin in it, ache in the
   eyes . . . (*To her.*) Is it really finished? I don't feel worthy
   of —
GALACTIA: Don't be silly!
CARPETA: Actually don't feel I deserve —
GALACTIA: Don't be so — what's the matter with you? Don't
   deserve — what are you —
CARPETA: Just — the honour —
GALACTIA: Be quiet, you'll spoil it for me! Stand there.
   There. Now, I will open all the shutters, and you — keep your
   eyes shut. Wait! Don't move! (*The shutters are flung open along
   the length of the room.*) Don't turn round! I feel utterly childish
   about this. I — I have never made a cult of this, of first
   showings but — flood in, daylight! Look, clear, liquid light
   and — (*The last one clatters open.*) Now, wait. (*Pause*) Open
   your eyes. (*Pause*) What? (*Pause*) Carpeta? (*Pause*) What, are

you — are you crying? You are crying! Oh, my dear, you're crying! Because it's good, is it? (*His sobs become audible.*) Is it that good? Tell me! **Oh, God, is it so good you have to** — (*He wails.*) Oh, wonderful, great lover, shh! (*Sound of hammering wood.*)

Scene Twelve

Some hours later. The studio is dismantled.

SUPPORTA: It is a great waterfall of flesh. It is the best thing you have ever done. But I don't think, forgive me, I want to be associated with you any more. Professionally, that is.

GALACTIA: I competely understand —

SUPPORTA: No, let me finish, mother, please —

GALACTIA: Absolutely get what you —

SUPPORTA: **You never let me finish.** (*Pause*) Because whilst it is your best work, I don't feel sympathy with what you —

GALACTIA: Quite! I am not in the least wounded by your rejection of me which —

SUPPORTA: Why do you —

GALACTIA: Which I thoroughly anticipated and therefore —

SUPPORTA: **Why won't you be hurt!** Always, you pretend to be prepared! I am giving up a professional relationship of twenty years, why don't you be hurt for just a minute? (*Pause*)

GALACTIA: Because it was obvious you would desert me, it was as clear as daylight to me I could not count on you any more.

SUPPORTA: I think you enjoy seeing people fail.

GALACTIA: Yes, I think I do. I expect it. I drive for it. And when it happens, all right, I'm gratified. I have shattered tolerance. You are a drapery painter, Supporta, you could not understand where I was headed and now you want — absolutely comprehensible! — to save yourself. Change your name or something. I don't care for your method anyway. Everything shines. Not all fabric shines, you paint too many highlights —

SUPPORTA: I think you are — I hate to say this — you are a little mad.

GALACTIA: Well, yes of course, you would reiterate the

popular opinion. I must help them, they are taking it off the stretcher, I have to supervise them or they —

SUPPORTA: I am not deserting you, I am saying —

GALACTIA (*to* WORKMEN): **Wait for me, there!** Listen, I am not injured. Set up a little studio, paint wedding pictures —

SUPPORTA: You always have to ridicule —

GALACTIA: Yes, dash it down! I haven't time to listen to your motives, and who cares about them anyway? If we all had to understand one another's motives! Christ! I will write you a cheque for your services — (*To* WORKMEN) **Don't do that, there, it's not a carpet!** (*To* SUPPORTA.) They are putting it on a barge, and the barge will sail up the canal, like some great bomb snuggled under tarpaulins, and they will unload it and carry it into the palaces of power, and it will tear their minds apart and explode the wind in their deep cavities, and I shall be punished for screaming truth where truth is not allowed. **It made Carpeta weep with its power!**

Scene Thirteen

A room in the palace.

URGENTINO: It is hanging. It is not framed, but it is hanging. In the gallery.

SUFFICI: Let me see it.

URGENTINO: No hurry! No hurry! Finish your drink. (*Pause*) Finish your drink. (*Pause*) There comes a point — with painting — at which no amount of intervention can significantly alter the outcome of the project.

SUFFICI: It is not what you —

URGENTINO: It is not what Venice — (*Pause*)

SUFFICI: Ah. (*Pause*)

URGENTINO: Because of what I can only describe as a — mental disorder — which prevents the artist satisfying the aspirations of her customer. (*Pause*)

SUFFICI: It's —

URGENTINO: It's a bit — it's not like anything I've seen before. Or want to see again for that matter.

SUFFICI: I see. And I — I am —

URGENTINO: In it. Yes. You are. You figure very prominently, but —

SUFFICI: I want to see.

URGENTINO: No hurry —

SUFFICI: I want to see. (*Pause*)

URGENTINO: Very well. It is an area of human activity in which control comes from within, in which the artist either exercises discretion, and wills discretion, or — I have got someone else doing one so it doesn't really matter what kind of mess she's made of — there. Feel free to be sick. (*Pause*) Spew up if you —

SUFFICI: **Shut up.** (*Pause*) The hands — the hands are utterly vile. They are not my hands.

URGENTINO: Nope.

SUFFICI: Look, look at my hands, look at them —

URGENTINO: Yes —

SUFFICI: **Look at them!**

URGENTINO: **I am looking at them!**

SUFFICI: That is not a likeness of my hands, is it?

URGENTINO: Of course it isn't —

SUFFICI: My hands which are beautiful in fact, despite my age, are beautiful and not claws as she has painted!

URGENTINO: Cesare —

SUFFICI: Not claws, are they!

URGENTINO: Cesare, you will have the servants running in —

SUFFICI: What is the point of making me attend three sittings if she goes away and copies some talons out of —

URGENTINO: Cesare —

SUFFICI: Some ornithological atlas!

URGENTINO: I have never seen you so animated —

SUFFICI: I am animated, I am animated!

URGENTINO: Quite rightly, but —

SUFFICI: Not because I am vain, I am the least vain of men, but because it is simply untrue —

URGENTINO: Untrue, yes —

SUFFICI: And consequently it is a lie, and I —

URGENTINO: Abhor a lie, I know you do —

SUFFICI: And the face —

URGENTINO: The face is worse —

SUFFICI: Whilst it looks like me —

URGENTINO: Vague resemblance — very vague resemblance —

SUFFICI: Is painted with contempt —

URGENTINO: Well, we don't know —

SUFFICI: It is contempt and you only have to see Garacci's
   portrait of me in the flower garden to see —
URGENTINO: This is a different genre, but yes —
SUFFICI: I am saying Gaacci understood me and this is — I am
   sorry to be so angry but —
URGENTINO: No, no —
SUFFICI: I am not normally angry but she simply cannot paint,
   she cannot be allowed to do this thing which is — in effect — a
   calculated offence to me and to the sailors who so heroically laid
   down their — what is this, what are all these bodies doing — it
   is all bodies, everywhere with gaping — I do not pretend to be
   an artist but it was not like that!

Scene Fourteen

A room.

URGENTINO: How are you feeling? (*Pause*) Are you feeling
   uncomfortable?
GALACTIA: Yes. (*Pause*) And good at the same time.
URGENTINO: How's that?
GALACTIA: Virtuous. And scared.
URGENTINO: Delicious combination. (*Pause*)
GALACTIA: Firstly, I am —
URGENTINO: Shut up —
GALACTIA: I am prepared to repay every penny of the fee
   I —
URGENTINO: Shut Up! I have seen a drawing of your breasts.
GALACTIA: What has that got to —
URGENTINO: Shut up.
GALACTIA: I don't see what that —
URGENTINO: **Shut up.** (*Pause*) This is my palace. This is my
   cushion. You have your empire, I have mine. I said I have seen
   a drawing of your breasts. It is on my desk, look. **What am I
   going to do with that painting?** (*Pause*) You should not think,
   because we are not artists, we are stupid. Because we are
   governors, or bureaucrats, stupid. Terrible error. Terrible
   vanity. Leads to the noose, the wall, the death chamber —
GALACTIA: I take full responsibility for —

URGENTINO: **I don't care if you take responsibility or not.** (*Pause*) What do you think that means? 'I take full responsibility — '? Arrogant! Sit there, on my cushion, on the armorial of Venice, in your steam of cleverness, unafraid long jutting woman's jaw, hate that! Really, humility would do you good. Please don't stare at me, look at the floor or something, what did you think you were doing, because the Committee is assembling and they are insulted, the Republic is insulted, don't you like the Republic? If you do not like it it is treason, don't tell me you didn't think of that?

GALACTIA: Not terribly.

URGENTINO: Not terribly, didn't terribly think of it, what are you —

GALACTIA: **Cry Of The Blood.** (*Pause*)

URGENTINO: There is a bridge over there. On one side of the bridge there is a carpet. And on the other side of the bridge there is bare stone. And on this side of the bridge there are cushions, and on the other side there is straw. And on this side there are windows, but on the other side it is dark. On this side we laugh, and on that side they cry. Do you know the bridge? (*Murmurs of approaching voices.*)

GALACTIA: The Bridge of Sighs.

URGENTINO: I cannot tell you how it excites me to think of your bare breasts against the wall, and my buttocks on this brocade . . . (*The committee enters the room.*)

GALACTIA: I am great. I am great because I conceded nothing, but utterly was myself. And all these artists hanging on the walls, were not themselves, but other people . . .

OFFICIAL: Sit down, please.

GALACTIA: I am prepared to refund to the State of Venice all monies I received for —

OFFICIAL: Silence, please, and sit down.

GALACTIA: I want to make this statement —

OSTENSIBILE: We do not want your statement —

GALACTIA: Why can't I make a statement?

OFFICIAL: Are you Anna Galactia, of Via —

GALACTIA: You know bloody well I am Galactia, everybody knows I'm Galactia, why else would I be here —

OFFICIAL: And are you the executor of the subject painting 'The Battle of Lepanto' which is hanging on the wall opposite the window there —

GALACTIA: Really, this is — what is the point of —

OSTENSIBILE: I think, ditch all that. Thank you. (*Pause*)

Signora, we do not understand your painting.

GALACTIA: It is a painting of a battle at sea.

OSTENSIBILE: It is a slaughter at sea.

GALACTIA: A battle is a slaughter.

OSTENSIBILE: No, it is the furtherance of political ends by violent means.

GALACTIA: I showed the violence.

OSTENSIBILE: But not the ends. So it is untruthful. The ends were the freedom of the seas, the affirmation of the Christian faith, the upholding of a principle. Why did you not paint those?

GALACTIA: How do you paint the upholding of a principle?

OSTENSIBILE: You show it by the nobility of the participants.

PASTACCIO: Do you believe in the principle, Signora? (*Pause*)

GALACTIA: I am a painter. I'm not —

OSTENSIBILE: Oh, now, you cannot hide behind your sensuality, your instinct —

GALACTIA: Why not?

OSTENSIBILE: That is dishonest, that is trying to slam the gate on our debate, isn't it?

GALACTIA: I painted death because all I saw was death.

PASTACCIO: So you admit to being partial? You admit to attending to one aspect of the truth?

GALACTIA: Yes. And I don't admit it, I embrace it.

PASTACCIO: You admit to attending to one aspect of the truth to the exclusion of the other?

GALACTIA: What other?

PASTACCIO: The nobility of the struggle.

GALACTIA: I deny its nobility.

OSTENSIBILE: You deny the virtue of the actions of the State of Venice?

GALACTIA: I — I suppose if you —

OSTENSIBILE: You obviously deny it. And the evidence is in the portrait of the Admiral, who is presented with an expression of the utmost callousness —

GALACTIA: Callousness?

OSTENSIBILE: Well, what else is it?

GALACTIA: I hadn't put a name to it.

OSTENSIBILE: I will do it for you. It is callousness.

PASTACCIO: You see, we have to get behind the picture, and you want us to look at the surface. You say, look at the surface, the brush strokes, the colour, the anatomy! Yes, all very good, that is your strength, who can quarrel with you on that ter-

ritory? You are supreme. But behind the painting we are all
equals. What are you saying? It seems to us you are saying you
revile the State of Venice. Do you want to argue with that?

OSTENSIBILE: Argue if you want. (*Pause*)

GALACTIA: What are you going to do with me?

PASTACCIO: Please, argue the point.

GALACTIA: No.

PASTACCIO: Why not?

GALACTIA: Because you will only win the argument.

PASTACCIO: How do we know until you have offered your
defence?

GALACTIA: No. I am not going to give you the satisfaction of
proving me wrong. If the surface of the painting is my territory,
the back of it is yours. You are specialists in arguments. I hate
arguments. What are you going to do with me?

OSTENSIBILE: I have never heard of an artist who did not
want to engage with his opponents, there is nothing they love
more than expostulating about their genius, what is the matter
with you? Defend yourself or we shall become irritated.

GALACTIA: You see, you must win.

OSTENSIBILE: It is not a question of —

GALACTIA: **Win. Win.**

OSTENSIBILE (*bitterly*): **Not a question of winning but of** —

GALACTIA: Hang the painting. Take it in the street, and hang
it.

OSTENSIBILE: Never.

GALACTIA: Why?

OSTENSIBILE: Because there is the little matter of public
morals, miss!

PASTACCIO: Hang it in the street . . . !

OSTENSIBILE: The artist's cry! The whine of the corrupter!

GALACTIA: Ah, real thing now, the real strangler!

OSTENSIBILE: The irresponsibility of your manner is of
course, only a mask, the posture of artistic freedom, look at the
way you dress, you have not washed that garment in God knows
how many —

GALACTIA (*disbelief*): How do you know when —

OSTENSIBILE: And your breasts quite clearly unsupported —

GALACTIA: How does he —

OSTENSIBILE: All calculated to make us think **artistic irresponsibility, well, no, we are not fooled!** (*Pause*) You are an
enemy of the Republic. You wish to destroy its unity and its
power for an end you will no doubt admit in time but the great

thing is **we are not fooled.** (*Pause*) I really do despise artists and that is why I am so perfectly qualified to sit on this committee. I despise artists as much as I love art, and I can look at that plane before me, glistening with colour and say it is an evil surface. There!

GALACTIA: I shall have to be punished, shan't I? You can't let someone say — on the back of the canvas — all your principle is actually dirt, and stench, and matted buttocks floating in the sea. I shall have to be broken in some way. (*Pause*) Well, won't I? (*A door slams in a prison.*)

Scene Fifteen

The prison.

GALACTIA: There's no light in here! Give us a candle!

GAOLER (*receding*):   No candles.

GALACTIA: No candles, no, of course not! A candle? What? Give you a bit of light, give a painter colour? Don't be charitable.

MAN IN THE NEXT CELL: **Shut up.**

GALACTIA: Shut up, he says. Voice from the depths. Shut up. **It stinks in here.** I do think you might change the straw, the previous occupant had crabs — no I haven't seen them, I speculate —

MAN IN THE NEXT CELL: **Shut up.**

GALACTIA: Shut up yourself! Get another room if you don't like it! It's not as dark in here as you might think. Now, that is interesting. It's like black, the colour black. People think there is only one black, but there is black and black, there is black the absence of light and black — are we under the canal here? **Ugh, I touched something!** (*She gasps with horror.*) I touched something. Oh, God, I . . .

MAN IN THE NEXT CELL: You have only been in there two minutes.

GALACTIA: Shut up, voice from the depths.

MAN IN THE NEXT CELL: **Two minutes.**

GALACTIA: Well, of course it's difficult, I expected it to be difficult. I am not surprised there is something disgusting on the floor, there would be and I — **Ugh** — (*The* MAN IN THE

NEXT CELL *laughs*.) Listen, my friend, you have the advant-
age of experience, you mustn't take such delight in — (*He
laughs on*.) All right, laugh on, laugh on, I never expected to get
an intellectual as a neighbour —

MAN IN THE NEXT CELL: **Who says I'm not an intellectual?
Who says I'm not?**

GALACTIA: Look at my squalor, look at my filth, this is what
happens to the one who loves the truth, I fully expected this, I
was prepared for it, no one visits me and when they do they tell
me lies, **no wonder**. How long have I been here, you cannot
count in the dark, the only proof that you have told the truth in
this life is that you are punished for it! Am I to be tortured? I
must be tortured, obviously, it would be inconsistent if I weren't
tortured, driven mad and and murdered in some corner. They
hate the truth, don't they, they yank the teeth out of its mouth
and kick the lips to blubber **understandably it's a dangerous
thing**. I shall say to the one who tortures me **I fully understand
your motives, it hurts you, doesn't it?** I shall say that, which of
course, only provokes more punishment, if you scream here can
the Doge hear you? What sort of face have you got? You sound
like you have a big nose.

MAN IN THE NEXT CELL: I have a big nose.

GALACTIA: Fancy that!

MAN IN THE NEXT CELL: I haven't seen my face for seven
years.

GALACTIA: Well, we don't get mirrors, do we, we might grow
vain, threading filthy straw through plaited hair and using shit
for powder, mind you I was an untidy bitch to start with, paint
up my fingernails and so on, though sometimes I like to show off
a bit, clean skirts and blouses, rather fragrant, but then I always
forgot something, hair washing or turned up with dirty feet. I
miss my lover, you lose your lover, don't you, lose your children, **calculated factor in the punishment**, have an awful need of
something physical and gross and old, banal thing up against
the — **will someone put a light on** . . . ! (*Pause. Breathless*.)

MAN IN THE NEXT CELL: Be still, because you have such a
long time to endure. Be still, and preserve yourself. (*Pause*)

GALACTIA: Yes . . .

MAN IN THE NEXT CELL: Because if you scream and struggle you will wear down what you have, which is little enough in
this bitterness. Be an animal in the straw. Be the toad.

GALACTIA: Yes . . .

MAN IN THE NEXT CELL: And slow your heart beat down.

GALACTIA: Yes . . .

MAN IN THE NEXT CELL: Lie, waiting. Hibernate the long winter of your offence.

GALACTIA: Thank you, yes . . .

MAN IN THE NEXT CELL: Anger, hang it up now. Prisons are such loud places. But only the quiet ones live. The noisy ones, they've carried passed my door . . .

Scene Sixteen

A studio in Venice.

URGENTINO: Ostensibile wants to charge her with being an agent of the Sultanate. He likes to win an argument and she refused to argue with him, so now he's furious and says she is a Muslim. She is not a Muslim, is she? The exaggerated sense of mission is something I cannot stomach in clergymen. Since she is quite obviously not an agent of anyone except herself it will involve torturing her to a confession. I do think that is vile. Torturing and bribing witnesses. It is all extremely ghastly and has a lot to do with the fact of celibacy. Torture! Really, what are you to do with them? I would like more red there, where the sun is setting . . . yes . . . there . . . perhaps orange, you say.

CARPETA: Orange.

URGENTINO: All right, orange. And she is in any case mad, I abhor a cliché, but you know it better than anyone. That figure is not very celebratory, I think —

CARPETA: This one —

URGENTINO: Holding the banner, yes, is not elated, is he?

CARPETA: He has got an arrow in his —

URGENTINO: Yes, but he is the standard bearer, isn't he, and standard bearers have to be elated because — that is why they are standard bearers, surely? There is altogether, and I'm sorry if I sound irritable, a certain lack of celebration in your work —

CARPETA: I have done everything you —

URGENTINO: Everything, I know, you have, you have —

CARPETA: Painting so quickly that —

URGENTINO: You have been wonderful, you have, and of

course it is hurried in some respects — the horn blowers look a
little — do you know Raphael?

CARPETA: Of course I know Raphael —

URGENTINO: Yes, well, he would have —

CARPETA: I'm sorry, I can't go on with this.

URGENTINO: More energy and — **what!** (*Pause*)

CARPETA: I can't go on with this. (*Pause*)

URGENTINO: You're being silly.

CARPETA: I —

URGENTINO: Yes, you are, now, listen —

CARPETA: Endless interruption and —

URGENTINO: Shh, shh!

CARPETA: Can't go on with it. (*Pause*)

URGENTINO: You are overwrought. The responsibility of
accepting a commission of this scale is obviously —

CARPETA: It's not that —

URGENTINO: Yes, it is that and —

CARPETA: **I want to see Galactia.** (*Pause*)

URGENTINO: Galactia? Why?

CARPETA: Because I love her and —

URGENTINO: You —

CARPETA: **Have to see her.** (*Pause*)

URGENTINO: I have taken a great risk in commissioning you
to do this work —

CARPETA: ı know and I —

URGENTINO: I took a great risk in commissioning her and I
took a great risk in commissioning you and I —

CARPETA: I am sorry I —

URGENTINO: I am sick of being messed about by artists.
(*Pause*) You did not say you were in love with her, you said —

CARPETA: I know, I —

URGENTINO: Said it was a little —

CARPETA: I know I did —

URGENTINO: A sordid little sexual transaction.

CARPETA: I wanted to —

URGENTINO: **Well, no you can't, not until you've finished it,**
you — (*He gropes blindly.*) It's not in my hands, it's the
Committee of Public Education you should make petition to,
not me —

CARPETA: You're the Doge —

URGENTINO: I am the Doge, but —

CARPETA: So you can —

URGENTINO: **This is a democratic country!**

RIVERA (*entering*):   Hello?

URGENTINO: **I hate you all.**

RIVERA: What are you —

URGENTINO: I wish I had never seen a painting in my life! I blame you for this!

RIVERA: Me?

URGENTINO: Yes, you! You encouraged me, Rivera! I have been — through my own sensitivity — been drawn into needless conflicts with people who, crazed by self-indulgence, will not, and perhaps, God help them, cannot, sympathize with the problems of governing a modern state! Whereas I am forever having to sympathize with them, they are in love, they have a mission, they have a headache, they are menstruating. **It is a most unequal relationship.** (*Pause*) I sometimes wish I was a brute.

RIVERA: No, no . . .

URGENTINO: Yes, a brute with brute senses. Sending regiments to toss pianos out of windows. Really. You cannot imagine how I long to send pianos flying out of windows! But I don't, do I? I don't, and I am made miserable. (*He turns on* CARPETA.) If you do not finish the painting, I will put you in a cell with her, there! And you can deliver babies on the filthy straw! (*He turns to* RIVERA.) Gina, Gina, come here, come here! (*They walk away.*) I am so upset, I cannot tell you. I am reduced to making threats against my favourite people, artists! Help me, tell me they are vaguely human, I am beginning to doubt my own perceptions . . . (*Whispers*) What is this painting like? The thing he's . . . tell me, is it —

RIVERA: Yes.

URGENTINO: What?

RIVERA: Shit.

URGENTINO: Is it? It is, isn't it! It is! I knew it was! Oh, God!

RIVERA: Sit down.

URGENTINO: Take me out of here — take me out — the smell of paint — I used to love a studio and now I could bring up my breakfast — he is a banal and gutless hack —

RIVERA: That is not fair —

URGENTINO: He is, he will not listen when I —

RIVERA: He has listened, he has listened too much —

URGENTINO: He has no imagination of his own, what do you expect me to do?

RIVERA: He is a very sound painter of religious subjects, he is not an epic painter —

URGENTINO: Why did he turn up, then? Imposter!

RIVERA: It is an offence against art to flatter minor artists with projects they are not equipped to handle —

URGENTINO: What am I to do, then!

RIVERA: Will you be quiet for a moment?

URGENTINO: I can't be quiet, I'm furious! (*Pause*) All right, what?

RIVERA: I have seen Galactia's painting.

URGENTINO: Ostensibile wants it burned!

RIVERA: Yes, but he won't. He will put it in a cellar. Now, listen to me, and I will tell you what I know, as a critic, and a loyal supporter of your party and your cause. In art nothing is what it seems to be, but everything can be claimed. The painting is not independent, even if the artist is. The picture is retrievable, even when the painter is lost . . .

Scene Seventeen

The prison. A door crashes back on its hinges. Pause.

CARPETA: Galactia . . . Galactia? (*Sound of scraping on stone.*) Is there a light in here? (*Movement*) Are you there? It's me, are you there or —

GALACTIA: Have you ever painted blind? (*She stops scraping.*) Actually it isn't dark. We make so much of light, but light's relative. I now think daylight is terribly crude.

CARPETA: Where are you, I —

GALACTIA: Clumsy thing you are, blundering in this little space. You can always find me by my smell.

CARPETA: I — I —

GALACTIA: It is a little fruity, isn't it? Like the badger's den and me the female badger, don't be frightened, look, I have drawn a man, in granite, with granite. It's you. In monochrome, but in this light who wants polychrome, or poly anything? Nothing's poly in a prison, it's all mono, mono dinner, mono supper, mono stench. This wall is covered with remarks, I could not read them for the first three months but —

CARPETA: Three months? You have not been here three —

GALACTIA: Then you find them, treasures! Whole biographies,

and sexual miseries, and me the first to make a picture! An artist always will, won't she, get decorating the cruel old wall of torture —

CARPETA: Listen, the Doge —

GALACTIA: The Doge? Kind Doge!

CARPETA: Has given me the letter of —

GALACTIA: Sweet, fat Doge! Listen —

CARPETA: No, you listen —

GALACTIA: **You listen to me.** (*She whispers, urgently.*) I find I am still fertile. I find, in this damp den, fertility back at my age! Lovely shock! Have you two minutes?

CARPETA: You aren't listening to me —

GALACTIA: I want a child, they are not allowed to execute the pregnant, I bleed again, you see, in this dark stillness, here, come here —

CARPETA: Look, I —

GALACTIA: Come, quick before they —

CARPETA: It isn't — I don't —

GALACTIA (*sarcastic*):   Oh, wonderful! Oh, reluctant Carpeta who was all over me once!

CARPETA: I can't actually see you and anyway —

GALACTIA: What does that matter? I want to lie in the straw like a badger, littering, quick do your stuff —

GALACTIA: **No.**

GALACTIA: Why are you here? Don't smile, why are you here? Have they burned the Battle?

CARPETA: No.

GALACTIA: **Liar!** Of course they have burned it and you have brought the ashes —

CARPETA: It is not burned —

GALACTIA: Of course it is burned, how could they tolerate it, it is too powerful for them, and I am too powerful for them, I am Galactia who told the truth and all you do is lie to me!

GAOLER (*entering*):   On yer way.

GALACTIA: Why do they lie to me? I tell you this, you with the bent back and the club fist, I like you best, you are no liar!

GAOLER: On yer way, I said. (*Pause*)

GALACTIA: What? (*Pause*) What is this?

GAOLER: Out. (*Pause*)

GALACTIA: Out? I live here.

GAOLER: Two minutes to get yer things —

GALACTIA: **What is this? All the truth tellers live here**.

CARPETA: You're free. This is the order, look —

GALACTIA (*snatches it*):   Show me —

CARPETA: Signed by the —

GALACTIA: **Can't see — In this light, can't** — (*She screws it up.*) **I cannot be released! How can they release me I am too dangerous!**

MAN IN THE NEXT CELL: Would you show a little slivver of consideration to the —

GALACTIA: **They are releasing me . . . !**

MAN IN THE NEXT CELL: Forgive me, I cannot work up any happiness for you, I have been here seven years, and it hurts me when someone goes out, it hurts me terribly, so please enjoy your freedom quietly.

GALACTIA (*quietly*):   What did you do, strange dark thing in the straw?

MAN IN THE NEXT CELL: Nothing. I did nothing. And that is why I shall never be released. (*Pause*)

GALACTIA: I'll paint you! I'll paint you and I will show your innocence!

MAN IN THE NEXT CELL: Please, you —

GALACTIA: **Truth of the imperial jurisdiction!**

MAN IN THE NEXT CELL: Please —

GALACTIA: **Expose the truth and back I'll come!**

GAOLER: Come on, you daft bitch —

GALACTIA: Don't clean it out, I'm coming back! (*Suddenly she sobs, falters.*) Hold me, hold me oh, daylight . . . !

Scene Eighteen

A public place. Subdued murmurs of a crowd passing in line before a National Treasure.

URGENTINO: To have lost such a canvas would have been an offence against the artistic primacy of Venice. To have said this work could not be absorbed by the spirit of the Republic would be to belittle the Republic, and our barbarian neighbours would have jeered at us. So we absorb all, and in absorbing it we show our greater majesty. It offends today, but we look harder and we know, it will not offend tomorrow. We force the canvas and the stretcher down the gagging throat, and coughing a little, and spluttering a little, we find, on digestion, it nourishes us! There will be no art outside. Only art inside.

OSTENSIBILE: **The message.** What about the **message.**

URGENTINO: Cardinal, your single-mindedness is a credit to your Jesuit professors, but you must stop hacking. The blunt, dull hack of Christian persecution, the urge to the bonfire. Hate it. With all respect, hate it . . . (*Murmurs of crowd.*)

PRODO: Thank you, thank you! That's me, I am the figure, thank you, same bolt, same head! Note the bolt which I endured for my nation, this is me here, a very reasonable likeness, I think you will agree, thank you, you see I shudder in an ecstasy of patriotic fervour . . . !

SORDO: It is a success.

LASAGNA: You mean it is popular. Yes, it is popular . . .

SORDO: I mean, people like it.

LASAGNA: Yes.

SORDO: They have nicknamed it **The Slag's Revenge.** Galactia has never kept a man. Several of the corpses look like Carpeta.

LASAGNA: And that's you, surely? With the javelin in the throat..

SORDO: And Bertocci, falling out of the rigging, yes!

LASAGNA: If it had been painted by a man it would have been an indictment of the war, but as it is, painted by the most promiscuous female within a hundred miles of the Lagoon, I think we are entitled to a different speculation.

SORDO: It is very aggressive. You and I, we wouldn't have been so aggressive. A woman painter has a particularly — female — aggressiveness, which is not, I think, the same as vigour. Do you agree with that distinction?

LASAGNA: Yes. It is coarse.

SORDO: Coarse, yes. Because she is so desperate to prove she is not feminine, a flower-painter, an embroiderer, she goes to the extremes and becomes, not virile, but shrill.

LASAGNA: It is shrill. It defeats its purpose by being shrill.

SORDO: She can paint, of course —

LASAGNA: She can paint, but it's excessive. And so is she.

SORDO (*pained*): And yet they seem to like it . . .

LASAGNA: Carpeta! Giulio and I have been speculating as to whether that object there — that figure with the head slewed off — is actually you. The Slag's Revenge, you see. It has your teeth.

CARPETA: I don't think it matters what —

SORDO: Humour, Carpeta —

CARPETA: What you or any other —
SORDO: Oh, come on —
CARPETA: It is a public picture and you can't dishonour it!
   (*Pause*) Sorry. Just — the little nausea, you know, the little
   belch of loathing at the fellow artists gnawing at each other's
   bones. Passing disgust at sound of tooth on bone. Gone now.
   Gone now! (*Popular noise, then silence.*)

Scene Nineteen

GALACTIA's *studio.*

RIVERA: May I come in? (*Pause*) May I, there is no light so
   I — (*She kicks something.*) Ow!
GALACTIA: I don't have lights.
RIVERA: Could I just draw —
GALACTIA: Don't draw the curtains.
RIVERA: Well, where are you —
GALACTIA: In my black hole. In my gaol. (*Pause*)
RIVERA: I'm sorry if —
GALACTIA: Sorry? You **pandered**. You **lied**. Got me out by
   licking and lapping. One hundred feet of pain and you **licked it
   smooth**.
RIVERA: They had no intention of leaving you in gaol, it was a
   gesture and —
GALACTIA: **Smothered my danger. Shameless conciliator.**
   (*Pause*) There are some words, in this mendacious time, this age
   of mendacity, which still bear filth and evil and the worst of
   those is **conciliator**! Unclean word!
RIVERA: I promise you a week was all they intended to —
GALACTIA: **Conciliator!** (*Pause*)
RIVERA: Yes . . . (*Pause*) You are terribly difficult to deal
   with. I thought — I honestly believed — you wanted the
   picture to be seen. I'm sorry. I really do not understand you —
GALACTIA: I am not meant to be understood. Don't you see?
   Oh, you miserable, well-meaning, always-on-the-right-side,
   desperate little intellect! Death to be understood. Awful
   death . . .

RIVERA: They are flocking to the exhibition. The hanging in San Marco. Doors are jammed and —

GALACTIA: Any soldiers trampled on their tunics? Much mutiny down the docks?

RIVERA: What?

GALACTIA: I can't hear rioting, but the curtains are thick . . .

RIVERA: In my catalogue I talk about the anatomy, which is — some people say they can touch the flesh, such is the realism of it, they — (*Pause*) Listen, it is art I am interested in. I have saved your art. Get up.

GALACTIA: Carpeta came. Holding a little bag. My lover, left his wife —

RIVERA: Get up, will you!

GALACTIA: Little bag in the doorway, and I thought, I do not need you, it is so terrible to know I do not need you any more . . .

Scene Twenty

The exhibition.

PRODO: The figure on the right is me. Same bolt, same head, thank you, who got this disability in service of my nation, sweeping the atheistic power from the sea —

GALACTIA: Doing all right, Prodo?

PRODO: Signora Galac —

GALACTIA: Shh!

PRODO (*quietly*): Signora, it has been a godsend, what with winter coming on —

GALACTIA: Nothing's in vain! Nothing is wasted! If one beggar is kept from starving, no effort is too extreme! What do they say, you know more than any critic, what do they say? Trash, do they say?

PRODO: Unfortunately I am obliged by the custodian to perch here at the right end of the picture, so they pass me as they enter, and they have no opinion. It is the other end, the exit, you should listen. One hundred feet later, a man might change his mind about many things. Some have catalogues, but most can't read. The ones who can't read gasp, the ones with cata-

logues go 'mmm'. So it's either gasp or mmm, take yer pick.
Excuse me, I must get on. (*He declaims.*) This is me, my
portrait at the moment of my agony, in service of my
nation . . . (GALACTIA *passes along the murmuring crowd.*)

GALACTIA: What do you think?

MAN: Me?

GALACTIA: Yes, what do you think of this? (*Pause*) Incredible or — (*Pause*) Or not? (*Pause*) Have you come far to —

MAN: The Piave —

GALACTIA: The Piave! You know I've never seen the Piave!
To see a picture — that is rather a long way to see — I'm not
trying to accost you, don't look for the custodian — **I am not
accosting you** — He thinks I — I just — (*Pause*) I painted it.
It's mine. All right? I did the — (*Pause*) No, I'm not mad.
Please don't look at me as if I'm mad — **I strenuously deny that
I am mad I just** — (*Pause*) He's holding my hands . . . he's
holding my hands . . . !

URGENTINO (*wading in*): Galactia comes, not to admire her
work — she is not so vain — but to admire the admirers! The
queue is fifty metres long and the man there has returned eight
times, ask him, it is a fact, he kneels there and he weeps. Look,
you have drawn tears from him, wrung water from his coarse
imagination! Do you feel powerful? I have such power, but no
such power. I can make men weep, but only by torturing them,
while you — don't resent me. In a hundred years no one will
weep for your painting, only respect it. Cold, dull respect.
Enjoy your peculiar authority! It is a great nation, is it not, that
shows its victories not as parades of virility, but as terrible cost?
My brother accepts he is a calculating man, but admirals must
be! You have winkled out his truth, he is full of admiration for
you, hands notwithstanding! Will you dine with us? I hate to
miss a celebrity from my table. (*Pause*)

GALACTIA: Yes.